Horary Astrology and Solar Returns

Unlocking Astrological Chart Reading, Divination, the Twelve Houses, the Sun Returning, and Planets in Transits

© Copyright 2024 - All rights reserved.

The content contained within this book may not be reproduced, duplicated, or transmitted without direct written permission from the author or the publisher.

Under no circumstances will any blame or legal responsibility be held against the publisher, or author, for any damages, reparation, or monetary loss due to the information contained within this book, either directly or indirectly.

Legal Notice:

This book is copyright protected. It is only for personal use. You cannot amend, distribute, sell, use, quote or paraphrase any part, or the content within this book, without the consent of the author or publisher.

Disclaimer Notice:

Please note the information contained within this document is for educational and entertainment purposes only. All effort has been executed to present accurate, up-to-date, reliable, and complete information. No warranties of any kind are declared or implied. Readers acknowledge that the author is not engaging in the rendering of legal, financial, medical, or professional advice. The content within this book has been derived from various sources. Please consult a licensed professional before attempting any techniques outlined in this book.

By reading this document, the reader agrees that under no circumstances is the author responsible for any losses, direct or indirect, that are incurred as a result of the use of the information contained within this document, including, but not limited to, errors, omissions, or inaccuracies.

Your Free Gift
(only available for a limited time)

Thanks for getting this book! If you want to learn more about various spirituality topics, then join Mari Silva's community and get a free guided meditation MP3 for awakening your third eye. This guided meditation mp3 is designed to open and strengthen ones third eye so you can experience a higher state of consciousness. Simply visit the link below the image to get started.

https://spiritualityspot.com/meditation

Or, Scan the QR code!

Table of Contents

PART 1: HORARY ASTROLOGY 1
   INTRODUCTION 2
   CHAPTER 1: HORARY ASTROLOGY AND DIVINATION 4
   CHAPTER 2: ZODIAC SIGNS BASICS 12
   CHAPTER 3: THE DECANS, AN EXTRA LAYER OF MEANING 32
   CHAPTER 4: 12 ASTROLOGICAL HOUSES AND 2 AXES 41
   CHAPTER 5: MAIN CHARACTERISTICS OF THE PLANETS 52
   CHAPTER 6: PLANETARY DIGNITIES AND JOYS 68
   CHAPTER 7: MAJOR PLANETARY ASPECTS 80
   CHAPTER 8: MINOR PLANETARY ASPECTS 89
   CHAPTER 9: PLANETARY TRANSITS 99
   CHAPTER 10: HOW TO READ ANY HORARY CHART 107
   GLOSSARY OF TERMS AND GLYPHS 117
   CONCLUSION 123
PART 2: SOLAR RETURNS 125
   INTRODUCTION 126
   CHAPTER 1: UNDERSTANDING SOLAR RETURNS 128
   CHAPTER 2: PLANETS, CARDINAL POINTS, AND MORE 134
   CHAPTER 3: WHEN PLANETS MOVE IN RETROGRADE 153
   CHAPTER 4: HOUSES AND ZODIAC SIGNS 101 160
   CHAPTER 5: YOUR SOLAR RETURN ASCENDANT 170
   CHAPTER 6: THE PLANETS IN THE HOUSES 185
   CHAPTER 7: THE PLANETS IN THE SIGNS 202

CHAPTER 8: SOLAR RETURN ASPECTS I – THE MAJOR ONES 214
CHAPTER 9: SOLAR RETURN ASPECTS II – THE MINOR ONES.......... 234
CHAPTER 10: INTERPRETING A SOLAR RETURN CHART 246
CONCLUSION 253
GLOSSARY OF ASTROLOGICAL TERMS AND SYMBOLS 255
EXTRA: YOUR SOLAR RETURN CHARTS 257
HERE'S ANOTHER BOOK BY MARI SILVA THAT YOU MIGHT LIKE 260
YOUR FREE GIFT (ONLY AVAILABLE FOR A LIMITED TIME) 261
REFERENCES 262

Part 1: Horary Astrology

An Essential Guide to Astrological Chart Reading, Divination, the Twelve Houses, Planetary Transits, Venus, Mars, Jupiter, Mercury, the Sun, and Moon

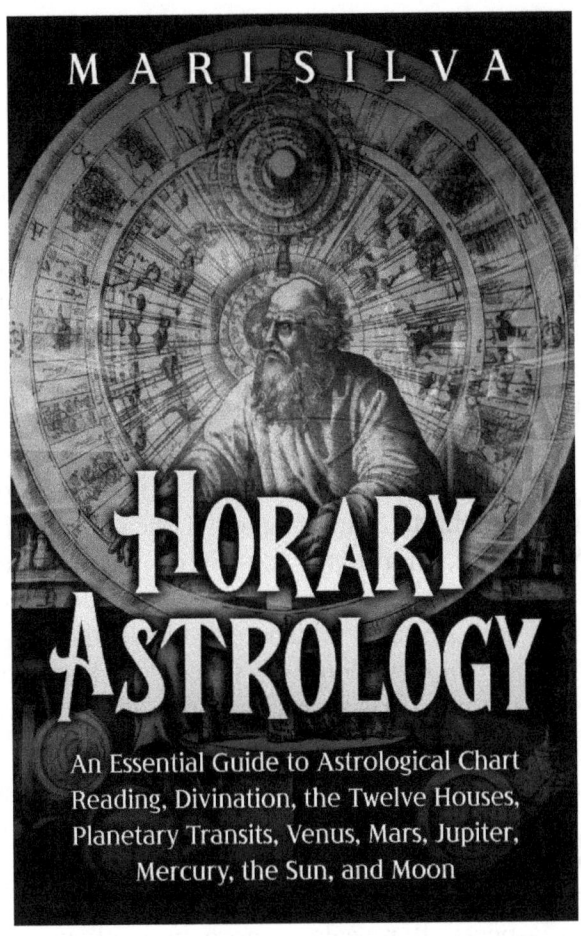

Introduction

As a branch of ancient astrology, horary astrology has been part of people's lives for thousands of years. As you'll learn from this book, horary astrology is a unique art. It relies on the same principles as other methods of discerning answers based on the position and interaction of heavenly bodies, but it's slightly different. Unlike traditional approaches to astrology, like natal astrology, the horary version is far more straightforward. You only need to know the position of the planets, stars, sun, and moon when asking a particular question to create and interpret a horary chart.

Of course, like other astrology, the zodiac signs are a fundamental part of interpreting your chart. The chapter dedicated to the characters explores them in-depth, thoroughly explaining their characteristics and importance. To accurately use horary astrology for divination, you must pay attention to the decans, which provide additional information associated with your inquiry. Since a specific zodiac sign rules each astrological house, the book has a chapter exploring the individual houses and the 2 axes, which are explained fully later in the book.

You'll learn the fundamental aspects of the planets. Empowered by this knowledge, you'll understand how these heavenly bodies provide accurate answers in horary astrology. The subsequent chapters are dedicated to planetary characteristics called "dignities" and "joys" and the major and minor planetary aspects. It reveals a more in-depth view of how each planet is associated with information seeking. Major and minor planetary aspects embody a unique system of energies, the source of the answer to the querent (one who consults an astrologer). Each planetary aspect has a distinctive role and impact on horary charts. The five principal planetary aspects (the Conjunction, the Sextile, the Square, the Trine, and the Opposition)have the most fundamental role in horary chart interpretation. While minor planetary aspects are less demonstrative than their major counterparts, they should be considered while doing horary divination.

How a planet moves across the sky paints a clearer picture of the querent's sought answer. The penultimate chapter defines the concept of planetary transits and explains how it differs from the aspects. It explores the information transits offer compared to aspects. The last chapter teaches you how to read a horary chart. It provides a beginner-friendly explanation of how horary charts are created, with step-by-step practical instructions and examples of what to consider when doing a horary reading.

If you're ready to embark on the unique and rewarding journey of learning astrological divination, keep reading!

Chapter 1: Horary Astrology and Divination

Astrology is an ancient science studying the influence of heavenly bodies on people's lives. It started thousands of years ago when astrologers and astronomers noticed many of Earth's events are determined by the position of the planets, sun, moon, and stars. Later, it was revealed that how the heavenly bodies were positioned when a person is born could shape their lives by influencing their personality, relationships, and other aspects of life. By identifying the astrological signs that ruled the planets when a person was born, astrologers could get clearer answers about the querent. Other factors, like the astrological houses and angles, affect the outcomes. These factors form an elaborate profile determining a person's life prospects.

Earth's events are determined by the position of the planets, sun, moon, and stars.
https://pixabay.com/es/illustrations/planetas-espacio-tierra-j%C3%BApiter-7612566/

Various past cultures used different astrological practices. Some have evolved, while others have remained the same. Nowadays, you can practice many forms of astrology. For example, you can look into prophecies through modern Western practices, like mundane astrology, interrogatory astrology, the ever-popular natal astrology, and horary astrology.

This first chapter introduces you to horary astrology. You'll learn about its history and position in the vast sea of divinatory practices. You'll be provided with explanations and examples of how this ancient divinatory form works in theory – and in practice.

History and Uses of Horary Astrology

The horary astrology origins can be traced to ancient Sumeria. When describing the art of capturing the moment in the horary chart, the Sumerians used the word "*kairos.*" For them, this term marked the time when the Earth and the heavenly bodies were frozen together, revealing answers related to a particular concern. The question was posed by their astrologers, who could discern the answers by looking up to the heavens.

Horary astrology was popularized in the 17th century by English Astrologer William Lilly, who created several publications about this art. Like many astrologers at the time, Lilly was proficient in medicine, herbology, architecture, and magic. He made astrology available to the masses through his work and publications. In modern times, people rely on natal astrology because they know their time of birth and can afford to pay astrologers for natal charts. However, this was far from the case in the 17th century. So, for people who couldn't afford to pay for complicated natal charts, horary charts represented a more suitable solution. They could receive guidance to resolve their issues and gain answers to burning questions without spending too much money. Lilly popularized the practice of reading the stars based on their current positions. This move was critical for the survival of astrological divination.

Lilly gained knowledge and experience through other astrologers' work who lived and practiced earlier in history. He studied the works of Guido Bonatti, an Italian astrologer who lived before 1300 CE. Bonatti spent much of his life examining the astrological systems created by the ancient Greek, Roman, Sumerian, Egyptian, and Arab civilizations. Bonatti collected the most essential information from these systems, synthesizing them into a system that established the foundation of modern astrology.

Lilly translated Bonattis's works (written in Latin) and other astrology-related texts from Greek, Sanskrit, and Near-Eastern languages with cryptic connotations.

William Lilly learned from astrologers and sorcerers who practiced this art in the Middle Ages. Astrology was forbidden due to its association with pre-Christian, pagan belief systems during that time. Despite this, people visited magicians and astrologers to seek guidance in practical matters. Revealing this, Lilly could pinpoint a unique quality of horary astrology - the connection between spirituality and applicable information. Unlike other astrology, horary astrology uses information about the heavenly object to provide information people can use in their current lives. It reminds people that heavenly bodies don't only affect each other in the skies, but they also have a bearing on life on Earth.

Contemporary horary astrology is efficient in answering people's day-to-day concerns. Although nowadays, many don't object to paying for detailed natal charts, they can create their own chart without studying complex planetary associations and links between the zodiac signs and houses.

Another reason people prefer to use horary charts over natal charts is they don't want to learn how the planets will determine their fate. Let's say you want to know if you should apply for a job you're interested in. In this case, you won't care about uncovering how your unique personality traits led to you finding that job. You just want to know whether submitting your application is a good idea.

Besides, not everyone wants to learn about the extensive strengths and weaknesses determined by the positioning and movements of heavenly objects at the time of their birth. Horary astrology provides precise answers without additional information. You must know the exact time of your birth to get answers to similar occurrences in a natal chart. Unlike the date and location of your birth, the time of birth isn't always recorded, even in modern times. So, if you don't know your exact birth time, horary astrology is one of the best ways to seek answers from the stars.

How Is Horary Astrology Used and Why

Horary astrology explores answers to questions based on the inquirer's current situation. The questions must be related to the present to reveal answers of the same nature. They cannot be related to the past or future because that goes beyond the scope of horary astrology. So, instead of asking questions like "Will I succeed in the job offered?" You should ask, "Should I take this job offer?" Similarly, you won't ask, "Was planning to move for a job the right decision?" Instead, ask, "Should I move – to be closer to my new job?"

The interpretation of a horary astrological chart is similar to a birth chart. Once you've asked the question, you can create a chart based on the current standing of the relevant heavenly bodies and interpret their positions to reveal the answer.

The horary chart won't reveal information about situations you've already explored through conscious information seeking. Unlike other divination forms, horary charts won't give you answers from previous lives or the life after this one. They won't offer explanations about death either. You can get answers about certain situations, but the questions must be open-ended. Asking questions requiring a yes or no answer leads to the risk of false results.

Your responses are determined by complex relationships between planetary positions. You shouldn't limit your questions to one-word answers. Even if your inquiry results in a simple answer, seeking information affected by several planetary positions is always better. Novice practitioners are advised to seek prophecies for other people. It takes time to master asking the right questions, let alone creating and reading a horary chart. If a practitioner is determined to seek questions about the future, they should limit their search to up to three months ahead. The planetary positions can determine nothing beyond that at the time of the inquiry. Once created for a specific question, horary charts are valid for three months. You shouldn't ask the same question again within this period; you'll likely get different results. If you do, your results are likely false. Recording the *time of the inquiry* helps you avoid this mistake.

The Connection between Horary Astrology and Divination

Horary astrology is an ancient divination system relying on the same principles as many other future-telling methods. Of course, there are several fundamental differences between horary astrology and other divination forms. The most notable difference is that the former is a passive method. You actively participate in divination when using Tarot cards, runes, and other oracular divination forms. You pick a card, rune, or other tool and engage with them through intuition. With the combined effort of your intuition and the tools chosen, you can get answers to your inquiries. In contrast, horary astrology requires a passive approach because you're essentially looking at the planets to reveal the answers.

Still, there are a few similarities between horary astrology and other divination forms. First, you must explore the concept of divination to understand these. When you perform an act of divination, you're engaging in a seemingly random act. However, in this universe, nothing is coincidental. Your experiences and environment tell you much more about the events you've set in motion with your actions than you're aware of. Every person has a secret history of their life, which is part of a complex energetic network. Engaging in a random act requires the participation of all the forces present in this energy field. As Austrian psychoanalyst Sigmund Freud suggested, people are only aware of a small part of their emotions and thoughts. The rest is hidden in the subconscious, the effects of their thoughts and feelings on their environment and outcomes. Prophetic practices use these forces to reveal the information the practitioner seeks by creating a connection between the subconscious and the energy field surrounding them.

For instance, you're sitting in a restaurant with your friends and want to know what brought you there. The obvious answer might be as simple as one of your friends wanting to celebrate their promotion and inviting you to the restaurant. You decide to dig deeper into the (still conscious) answer. With a little introspection, you may reveal that your recent move to that city is why you're at the restaurant at that specific moment.

When seeking answers through divination, you must understand not all solutions lie in the universe's secret forces. You may not know the answer, but it can become obvious by taking a little time to identify it. For instance, pulling a card from a deck doesn't necessarily mean you were drawn to it because your subconscious was telling you it reveals critical answers. You could have picked it because you knew it had a bent edge - you merely weren't aware of this knowledge.

Horary astrology works the same as other prophecy forms. It extracts information from the energy system by looking at the heavenly bodies in a particular configuration. This configuration is associated with feelings and thoughts and reveals knowledge you otherwise wouldn't have accessed. Using the same example of the restaurant scene, the true answer to your question lies in the planetary configurations at the moment you ask the question. It's like taking a picture of the planets when the thought of questioning why you're at the restaurant comes to mind and freezing the related universe's forces in time. Since these forces are fluid and in constant motion creating a photograph is a way to make them accessible to the conscious mind.

Your natal chart reveals talents, potential, and indications taking the form of actions and thoughts. These are the results of a complex energy process, which astrology (and the divination methods based on it) seeks to explore. Horary astrology focuses on creating a clearer picture. Unlike the natal chart that can change during your life, a horary chart is frozen at that moment. Since the information you gain is based on a particular moment, the astrological symbols are far less fluid.

Horary astrology relies on the same principles as many other astrology forms. One of the most influential aspects of this divinatory practice is the moon's position and characteristics. On a horary chart, as the querent, you are represented by the sign's ruler residing in the first house cusp. Planetary rules of the houses and other aspects determined by the present house cusps crucially impact creating and interpreting horary charts.

Generally, when you read a horary chart, you first appoint your inquiry to a specific house in the chart. For example, if you're looking for a lost animal, you would assign this question to the sixth house, which rules over animals smaller than a goat. On the chart, you'll see this house's cusp residing in a particular sign. A specific planet will rule the sign at that moment. The place of the planet will hold the answer, symbolizing the location of the lost animal. Likewise, the planet's characteristics, determined by the horoscope, will tell you if the missing animal is injured, ill, or in danger. So, the answer to a simple question provides complex results determined by multiple factors. Your inquiry's intention, the intentions of others related to the inquiry, and the options associated with the questions affect your answers.

Horary Astrology at Work

Here is an example of how honorary astrology works in practice:

Charley explained, "I was down with the flu, but I was already making plans for a dinner party I was supposed to hold for my friends the next week, thinking my symptoms would clear up by then. I asked whether I should hold the party on a particular day. However, my chart revealed some unforeseen compilation. It warned me that it's not wise to plan a party because, based on the current planetary position, I was looking for a much longer recovery period than anticipated. I normally don't rush to the doctor with flu-like symptoms, but the warning made me think twice about looking after my health. So, I made an appointment. After some testing, the doctor revealed that I suffered from a serious bacterial infection requiring immediate treatment. I was disappointed to have to cancel my dinner party, but my friends were understanding. And I was grateful for the revelation that saved me from more serious health complications."

As the following testimony suggests, horary charts can reveal answers to questions related to lost objects:

"I was rushing out one winter morning and couldn't find my favorite pair of gloves. They were a birthday present from a dear friend, and I also liked wearing them. I was looking for them in my bag, coat, and closet, thinking I'd put them in either of those places. Since I was in a hurry, I had to settle for another pair before heading out. When I returned home, I decided to look for the gloves again - this time with a little divinatory help. Thinking I'd already looked everywhere else in the house, I asked whether I should look for the gloves in the garage. Based on the planetary chart at the moment of the inquiry, the answer was a clear yes. After going into the garage, I found the gloves. They were on the shelf next to the snow shovel I used the last time I wore the gloves. I took them off, so they wouldn't get dirty while clearing the pathway in front of my home." explained Lewis.

Horary astrology can answer questions on financial matters - as long as they're about you personally:

"When the global pandemic hit, the stock market went into a deep dive. Since I had substantial savings, a friend of mine suggested that I invest it in stock. With the stock prices plummeting, it seemed like a good investment. When the market starts to recover, I could sell my shares for a much higher price. However, I was skeptical about investing my money as I wasn't sure how the economy would fare later on. After consulting the horary chart, I learned that investing in stock was not a good idea, as the market would go further down. I decided against investing, and as it turned out, it was a good decision - the energy crisis caused stock prices to go even lower." Maxine.

Besides answering questions, horary charts can give you clarity over certain situations:

"I recently had a job interview for a position I had coveted for a long time. As time passed, I realized I wouldn't get a call back from the recruiter. I was considering applying for different positions but was hesitant as I was still hoping to get the job I wanted. After consulting the horary chart, I learned that while the recruiter considered me a good fit for the role, the employer didn't, thus giving someone else the position. However, the chart also showed that the person who got the job would soon leave it. About a month later, I received a call from the recruiter asking if I was still interested in the position." Carla.

Chapter 2: Zodiac Signs Basics

You are probably familiar with zodiac signs and have used them to understand your personality and your compatibility with someone or not. However, astrology signs are significantly important in horary astrology, albeit differently. Each zodiac sign brings a different energy to answer your questions.

Wheel of zodiac signs.
https://openclipart.org/detail/326713/vintage-zodiac-wheel-colour

Generally, zodiac signs are the twelve constellations in astrology, called "sun signs" because the sun passes through each one during a specific time of the year. Your sign is determined by the sun's position in the zodiac sign on the day you were born, impacting your personality and life. It can give detailed information about your personality, like your negative and positive traits, mood, relationships, challenges, etc.

In horary astrology, a zodiac sign in your chart can hint at an answer to your question. For instance, if you lose your cell phone and you get Gemini, your phone could be in your office or a place near your office. Since Gemini is the sign of communication, its presence can hint at an answer to communicating or socializing.

Three Types of Signs

1. Cardinal
2. Fixed
3. Mutable

This chapter covers each in detail so you can understand how zodiac signs connect to your horary astrology reading.

Cardinal Signs

The first types are the "cardinal signs," consisting of Capricorn, Libra, Cancer, and Aries. These signs symbolize initiation, innovation, transformation, change, and new experiences, associated with changing seasons. Capricorn is connected to winter, Libra represents the changes in fall, Cancer reflects the warmth of the summer, and Aries is linked to spring. If you get a cardinal sign in your horary reading, it means that this is the best time to take action and make things happen.

Aries

Glyph

Aries glyph represents the ram horns which influence the sign's energy and attitude of taking charge. The ram pushes through and moves everything in its way to achieve its goals. Similar to the ram, Aries is a symbol of strength and drive. People born under this sign are prone to explosive and strong emotions like aggression and losing their temper.

Rams represented new beginnings in ancient cultures.

Keywords

Aries hints at an answer related to any of these traits in a horary reading.

- Impulse
- Impatience
- Bravery
- Straightforwardness
- Determination
- Confidence
- Taking action
- Taking risks
- Boldness
- Passion
- Seeking attention
- Resolution
- Aggression
- Leadership
- Creativity
- Positive energy
- Self-confidence
- Selfishness
- Anger
- Competitiveness

Horary questions could ask about a lost item. If you get Aries in your reading, you'll find what you are looking for in any of these locations.

- On a hill or in a sandy area
- Unfrequented places
- Plastering in the home
- Ceilings
- Roof coverings

Element

Aries' element is fire, which drives the sign's fiery, impulsive, direct, energetic, and curious personality. The fire burning inside an Aries pushes it to fight and lead, providing answers related to fights, arguments, leadership, and promotions.

Modality

As a cardinal sign, Aries has a take-charge personality and prefers to lead rather than follow. Regarding questions about taking the initiative, a modality sign can show you the way.

Ruling Planet and House

Mars is Aries' planet. Mars is the God of War in Roman mythology, making it ideal for the competitive sign willing to win at all costs. It drives their aggression, impulse, and inner fire. Mars represents trouble in your relationships, like conflict and disagreements. Aries belongs to the first house in astrology and provides answers associated with self-worth, appearance, identity, vitality, and self. It indicates the desire to create a union in relationships.

Polarity

Aries has a positive polarity. Positive signs have an outward energy and impeccable self-expression skills. They are compatible with negative polarity signs as opposites attract.

Cancer

Glyph

The cancer symbol is the crab. It reflects its self-protective personality. The glyph can also resemble breasts, symbolizing its mothering and nurturing nature. They often provide answers connected to practicality, spirituality, and empathy.

Keywords

- Imagination
- Intuition
- Sympathy
- Caution
- Shrewdness

- Protection
- Clinginess
- Oversensitivity
- Inability to let go
- Loyalty
- Care
- Moodiness

Vengeance Finding a lost item:
- Kitchens
- Near water or ponds
- Cisterns
- Bathrooms
- Wash houses
- Utility rooms

Element

Cancer is a water sign and reflects the sign's maternal and emotional side. People born under a water element are warm and kind-hearted individuals. These traits make them caring, empathetic, and attached to their partners. A water sign in your horary reading indicates a positive outcome when asking about relationships.

Modality

Cardinal cancer enjoys forming emotional bonds, giving hints to questions about emotions or family relationships. It focuses on the subconscious and creativity.

Ruling Planet and Houses

Cancer is a Moon sign. Like the moon impacts the ocean, Cancer has ebbs and flows or highs and lows of emotions, and their mood changes fast. With relationship questions, a well-placed Moon is a sign that your relationship with your significant other will develop.

Cancer is ruled by the fourth house in astrology, symbolizing foundations, family, and home. It is associated with answers about upbringing and emotional security.

Polarity

Cancer has a negative polarity. Their energy is more receptive and inward, influencing the sign's imaginative, intuitive, and oversensitive personality.

Libra

Glyph

Libra's symbol is the scales. They symbolize Libra's love for balance, harmony, equality, and justice. The glyph can represent the setting sun, reflected in the sign's peaceful, calm, and relaxed personality. Libra provides answers connected to equality and justice.

Keywords

- Art
- Compromise
- Respect
- Indecisiveness
- Likability
- Diplomacy
- Fairness
- Kindness
- Accommodation
- Justice
- Social
- Self-indulgence
- Flirtation
- Gullibility
- Change
- Indecisiveness
- Peace
- Idealism
- Charm

Romance Finding a lost item:
- Closets
- Little houses
- Chambers
- Upper floors
- Barns
- Windmills

Element

Air signs are social butterflies who enjoy freedom and adventure. They often live in their own world but are intelligent and intellectual individuals. Anxious and frequently over-thinkers, they always obsess over the past and what could have been. They hint at answers connected to intellect, socialization, and overthinking.

Modality

Libra is the sign of love and romance, and their cardinal modality drives them to initiate relationships. They can usually provide answers connected to relationships, love, and romance.

Ruling Planet and House

Venus is Libra's ruling planet. Venus is the Goddess of Love and beauty in Roman mythology, traits associated with Libra, who is attractive inside and outside. The planet influences their love for harmony, honesty, commitment, and relationships. Since it's associated with love, Venus, in a horary reading, indicates sweethearts, which is a positive sign if you wonder how your relationship with someone will develop.

Libra falls under the seventh house in the zodiac. It is the house of partnerships but not only romantic; they can also be friendships and business partnerships. If Venus is in your seventh house in a horary reading, the person you ask about is interested in you.

Polarity

Libra's positive polarity influences this social sign's ability to express itself easily.

Capricorn

Glyph

The glyph is an illustration of a sea goat with horns and represents the sign's ability to rise above strong emotions, grow, and go after its goals. It indicates answers related to intense feelings and making dreams a reality.

Keywords
- Humor
- Patience
- Ambition
- Discipline
- Practicality
- Carefulness
- Grudge
- Pessimism
- Sensitivity
- Inner reflection

Self-criticism Finding a lost item:
- Barren fields
- Wood stores
- Cow sheds
- Near thresholds
- Dark places
- Low places

Element
Capricorns are Earth signs, influencing their hardworking and ambitious personality. They have a take-charge personality, so they usually hint at answers connected to leadership and achieving goals.

Modality
The cardinal Capricorns are go-getters who usually plan for the future. This sign can provide answers to questions related to long-term goals.

Ruling Planet and House

Capricorn's ruling planet is Saturn. It symbolizes the sign's determination, responsible, and hardworking nature. This planet hints at answers associated with limitations and learning lessons. Saturn is a symbol for older and mature men in a horary reading.

Capricorn falls under the tenth zodiac house. The sign answers about reputation, status, goals, and career.

Polarity

Capricorns have a negative polarity, and their energy is usually quiet and inward.

Fixed Signs

The second types are the "fixed signs," Aquarius, Scorpio, Leo, and Taurus. As the name indicates, these signs are fixated on their goals and traditions. They are responsible individuals who always finish a project they start. People born under fixed signs are dependable, reliable, loyal, and devoted. They prefer a routine life and struggle with change and disruptions.

Taurus

Glyph

The Taurus symbol is the bull; its glyph is the animal's head with curved horns. Bulls are associated with power, virility, tenacity, stubbornness, and strength. Like their animals, people born under this sign are persistent, hardworking, and never retreat from challenges. This sign will give you answers about power, hard work, and tenacity.

Keywords

- Reliability
- Patience
- Security
- Determination
- Persistence
- Greed

Resentfulness Inflexibility Self-indulgence Finding a lost item:
- Stables
- Sheds
- Agricultural outhouses
- Cellars
- Low rooms

Element
Taurus's element is Earth. These individuals are grounded in their beliefs, opinions, and thoughts. It represents practicality and sensibility in a horary reading.

Modality
Fixed Taurus' are materialistic, but they work hard so they can afford the luxurious lifestyle they enjoy.

Ruling Planet and House
Taurus's ruling planet is Venus, the planet of sex, beauty, and money. Venus influences the sign's sensual nature. They eat the best food, dress in the most luxurious clothes, and enjoy spoiling themselves. This sign can provide answers related to commitment and loyalty.

Taurus belongs to the second house, associated with finance, values, and possessions. It can provide guidance with questions associated with money or financial decisions.

Polarity
Taurus has a negative polarity.

Leo

Glyph

Leo's symbol is the lion, influencing their bold, loyal, confident, and playful personality. Its glyph is a lion's tail, mane, and head. The circle represents the sun signifying their strong personalities and presence. Creative, dominant, and confident, Leos can hint at answers connected with high self-esteem and leadership skills.

Keywords
- Faithfulness
- Kindness

- Self-confidence
- Open-mindedness
- Enthusiasm
- Generosity
- Creativity
- Intolerance

Patronizing Ego Bossiness Finding a lost item:
- Chimneys
- Places
- Building
- Parks
- Woods

Element

Leo is a fire sign which shows in their warm personalities. They are in touch with their emotional side but prefer to hide their weaknesses and instead show off their strengths to the world. Like fire, they burn with passion.

Modality

Fixed Leos have very powerful personalities, so they prefer to lead rather than follow.

Ruling Planets and Houses

Leo's ruling planet is the Sun. It is impossible not to notice a Leo in a group of people since they shine brightly, just like their ruling planet. They are full of energy and never stop giving. The Sun symbolizes confidence and the development of a relationship in a horary reading.

Leo falls under the fifth house, associated with pleasure. It encourages self-expression, joy, and hobbies. Leo can provide answers connected with having fun and enjoyment.

Polarity

Leo has negative polarity. Their energy is like the sun shining through every part of their being.

Scorpio

Glyph

Scorpio is symbolized by a scorpion. People born under this sign are observant and quiet, but they will not react well if you threaten them. Its glyph is the letter "M" with a tail, symbolic of Scorpio's destructive and creative nature.

Keywords
- Magnetism
- Excitement
- Passion
- Power
- Intuition
- Emotion
- Force
- Determination
- Secretiveness
- Obsessions
- Compulsion
- Resentfulness
- Jealousy
- Courage
- Confidence

Finding a lost item:
- Dare places
- Ruins
- Bathrooms
- Kitchens
- Sinks
- Gutters
- Mudded areas

Element

Scorpio is a water sign. Like the seas and oceans, Scorpio is mysterious and secretive. They struggle with opening up, and you can drown if you try swimming in their deep waters. Scorpio symbolizes hope and a future in a relationship in a horary reading.

Modality

Fixed Scorpios have intense emotions, and their feelings can be stuck because of their inability to open up and express themselves. In a reading, they hint at answers about privacy, secrecy, and lack of self-expression.

Ruling Planets and Houses

Pluto, the farthest planet from the sun, rules Scorpio. It is associated with darkness, representing Scorpio's dark personality. It represents rebirth, death, the subconscious, and intensity. Scorpio can provide answers connected with privacy and the shady side of personalities. It hints that a relationship can have a future in a horary reading.

Scorpio falls under the eighth house, which is associated with psychological processes.

Polarity

Scorpio has a negative polarity.

Aquarius

Glyph

Aquarius' symbol is a water bearer pouring water from a jug. This image represents the streaming of knowledge to quench thirst. The glyph symbolizes two lightning bolts, depicting the sign's limitless perspective; these individuals make their own rules and refuse to live a life dictated by others. Aquarius hints at answers related to standing out, being different, and living life on your terms.

Keywords

- Intellect
- Independence
- Inventiveness
- Originality
- Loyalty

- Honesty
- Friendliness
- Detachment
- Lack of emotion
- Unpredictability

Creativity Idealism Intelligence Finding a lost item:

- The upper part of a room
- Roofs
- Attics
- High places
- Hills
- Uneven places

Element

Aquarius is an air sign. They are full of unconventional ideas and don't shy away from sharing with the world. Although clever individuals, their heads are in the clouds. They enjoy new experiences, meeting new people, and visiting new places.

Modality

Fixed Aquarius' are intelligent individuals who value their intellect. They are quirky and unconventional but stand firm by their convictions and beliefs.

Ruling Planet and House

Uranus rules Aquarius and symbolizes individuality, awareness, and innovation. People born under this sign represent these qualities. Uranus encourages them to think differently and develop new ideas. Getting Uranus is bad news as it represents divorce, separation, and division in relationship questions.

Aquarius falls under the eleventh house, representing hopes, dreams, and friends. It is often referred to as the house of the future. Aquarius is associated with answers related to ideas to improve the future and world.

Polarity

Aquarius is positive polarity.

Mutable Signs

The third types are the "mutable signs, " which are Pisces, Sagittarius, Virgo, and Gemini. They are the opposite of fixed signs because they seek chaos and change. They love trying new things and never say "No" to new experiences. People born under this sign are spontaneous and crave variety in their lives.

Gemini

Glyph

Gemini's symbol is the twins. Its glyph is two joined lines, representing neutrality and duality. People born under this sign are communicative, social, restless, and enjoy having fun. Gemini gives answers related to communication.

Keywords
- Communication skills
- Youth
- Eloquence
- Intellect
- Wit

Inquisition Inconsistency Superficiality Finding a lost item:
- Paneled rooms
- High places
- Chests
- Communication equipment
- Offices
- Areas near offices

Element

Gemini is an air sign. They enjoy connecting with others and expanding their social network. They always have information to share and participate in idle gossip. Having this sign in your answer signifies socializing and making new friends.

Modality

Mutable Gemini is an expert at collecting and spreading information.

Ruling Planet and House

Gemini's ruling planet is Mercury. Mercury was the messenger of the gods in Roman mythology, which is ideal for the sign that enjoys gossiping and sharing information. It influences the people born under this sign to think and learn. Gemini appearing in an answer hints at intellect and sharing information.

Gemini belongs to the third house, associated with intellect and communication. It influences Gemini to think and develop ideas.

Virgo

Glyph

Virgo's symbol is a virgin maiden. The glyph is the letter "M," with the last part twisting inward, representing modesty and introspection.

Keywords
- Intelligence
- Practicality
- Modesty
- Analysis
- Diligence
- Reliability
- Fuss
- Worry
- Perfection
- Harshness
- Over criticism

Finding a lost item:
- Storage areas
- Studies
- Closets
- Dairy houses

- Barns
- Drawers

Element

Virgo is an Earth sign. They are sensible individuals who take their time before deciding. You'll often get answers related to practicality and planning from a Virgo.

Modality

Mutable Virgo is a skilled individual. They are associated with flexibility and the ability to change.

Ruling Planets and Houses

Virgo's ruling planet is Mercury, the planet of travel, technology, and communication. It influences Virgo's productive, reasonable, and logical nature. The sign hints at answers connected with logic and reason.

Virgo belongs to the sixth house, representing routine, health, responsibility, duty, and service.

Polarity

Virgo has negative polarity.

Sagittarius

Glyph

Sagittarius is symbolized by a centaur, representing this sign's paradoxical and dual personality. Its glyph is an arrow signifying Sagittarius's ability to consistently hit its mark without fail.

Keywords

- Philosophy
- Intellect
- Straightforwardness
- Honesty
- Sense of humor
- Freedom
- Optimism
- Restlessness
- Superficiality

- Irresponsibility
- Carelessness

Finding a lost item:
- Hills
- Stables
- Near radiators or fire
- Upper rooms
- High grounds

Element

Sagittarius is a fire sign. They are hot-headed and the first to take action. They are passionate and assertive individuals who are goal-oriented and make quick decisions. It is often the sign that provides answers related to taking charge and achieving goals.

Modality

Mutable Sagittarius are enthusiastic individuals. Flexibility is key with this sign, and they go with the flow.

Ruling Planet and House

Jupiter rules Sagittarius and symbolizes good fortune, knowledge, and spirituality. It influences the sign's adventurous spirit and desire to see the world. It is associated with answers related to positivity and spontaneity. Sagittarius falls under the ninth house, associated with various qualities such as adventure, wisdom, and knowledge. When Sagittarius is in your reading, it can signify getting out of your comfort zone and trying new things.

Polarity

Sagittarius has a Positive polarity.

Pisces

Glyph

Pisces is represented by fish, and its glyph is of two fish facing different directions. It represents the sign's ability to live in both the real and its own world.

Keywords
- Sympathy
- Intuition
- Selflessness
- Kindness
- Compassion
- Sensitivity
- Imagination
- Gullibility
- Vagueness
- Secrecy
- Idealism
- Escapism
- Dreams
- Creativity

Keywords when you lose an item:
- Fishponds
- Rivers
- Damp areas
- Near wells
- Kitchen
- Bathroom

Element
Pisces is a water sign. These people are deep, emotional, and sensitive. Like the ocean, they have an air of mystery and hold their secrets close to their hearts. They are associated with answers about imagination, privacy, and dreams.

Modality
Mutable Pisces are dreamers with a vision for themselves and the future.

Ruling Planet and House
Pisces's ruling planet is Neptune, the god of the seas in Roman mythology. The planet symbolizes spirituality, imagination, and dreams. It

is associated with answers about fantasy, dreams, and deep emotions. It hints at answers connected with self-deception, deceit, and relationship confusion.

Pisces belongs to the twelfth and last house of the zodiac. It represents seclusion and mysticism.

Polarity

Pisces has negative polarity.

The more you learn about zodiac signs and their characteristics, the more you understand horary astrology and find answers to your questions. Everything each sign represents can relate to an answer in a horary reading.

Chapter 3: The Decans, an Extra Layer of Meaning

Decans, called "faces" or "decanates," are unique astrological factors in horary astrology. Therefore, they should be considered during horary divination. The 360 degrees of the zodiac wheel is divided into 36 segments - each corresponding to a decan or segment, splitting each zodiac sign into three parts. Each decan occupies 10 degrees on the zodiac wheel and adds unique meaning to the traits, situations, and outcomes determined by a particular zodiac sign.

Each decan occupies 10 degrees on the zodiac wheel.
https://pixabay.com/es/illustrations/astrolog%c3%ada-simbolos-acuario-aries-6808362/

How to Identify the Decans on a Horary Chart

Over the history of the practice, people identified decans on astrological charts in many ways. The most popular approach associated with horary divination is the triplicity method. It splits each sign into thirds and assigns heavenly bodies to them. The association is made based on the traits of other signs with the same triplicity. According to this, the first 10 degrees of each zodiac sign belongs to the sign's fundamental characteristics. The second 10 degrees are linked to the next sign in the zodiacal wheel with the same element or triplicity. The last 10 degrees are associated with a third sign with the same triplicity.

Here is a list of decans on the astrological chart based on this method:

Aries
- 1st decan - 0-9 degrees
- 2nd decan - 10-19 degrees
- 3rd decan - 20-29 degrees

Taurus
- 1st decan - 0-9 degrees
- 2nd decan - 10-19 degrees
- 3rd decan - 20-29 degrees

Gemini
- 1st decan - 0-9 degrees
- 2nd decan - 10-19 degrees
- 3rd decan - 20-29 degrees

Cancer
- 1st decan - 0-9 degrees
- 2nd decan - 10-19 degrees
- 3rd decan - 20-29 degrees

Leo
- 1st decan - 0-9 degrees
- 2nd decan - 10-19 degrees
- 3rd decan - 20-29 degrees

Virgo
- 1st decan - 0-9 degrees
- 2nd decan - 10-19 degrees
- 3rd decan - 20-29 degrees

Libra
- 1st decan - 0-9 degrees
- 2nd decan - 10-19 degrees
- 3rd decan - 20-29 degrees

Scorpio
- 1st decan - 0-9 degrees
- 2nd decan - 10-19 degrees
- 3rd decan - 20-29 degrees

Sagittarius
- 1st decan - 0-9 degrees
- 2nd decan - 10-19 degrees
- 3rd decan - 20-29 degrees

Capricorn
- 1st decan - 0-9 degrees
- 2nd decan - 10-19 degrees
- 3rd decan - 20-29 degrees

Aquarius
- 1st decan - 0-9 degrees
- 2nd decan - 10-19 degrees
- 3rd decan - 20-29 degrees

Pisces
- 1st decan - 0-9 degrees
- 2nd decan - 10-19 degrees
- 3rd decan - 20-29 degrees

Interpreting the Zodiac Signs Decans

Aries

Decan 1 - Ruled by Mars, the Aries' faces are impulsive actions, ambitions, passion, and relentless pursuits. In divination, it could mean you'll develop innovative ideas, face your challenges without fear, and be outspoken about your desires. It embodies the typical characteristic of Aries - the action-oriented sign that never slows down. You must learn to take a softer approach to life. Otherwise, you'll always let your negative emotions lead you instead of being the leader you desire to be.

Decan 2 - Governed by the Sun, this decan indicates a more sensual and fluid lifestyle. This face has the bold confidence of the Aries signs and the natural optimism leading to passionate pursuits. Despite this, you'll still be restless deep down. You feel you can achieve more. In divination, this decan depicts creative pursuits and the desire to catch the eye of those around you.

Decan 3 - Under the reign of Venus, the third face of Aries indicates independence, bossy behavior, and lots of good luck. If this decan arises in your horary chart, it indicates that you are probably occupied with something that inspires you. Or, you may opt for traveling and engaging in nomadic pursuits.

Taurus

Decan 1 - Governed by Mercury, the first face of Taurus is all about aesthetics. As a typical Taurus, while ruled by this sign, you'll be charming, sociable, and ready to speak your mind - although you may come off as slightly materialistic. When this face appears on the horary chart, you'll strive for predictability and show loyalty in your relationships. Your senses are heightened, enabling you to find the smartest way to resolve your problems.

Decan 2 - Headed by the Moon, this decan reflects the need for perfection. You'll communicate your desires to larger groups and be very detailed. In horary divination, this face of the Taurus indicates that you may come off as too rigid or calculated in others' eyes during your inquiry. Being more helpful would help you to avoid issues.

Decan 3 - Ruled by Saturn, this decan showcases practical and reliable pursuits. You'll be determined to show off your loyalty and seriousness about your relationships. Fortunately, you'll be successful, but you probably already know this. You're following the same path that led you to past success for a reason. You may come into money or have other achievements.

Gemini

Decan 1 - Under Mercury's rule, this decan reflects a period of quick thinking and extravagant, sociable behavior. You'll be flexible and ready to talk about anything, albeit unable to focus on one subject for long. Showing characteristics of a typical Gemini sign, this is the time to enjoy what the world offers. However, don't be surprised if your behavior causes conflict with those preferring a more peaceful life.

Decan 2 - Governed by the planet Venus, the second face of Gemini is more expressive and charming. In horary divination, it can indicate that you'll seek attention by expressing your opinions. You'll strive to absorb as much knowledge as needed to obtain your goals. This face denotes a more conflict-averse behavior, although you must be careful with whom you form relationships.

Decan 3 - Ruled by Uranus, this face showcases open-minded behavior. It denotes the opportunity to apply your out-of-the-box thinking skills. You'll be optimistic, creative, adventurous, and ready to help others, even if the only thing you can do is listen to their problems. You may feel rebellious, especially if your independence or social status is threatened.

Cancer

Decan 1 - Governed by the Moon, the first face of Cancer denotes emotional and intuitive behaviors. In horary divination, this decan means you'll be connected to your intuition, prompting you to make good decisions and avoid conflicts. You'll nurture your talents, relationships, and those around you. It can indicate an emotional period. Depending on the nature of the emotions, your life can change in either direction.

Decan 2 - Under Pluto's rule, the second decan of Cancer is far more practical and suggests the need for deep considerations. You may be more stubborn and sentimental than usual in the upcoming period. Yet the same qualities allow you to care for yourself and others. Pay attention to the negative aspects of this decan, including the possessive and brooding behaviors, and change them as soon as you notice them.

Decan 3 - Headed by Neptune, this decan is about fantasy and connecting to your subconscious desires. You may be harboring romantic or dreamy illusions, and now it's time to act on them. In horary divination, this face can signify you'll forgive someone who has hurt you. You may deepen your spirituality to find peace and move past your hurts.

Leo

Decan 1 - Ruled by Saturn, this decan is a harbinger of a bright and playful period. However, it can indicate you'll be prideful and may need to keep your ego in check. You'll place a high emphasis on your appearance and reputation. Still, in a horary chart, this decan is considered a good sign as it denotes loyalty to your loved ones and sensitivity to their needs.

Decan 2 - Governed by Jupiter, the second face of Leo is a sign of positive things to come. You'll enjoy your freedom, rebelling against rules, and be ready to have the time of your life. You'll seek attention by reaching out to others, seeking to entertain and connect with them. You may accompany someone on their travels and offer them great ideas or performances they're sure to enjoy.

Decan 3 - Under Mars's rule, the last face of Leo is more daring and aggressive than the previous one. This decan represents stubborn behavior, passion, and kindness toward others in horary astrology. You'll follow through on any mission because you'll be forever optimistic about the outcome. Depending on the nature of your inquiry, you may be driven by larger goals forcing you to take a leadership position.

Virgo

Decan 1 - Ruled by the magnificence of the Sun, the first decan of Virgo represents the true nature of this sign. It is the face of a detail-oriented, ambitious, and ever-so-practical sign. In horary divination, it indicates a period obsessed with self-improvement. You'll have trouble with criticism and messy situations. Still, you'll be reliable and always ready to help those in need.

Decan 2 - Governed by Saturn, this face shows a more stand-offish and materialistic side of Virgo. It indicates a fierce determination to follow through with plans and focus on the bigger picture. Despite being honed on in your tasks, you'll still have time to please those around you - mainly because you know they can bring you closer to your goals and cover you with the praise your strive for.

Decan 3 - Under Venus's rule, the last face of Virgo is more whimsical and artistic. It indicates you'll exhibit mature behaviors and be generous, warm-hearted, and loving with those around you. Unlike this sign's previous faces, this one seeks attention. It can signify you'll be more likely to be shy about enjoying sensuality. You'll have no trouble expressing your creativity by improving your aesthetics.

Libra

Decan 1 - Ruled by Venus, this decan indicates your need to make a statement in life. You'll seek luxury, love, and beauty. Whatever you obtain, you'll guard jealously, although you do not wish to engage in conflicts. You'll aim for balance by helping others attain the same goals. Be careful, as you may struggle to remain grounded, particularly in an unstructured environment.

Decan 2 - Under Uranus's rule, the second face of Libra is about fighting the status quo. It denotes wanting to be original in horary astrology. This decan indicates you'll be determined to create unique ideas and stand out from the crowd. Unlike the typical Libra sign, this face is more rebellious. It focuses more on the big picture rather than getting along with others.

Decan 3 - Governed by Mercury, this decan suggests a socialization period. You'll seek to balance your life, mediate conflicts, and entertain others. You'll be a free spirit, happy to make new acquaintances, but also a little vain. You'll likely keep your mind busy, and if you can't find company to help you stay engaged, a good book will do equally well.

Scorpio

Decan 1 - Ruled by Pluto, this decan presents a dependable and loyal mindset. You'll be committed to your goals and others. During this time, you're unlikely to change your mind. You'll leave little room for misinterpretation of your thoughts and emotions. However, you may have periods of dark brooding preventing you from connecting to people. These moments will be more about inner transformation than anything else.

Decan 2 - Governed by Neptune, the second face of Scorpio is a selfless yet moody and impatient sign. In horary, this decan indicates periods of daydreaming, and you'll take everything lightly. It can suggest you're becoming sensitive to energetic influences and less centered. While having your head in the clouds may not benefit your long-term goals, you can use this time to give in to your artistic urges.

Decan 3 - Under Moon's rule, this is the most intuitive and sensitive face of the Scorpio sign and the most popular. You'll be seen as a nurturing person, always ready to be there for those in need. You'll have great empathy for others' feelings, yet be cunning enough to protect yourself and your loved ones from being swept away by other people's problems.

Sagittarius

Decan 1 - Governed by Jupiter, this decan showcases the typical Sagittarius sign. It shows optimism and an independent and adventurous spirit. Horary divination indicates that although non-committal, you'll be lucky in many areas of life. You'll strive to cherish your independence by staying open-minded and curious about new ideas for making it on your own. You may seek new adventures and knowledge.

Decan 2 - Headed by Mars, the second face of the Sagittarius sign is far more disciplined, loyal, and dependable than its predecessor. However, it indicates you'll be action-oriented and likely to take a more aggressive approach. The latter can seem controlling. Fortunately, you'll know how to make up for it with humor. You'll seek new ways to express yourself and succeed in competitions.

Decan 3 - Ruled by the Sun, the last decan of this sign is the freest. Depending on the context of your inquiry, it can indicate you'll meet new people, make an impulsive decision, or create new experiences. You may be focused on your appearance and social status and seek to charm everyone you meet. Your ability to express yourself creatively will help you with the latter.

Capricorn

Decan 1 - Ruled by Saturn, this decan highlights the textbook Capricorn characteristics - old-fashioned and glamorous thinking, occasionally laced with impatience. You'll seek a distinguished status and won't let any grueling task, challenging goal, or your goals stop you. However, you'll make your own rules, which can come off as disrespectful. Your aspiration to have a structured life can be your biggest weapon to obtain success.

Decan 2 - Being governed by Venus, the second face of the Capricorn sign is far friendlier than the first. It denotes you'll be agreeable, enthusiastic, and energetic, albeit a little too proud of yourself. You'll likely seek sensual and hedonistic pursuits and enjoy the beauty of life by finding balance in everything. You'll work hard, but have plenty of rest, too.

Decan 3 - Headed by the planet Mercury, this decan is mysterious yet curious, vibrant, and endlessly thoughtful. This period indicates you'll be curious, helpful, and tender-hearted. People will turn to you with their problems without the risk of being judged, and you'll only care about the truth, not the reasons someone fell off track.

Aquarius

Decan 1 - Under Uranus's rule, the first face of the Aquarius sign indicates defiance and making radical yet innovative moves. You give in to artistic pursuits; some may even make you look eccentric. However, soon others will follow your example and fully support you. You'll have a vision for making the world a better place. You may struggle with restrictions and reclaim your independence.

Decan 2 - Governed by Mercury, the second face of this sign is rather versatile. Sometimes it indicates you'll be restless and seek your own intellectual stimulation. At other times, it symbolizes a social butterfly who enjoys communicating with others and is fulfilled by endless conversations. You may come up with great ideas to sell to anyone or advice people will listen to.

Decan 3 - Ruled by Venus, this decan is the most affectionate face of Aquarius. It indicates a period of good judgment and aspirations for autonomy and balance. Your romantic side will flourish, and you'll have no trouble fitting in with like-minded people. Unlike the sign's previous two decans, this one is more about following trends than creating them. Still, you'll prioritize the beautiful parts of life.

Pisces

Decan 1 - Governed by Neptune, the first face of the Pisces sign denotes friendly, kind, and devoted behavior. You are likely to be creative and use your imagination to its fullest. You'll harbor tender, romantic aspirations and become concerned with hypothetical situations. The decan warns you to occupy yourself with creative pursuits to avoid over-romanticizing people and experiences, allowing you to give in to creativity while remaining grounded in reality.

Decan 2 - Headed by the Moon, this decan symbolizes independence and genuine aspects of the Pisces sign. You can expect an emotional period with unpredictable turns. You'll keep your personal space protected and remain reclusive for the moment. Despite this, you'll maintain your well-being and that of your loved ones. You'll have a chance to listen and care for others.

Decan 3 - Under Pluto's rule, the last face of the twelfth sign is the embodiment of empathy and exceptional listening skills. However, your thoughts and emotions will remain secretive and mysterious. You will likely make a good impression by persisting with your goals and taking on challenging tasks. This decan can symbolize necessary alone time.

Chapter 4: 12 Astrological Houses and 2 Axes

Since a specific zodiac sign rules each astrological house, this chapter helps you to explore them. The illustration of the zodiac wheel with the astrological houses, the IC-MC (Imum Coeli - Medium Coeli) axis, and the AC-DC (Ascendant - Descendant) axis represents the frame of a horary chart. This wheel is split into four quadrants, adding another layer of meaning to the interpretation of the houses. The houses in the first quadrant are associated with drive and motivation. The houses in the second quadrant are linked to instinct and intuition. The houses in the third quadrant are the embodiment of knowledge and thinking. The houses in the fourth quadrant are tied to a person's being or existence. The chapter discusses the axes and their significance in horary divination.

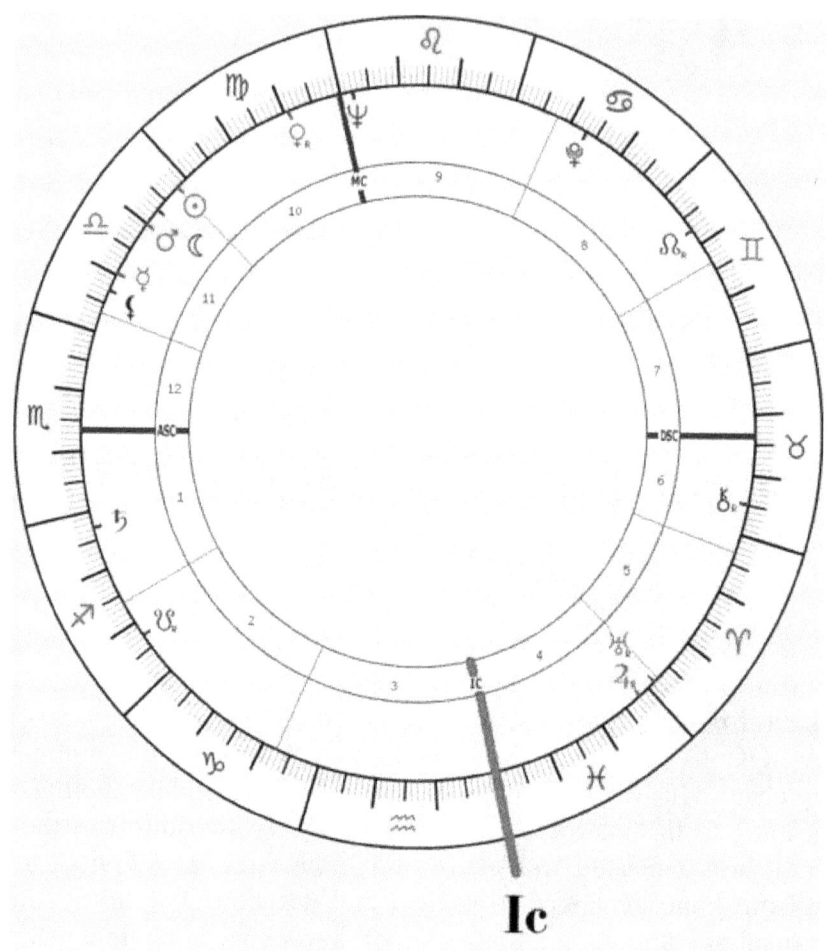

The axis on the wheel.

Coddod, CC BY-SA 4.0 <https://creativecommons.org/licenses/by-sa/4.0>, via Wikimedia Commons
https://commons.wikimedia.org/wiki/File:Imum_Coeli_Bearzot.png

The 12 Houses

1st house
  Zodiac sign: Aries
  Keywords: Health, life, body.
  Correspondences: Eyes, head, life-changing events, and red.
  Ruling planet: Mars - suggesting a strong sense of self and ego-driven decisions.

It can answer questions about yourself, including your body image and physical appearance, mental health, and overall fitness and vitality.

This house is the domain of first impressions, your image, and your appearance. It can signal you'll be ready to make a fresh start after a bad experience. Pay attention to the surrounding information, as the event you'll need to recover from might still happen; it's not an event from the past. It could be an accident or health event you'll struggle to overcome. Besides the new start for yourself, the house can reveal something about your relatives' lives. You may spend time with your grandparents, nieces, nephews, or grandchildren and learn about their personalities.

Mars in this house is weak in Sagittarius and Pisces and strong in Virgo and Gemini.

2nd house

Zodiac sign: Taurus

Keywords: Finances, livelihood, items, movable possessions.

Correspondences: Bright green color, events in professional life, neck, and shoulders.

Ruling planet: Venus - indicating unique values.

It can answer questions about finances, movable possessions (including clothes, vehicles, and other items), and allies (business partners or lawyers).

Due to Taurus's strong influences, the second house is linked to your material possession, income, financial status, and environment. It can refer to an experience you'll receive through your senses or something you'll see, taste, smell, touch, or hear. If you struggle with a self-esteem issue, you'll have a chance to get a confidence boost. You may get a promotion or acknowledgment for your hard work. Or you may be able to afford to buy something you've wanted for a long time. On the other hand, the house can bring bad news about financial losses and a close relative's health.

Venus in this house is strong in Taurus, Libra, and Pisces and weak in Aries, Virgo, and Scorpio.

3rd house

Zodiac sign: Gemini

Keywords: Neighbors, siblings, journey, spiritual exploration.

Correspondences: The nervous system, hands, throat, lungs, breath, social events, and yellow.

Ruling planet: Mercury - highlighting communication in relationships with yourself and others.

It can answer questions about your siblings, other relatives, neighbors, and others in your neighborhood, roommates, and people you have met online. It can reveal information about early education, traveling, and contracts.

Under the chatty Gemini's rule, the third house governs all interactions. In Horary astrology, this signals you'll be actively communicating in person and on mobile devices. Whether this communication occurs in a school, neighborhood, or another place, you'll get your point across efficiently. You may be signing new contracts with recent acquaintances or receiving packages or deals. Sometimes, you'll have to deal with rumors and gossip generated by or related to your family, friends, or community.

Mercury in this house is weak in Sagittarius and Pisces and strong in Gemini and Virgo.

4th house

Zodiac sign: Cancer

Keywords: Building, home, land, parents.

Correspondences: White and silver, events at home or the family, the chest area, and the stomach.

Ruling planet: The Moon - indicating the connection to home.

It can answer questions about your family and parents (more precisely, your father). Or you can gain resolution for issues about immovable possessions (house, land, or other fixed property).

Governed by Cancer, the fourth house represents a good basis for all planetary and sign aspects. You may receive surprising information about your home, security, or privacy. If you have elderly or ill parents or children, you may receive bad news about them. Or your role as a caretaker of your children will be threatened by income loss. You may need a little TLC because you've been too harsh lately. Sometimes, the house will relate to a family member's finances or conflict and provide a possible resolution for putting things to rest.

The Moon in this house is strong in Taurus and Cancer and weak in Scorpio and Capricorn.

5th house

Zodiac sign: Leo

Keywords: Sex, children, game, gambling, please.

Correspondences: Gold, joyful events, the heart, the upper back, and the spine.

Ruling planet: The Sun - linked to the pleasurable side of life.

It can answer questions about your relationships with your children, sentiments about having children, or the childish behavior of others. It can reveal information about romance, sex, hobbies, and gambling.

The fifth house is headed by Leo, the most dramatic sign of the zodiac. It relates to creative and fun experiences. You may get to express your creativity through hidden or existing talents. This house in horary is the sign of colorful experiences to come or possible romance on the horizon. Sometimes, you may receive surprising news about your children (or future children), lovers, and hobbies. The house can relate to your person as someone's child, meaning you'll receive information about your mother and father (possibly about their deaths or finances).

The Sun in this house is strong in Aries and Leo and weak in Libra and Aquarius.

6th house

Zodiac sign: Virgo

Keywords: Illness, injury, litigation, open enemies, servants, and small animals.

Correspondences: The abdominal area, digestive system, spleen, stressful events, and dark green and brown.

Ruling planet: Mercury - suggesting a link to physical and mental health.

It can answer questions about illness, injuries, accidents, health in general, and small animals. It can reveal information about your place of work and relationships with co-workers and hired employees, including those you employ for one-time jobs (like professionals for specific projects in your home).

The sixth house is the center of health, property, and service. Under the communicative Mercury's rule, the house governs professions thriving on schedules, organization, helpfulness, routines, and serving others. If you have relatives or friends working in medicine, the army, or the police among your close acquaintances, the message from this house may be about them. You can expect changes if you have pets and property owned by you or a family member. Or, if you're about to embrace a healthier, natural lifestyle, you may receive guidance about a suitable diet and exercise plan.

Mercury in this house is weak in Gemini and Virgo and strong in Sagittarius and Pisces.

7th house
Zodiac sign: Libra

Keywords: Partners, spouses, marriage.

Correspondences: Light blue and pink, events related to romantic life, the lower back area, kidneys, butt, and skin.

Ruling planet: Venus - linked to romantic and business relationships.

It can answer questions about feelings and bonds in relationships and marriage. You can learn about the intricacies of other partnerships, including business connections and adversaries from your personnel or professional life.

The seventh house represents the home of relationships and connections to other people. This house can bring you news about your romantic or business relationships in horary. You may seal that business deal you've been working on lately or sign a contract with a new client or partner. Changes in your relationship dynamics or marriage (current or previous) may force you to take legal action. Sometimes, it will be about your existing legal matters, including court battles against someone who committed a crime against you or your loved ones.

Venus in this house is weak in Aries, Virgo, and Scorpio and strong in Taurus, Libra, and Pisces.

8th house
Zodiac sign: Scorpio

Keywords: Death, inheritance, debt, fear, illness, and other people's finances.

Correspondences: The hips, reproductive system, deaths, other mournful events, and black.

Ruling planet: Pluto - indicating a strong association with death and sex.

It can answer questions about shared resources you can or will have access to. For example, you can learn about inheritance, grants, tax returns

- and debts you must pay. It can reveal information about your partner's finances and fears about death.

Often called the weak house, the zodiac's eighth house is shrouded in mystery. It governs birth, death, transformation, secretive forces, sex, shared energies, and bonds. You might receive bad news about your or your partner's finances or health or suffer their loss due to death or betrayal. In contrast, the information revealed by this house may be about an upcoming financial benefit. With Pluto's energy comes death, but with death often comes renewal energy like an inheritance to ease your hardship. On the other hand, if you owe someone, they may be ready to collect their dues, which further diminishes your self-worth.

9th house

Zodiac sign: Sagittarius

Keywords: Travel, being abroad, foreign people and experiences, wisdom, teachers, spirituality, and religion.

Correspondences: Purple, events about travel and foreign cultures, the liver, thighs, and legs.

Ruling planet: Jupiter - a powerful link to spirituality and knowledge.

It can answer questions about long-distance relationships and travel plans, especially if these involve foreign lands or cultures. It can provide guidance regarding higher education, learning options, material (including books you can learn from or which university or college to choose), religion, teachers, philosophy, spirituality, and books.

Under the ever-inspired Sagittarius's rule, the ninth house is the embodiment of the open mind. In horary divination, this house opens a world of possibilities. Ensure you consider how it relates to your questions. You can discover new adventures, from travel to foreign languages to education to adopting a new religion or code of conduct. Whatever you do, it's guaranteed you'll stay motivated and optimistic about where your path leads. This house is likened to luck, but you may need to take some risks to attract it. Sometimes, it will be about second-degree family members (including grandchildren and in-laws), professors, or publishers.

Jupiter is weak in Gemini, Virgo, and Capricorn and strong in Cancer, Sagittarius, and Pisces.

10th house

Zodiac sign: Capricorn

Keywords: Career, action, work, reputation, and employers.

Correspondences: Gray and brown, promotions and other positive work events, the joints, skeletal system, and teeth.

Ruling planet: Saturn - suggesting ambition and perseverance.

It can answer questions about your career, property, public image, or your partner's property or image. It can help you explore your relationship with authority figures (including law enforcement and government) and your mother.

The tenth house is particularly institutionalized, not surprising since it's ruled by the natural-born achiever Capricorn. Like its ruling sign, the house shows relevance in structures, tradition, achievements, rules, awards, and discipline. It can be a harbinger of fame, the rise of a public image, or the signal you'll make an authority figure you admire (like your father or boss) proud. This house is linked to your professional life and career, reflecting your effort to present your desired image. Sometimes, it can be associated with an authority figure's health, your health, or your child's health.

Saturn is strong in Libra, Capricorn, and Aquarius and weak in Aries, Cancer, and Leo.

11th house

Zodiac sign: Aquarius

Keywords: Hope, good fortune, wishes, friendships.

Correspondences: Blue, lucky events, the circulatory system, shins, calves, and ankles.

Ruling planet: Uranus - associated with relationships with friends and acquaintances.

It can answer questions about getting along with friends and communities and reveal how to make your hopes and wishes come true. You can learn about forming alliances or whether you should join certain memberships and groups.

The eleventh house governs fortune and wishes in relationships about humanitarian causes, networking, friends, and other social groups. It can show you if you'll be susceptible to rebellion against society's rules or remain the team player you currently are. Ruled by the highly sociable

Aquarius, this house can be about making connections with large groups of people or catering to their desires through technology, social media, or other platforms. You may seek innovative ideas, surprising luck, and eccentric behavior. The house is linked to money you inherit from your mother's side, a close family member's health, and new additions to the family (including through marriage, adoption, or foster care).

12th house

Zodiac sign: Pisces

Keywords: Imprisonment, exile, hidden enemies, large animals, black magic.

Correspondences: The lymphatic system, feet, sudden events, and light green.

Ruling planet: Neptune - Implying that the house is associated with secrets, fears, and mystery.

It can answer questions about hidden, mysterious, or fearsome and clinically sounding places, including prisons, retreats, hospitals, and monasteries. You can get resolutions related to a recent loss, people who secretly want you to fail, large animals, or things you do to undermine yourself.

This house represents the final phase of the process. It's about tying up loose ends and marking endings (in old age and projects). However, it can be about beginnings, the afterlife, dreams, and artistic pursuits. It can be a sign it's time to surrender to the changes brought by the end and await the renewal. Sometimes, this house can denote isolation and hidden or cold places where people usually feel isolated. It doesn't necessarily mean you'll end up in prison, a hospital, or a similar institution. It means you're unaware of a close person's isolated (hidden) intentions.

The Two Axes and Their Four Points

The two axes in the horary chart represent the connection between 4 crucial points of the astrological wheel. These are the Ascendant and the Descendant (connected with the AC-DC axis), the Imum Coeli, and the Midheaven (linked with the IC-MC axis).

The Ascendant (AC) and the Descendant (DC) are at opposite ends of a horary chart. The former lies at the beginning of the first house, while the latter is positioned at the cusp of the seventh house. The AC-DC axis ties two contradictory forces or aspects of life together.

At the verge of the House of Self, the Ascendant is the domain of personal traits and perceptions. It showcases qualities you can objectively see and accept in yourself. Most people are proud of these and happy to show them off. The AC represents the center of a person's planetary characteristics and is often driven by the person's ego. Due to this, it will always be a constructed image. How you wear your hair, dress, makeup, how you hold your body, and your facial expressions reflect this desire to show a particular picture. While this may make people think they know who you are, they only get what you want to show them. It's like a mask of traits you believe will make you more desirable and accepted.

The Descendant shows the other side of the story. It is the cusp of the 7th house of relationships and hidden qualities. The DC is linked to what lies in the shadow of your perfectly constructed image - the traits you dislike about yourself and refuse to accept. Many people have characteristics they ignore, repress, or disassociate from, just to conform to their relationships. The latter is the theme of the 7th house and is a massive driving force shaping people's lives. However, no matter how irritated by the traits, you refuse to acknowledge them and are still drawn to them. Mostly you'll be attracted to people with these characteristics. The culprit is the AC-DC axis. In horary astrology, this axis reminds you of connections you can't deny. As your relationship deepens, everybody you meet during the rule of the 7th house will notice your true self even if you can't. You can unveil your shadow self by studying your relationships with others and observing your behavior through other people's perspectives. Working with the horary chart by asking questions about your relationships can help you realize your true self.

The role of the AC-DC axis is to create the balance necessary for your overall well-being. The 1st house isn't only about appearance; it's also about physical and mental health. Your health enormously impacts your ability to establish good relationships and vice versa. You inevitably attract people who are more like your descendant and create relationships with them, improving your quality of life. By bringing these two aspects together, elevate yourself and grow into someone who doesn't rely on others for acceptance but can stay true to yourself.

As the cusp of the 4th house, the Imum Coeli is associated with family, home, and other foundational aspects of life. If you are around your IC on your horary chart, you can expect to see the ruling planet's effect on your environment. You'll see them in your home, those your share your environment with, and your feelings about your living arrangements. The

IC affects how you feel about a place you've just moved into, whether you're ready to settle in one place or what you consider home. It can affect your perception of your past environment - how you grew up, your experience in your environment, and much more.

The Midheaven (MC) is the cusp of the 10th astrological house. It showcases your sentiments and thoughts about your career, reputation, and social standing. The MC is responsible for the impression you leave on people who haven't met you but have heard about your accomplishments. It's infused with the traits of the ruling planet, allowing these to seep into your professional and public profiles. Different aspects of the ruling matters can affect your professional life, effectively including other people's opinions about you in your work environment. You typically won't be aware of this influence unless you look into the IC-MC connection on the horary chart. In horary, the IC-MC axis represents the link between home and work - two interconnected aspects balancing your life. Together, they represent your legacy, left by the ancestors who worked very hard for their achievements. These can be long-lost ancestors or even your parents. In some cases, the linkage is related to you as a parent.

Chapter 5: Main Characteristics of the Planets

The characteristics of planets in horary astrology are often confusing for beginners. However, understanding and recognizing the significance of each can go a long way toward improving your predictive accuracy. Every planet has its special meaning and effects when it appears in a chart, from Mars representing strength and ambition to Saturn representing responsibility and tradition. Navigating these different qualities is key to accurately analyzing how the planetary movement will affect someone's life. This chapter explains each planet's significance, offering insight into their meaning in practice and how to understand their movements and how they interact with each other.

Planets and Their Significance in Horary Astrology

Sun

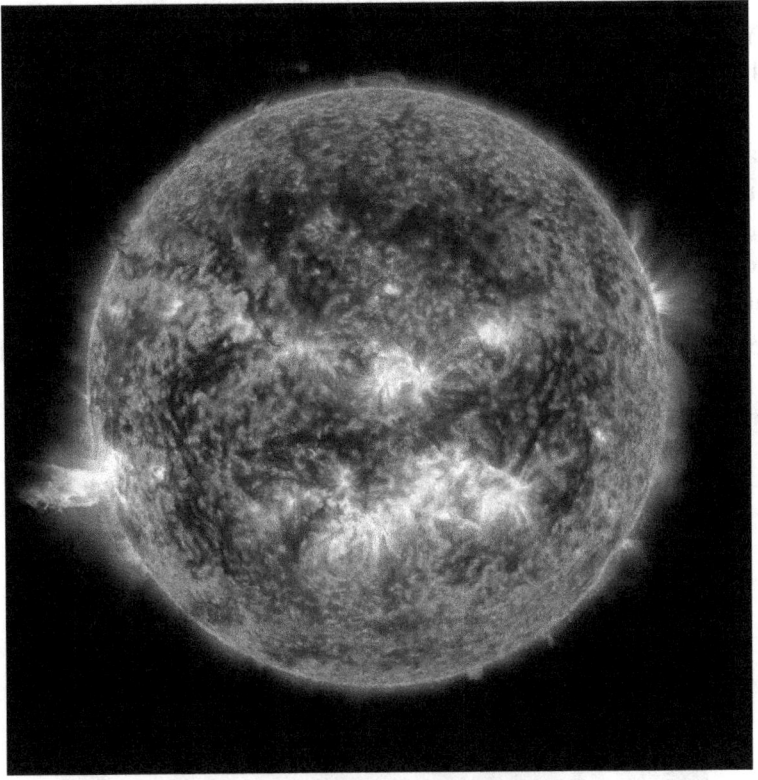

The sun plays a pivotal role in horary astrology.
NASA Goddard Space Flight Center, ATTRIBUTION 2.0 GENERIC, CC BY 2.0
<https://creativecommons.org/licenses/by/2.0/>
https://www.flickr.com/photos/gsfc/9103296900

The Sun is one of the most important planets in a chart in horary astrology. It represents the querent, their soul journey, and their power or authority. The Sun can represent achievement, success, and recognition, which often positively influences a question regarding those aspects. Symbolically, it indicates wealth, honor, and fame due to hard work and dedication. The sun's impact in horary astrology signifies luck or favorability for querent's actions.

Meaning and Interpretation of the Sun in Horary Astrology

The Sun is interpreted as a signifier of leadership qualities and self-assertiveness. It can indicate taking control of your life and making decisions independently or with confidence. The Sun in a chart can mean energy is abundant, so new projects undertaken by the querent could succeed with effort. Whether taking on a business venture or starting something personal, like building a family home, the Sun is important in giving hope for success in these pursuits.

The sign under which the Sun falls will show how best to take advantage of its power during a situation. For instance, if the Sun is in Aries, it might symbolize entering into bold actions with an assurance that luck will favor them regardless of the obstacles. In contrast, if the Sun is in Capricorn, it could suggest working hard toward achieving goals with meticulous planning and persistence, but within realistic limits.

Overall, through horary astrology, the Sun gives an understanding of how a person should approach life's challenges with optimism while staying mindful.

Moon

The moon represents changing moods and the concept of stability in horary.
https://www.pexels.com/photo/photo-of-moon-47367/

The Moon is associated with the ocean, emotions, feelings, and femininity. It is a symbol of fluidity, transformation, and movement. In horary astrology, it represents changing moods and reassurance or stability. It reflects a person's inner world, hidden thoughts and desires, and past influences and patterns still affecting the present. The Moon has been connected to many goddesses, such as Hecate, Diana, and Artemis, who symbolize fertility, growth, and abundance. The Moon is closely tied to motherly love, empathy, and intuition. It moves quickly between the points of its orbit while reflecting light from the Sun onto the Earth.

Meaning and Interpretation of the Moon in Horary Astrology

The Moon is a significator for the querent's feelings, thoughts, desires, and emotions. It reflects how a person feels at the present moment and acts as an indicator of future events. The Moon can signify a person's moods, attitude toward life, and level of contentment. Horary astrology can represent relationships, changes, or transitions that will occur soon. Depending on its placement in the chart, it might point to financial gain or loss. Furthermore, when considering a relationship (business or romantic), both parties are represented by two different Moons depending on which house they occupy.

The South Node in Horary Astrology

The South Node of the Moon signifies the querent's past influences and patterns. It reflects how they felt in the past, including their childhood experiences and family relationships. The South Node can indicate things holding them back, like outdated beliefs or habits no longer serving them, and it points to people from the past. When interpreting the South Node in horary astrology, looking at its placement in relation to other planets and determining which areas of life it affects is critical.

The North Node in Horary Astrology

The North Node of the Moon represents the querent's current direction, goals, and desires. It points to the areas of life where a person is growing and evolving. The North Node is a guiding light, showing the querent's true potential and what they can achieve. This node reflects the querent's relationship with their higher self, including spiritual guidance or insight through interpreting it in a horary chart.

The Moon is significant in horary astrology as it indicates someone's feelings, emotions, and thoughts. It relates to changes occurring within a person and their relationships and transitions soon taking place in life.

Mercury

Mercury in horary astrology is crucial since it is associated with communication, commerce, and travel. The meaning and purpose of Mercury in horary astrology is to understand how a person's thoughts, words, and actions will be affected by their environment.

Mercury is the messenger of the gods.
https://pixabay.com/es/illustrations/mercurio-planeta-espacio-universo-5556108/

Meaning and Interpretation of Mercury in Horary Astrology

In horary astrology, Mercury is known as the Messenger of the gods. It symbolizes intellect, reason, wit, understanding, and creativity. Its main purpose is to provide insight into a person's mental state to manage emotions and behavior better. It helps develop self-awareness to make sound decisions based on the best interests rather than impulse or emotion.

Mercury's meaning and interpretation in horary astrology go beyond communication-related matters. It brings change and transformation through its symbolism of ideas and movement. This planet drives ambition and can help individuals overcome obstacles or start new projects. It teaches thinking outside the box and encourages exploring different perspectives of a situation or problem. Furthermore, its influence encourages people to take action, helping them to act on their ideas quickly instead of waiting too long or getting caught up in analysis paralysis.

Venus

Venus represents the feminine principle and can offer insight into the core needs of relationships. Venus represents beauty, harmony, love, money, friendship, and partnerships. The placement of Venus in a chart can reveal a lot about an individual's preferences and overall attitude.

Venus represents values and desires.
https://pixabay.com/es/illustrations/venus-planeta-espacio-universo-5556107/

Meaning and Interpretation of Venus in Horary Astrology

Venus indicates the querent's values and desires and how they seek them out in horary astrology. It shows the curiosities they possess, making them unique. Moreover, it indicates relationships they will likely attract or become involved in. Are they fleeting or long-term? Do they bring joy or sorrow?

Venus symbolizes creativity, gracefulness, balance, and abundance. It stands for fertility in its traditional sense (giving birth) and less literal sense (creating art). Therefore, Venus's appearance in a chart suggests potential success and reward through creative expression or ventures.

The interpretation of Venus in horary astrology depends on what part of its symbolism resonates with the querent's life at the moment. Suppose another point in the chart indicates a lack of harmony or interpersonal conflict. In that case, it suggests the querent should cultivate more balance in their relationships. It could be through strengthening the bonds with others similarly interested in harmony and peacekeeping efforts. On the other hand, if money is an issue, then Venus could indicate that now might be a good time to take action toward earning additional income or making investments with steady returns over time.

Mars

Mars is often called the "Lesser Malefic" in horary astrology. It symbolizes action, energy, and assertiveness. Its aspects can directly bring results and can often create accidents or spur quarrels and injuries. Due to its fiery nature, it is a powerful force of transformation, pushing the querent forward toward their goals yet creating obstacles along the way. Mars symbolizes physical effort, courage, ambition, and taking risks to succeed. It encourages people to face their fears while maintaining determination and focusing on the desired outcome.

Mars represents strength and passion.
https://pixabay.com/es/illustrations/marte-espacio-planeta-planetas-7723123/

Meaning and Interpretation of Mars in Horary Astrology

Mars is associated with masculine energy and embodies strength, power, passion, and aggression, positively or negatively. For example, regarding love, if someone is looking for a new romantic partner, they must have the courage to make themselves visible; otherwise, nothing will happen. Mars represents this part of people that helps them overcome inhibitions or doubts so they can confidently move forward.

It is necessary to recognize that the planet is about taking decisive action using willpower and perseverance to reach objectives and understand Mars's horary purpose. It enables a person to break through difficulties but warns against being reckless or careless since it has a destructive side, which could lead to dangerous consequences. Ultimately it teaches how channeling energy into productive means can help bring forth positive outcomes, even in difficult situations!

Jupiter

In horary astrology, Jupiter is called the *Greater Benefic* and represents luck, opportunity, growth, long journeys, higher education, and prophecy. Jupiter reflects querent's ambitions, wishes, and desires and relates to long-term prospects or opportunities likely to benefit them. In horary astrology, it can indicate the outcome of an event or situation or give insight into a possible future development.

Jupiter represents wealth and success.
https://pixabay.com/es/photos/j%c3%bapiter-planeta-espacio-6938302/

Meaning and Interpretation of Jupiter in Horary Astrology

The symbolism associated with Jupiter includes material wealth (including money) and success through hard work. In horary astrology, Jupiter denotes honor, respect, and prosperity. It represents truthfulness and justice but can be excessive when too strong or unbalanced due to unfavorable aspects from other planets.

Jupiter is associated with optimism and hope in horary astrology. It can indicate potential good fortune and abundance or a period of good luck. However, it can represent bad judgment, leading to overindulgence and wastefulness if not managed properly. Aspects of Jupiter can suggest the need for individuals to take risks or become more adventurous to achieve their goals.

Jupiter's influence on a chart provides insight into how an individual can approach life's opportunities and challenges. Its placement indicates their luck and ability to make wise decisions with difficult choices. A strong Jupiter position suggests that an individual will likely be blessed with luck, whereas a weak placement could indicate being more cautious to reap the rewards.

Overall, Jupiter represents the ability of individuals to recognize and use good fortune when presented. It encourages taking risks and trusting that decisions will lead to prosperity. Understanding its symbolism, meaning, and interpretation can help align people's actions with potential success.

Saturn

Saturn is the greater malefic in horary astrology and has a powerful influence over the chart. It rules burdens, karmic lessons, ambitions, debts, delays, poverty, obstacles, and death. Traditional texts associated it with fathers, old people, and various restrictions. It symbolizes hard work, discipline, and perseverance in pursuit of goals. When Saturn is prominent in a chart, it can indicate struggles and difficulties that must be overcome before real progress can be made.

Saturn represents ambition and dedication.
https://pixabay.com/es/illustrations/saturno-planeta-espacio-universo-5550180/

Meaning and Interpretation of Saturn in Horary Astrology

Saturn symbolizes heavy burdens that must be met through dedication and hard work in horary astrology. It symbolizes ambition and dedication to long-term projects or goals. As the Greater Malefic, it represents setbacks or hardships to achieving ambitions. However difficult these times might be, they can teach valuable lessons if individuals embrace them with courage and resilience. Saturn reflects the capacity for delayed gratification, an important quality when planning projects or working toward long-term goals.

The interpretation of Saturn in a chart depends on its dignity (exaltation or detriment) and whether angular, cadent, or intercepted within the chart wheel. Saturn indicates obstacles that must be overcome, but this will depend on other aspects within the chart. If other planets are helping bring success, then these challenges will not seem so daunting and will eventually lead to success. If no aspects from other planets indicate success, then these difficulties could become more serious over time, leading to delays or even failure.

When Saturn is well placed within a chart, it can indicate good things coming from hard work or effort put into long-term projects, like building a business or raising a family. Despite setbacks, these long-term investments will eventually lead to great rewards if the individual stays focused on their goal throughout the challenges encountered on this journey. If Saturn is poorly placed, it can suggest obstacles or hardships might hinder efforts, leading to delays or complete failure. Caution should be exercised when embarking upon new ventures unless they have strong indications from other planets that success will ensue despite adversity. Finally, when interpreting Saturn, remember "no pain, no gain." Often-encountered obstacles teach many valuable lessons if people confront them with courage and resilience.

Uranus

Uranus's position holds great significance in horary astrology, symbolizing a wide range of meanings and interpretations when in various houses or aspects. For a deeper understanding, delving into Uranus's complex and multifaceted nature and how it affects the horary chart as a whole is essential.

Uranus represents revolution.
https://pixabay.com/es/illustrations/urano-planeta-espacio-5559037/

Uranus, the seventh planet from the Sun, holds a unique position in astrology as it is renowned for its association with sudden changes, revolution, and upheaval. Known as the planet of awakening, Uranus symbolizes the emergence of new ideas, inventive thinking, and breaking free from established norms. Its influence is evident in technology, science, and societal revolution realms. Uranus represents the urge for individual freedom, intellectual independence, and breaking the shackles of tradition and conventionality.

Meaning and Interpretation of Uranus in Horary Astrology

In horary astrology, the position of Uranus becomes especially significant when deciphering a horary chart or having a snapshot of the heavens at the specific moment when the astrologer studies the querent's question. The chart is analyzed to obtain answers and insights into the individual's doubts and queries about their life.

Depending on the house in which Uranus resides in the horary chart, the planet's influence could have various implications for the querent. For instance, in the first house, Uranus indicates that the querent is experiencing a radical change in their personality or identity. On the other hand, if found in the sixth house, Uranus could suggest an unexpected shift in the person's work or health conditions.

Additionally, the aspects Uranus forms with other planets in the horary chart can further intensify or mitigate its influence. For example, a harmonious aspect between Uranus and Venus may symbolize sudden positive relationship changes or creativity. A challenging aspect between Uranus and Saturn could imply resistance to change or a clash between the old and the new.

One of the fascinating dimensions of Uranus in horary astrology is its link to unpredictability and surprises. The energy of Uranus brings a hint of chaos, prompting the querent to embrace change and adapt to new, unexpected circumstances. The presence of Uranus in a horary chart suggests that standard methods of inquiry and established thought patterns may not be sufficient to resolve the issue. Alternatively, it could hint at a ground-breaking solution or innovative approach the querent has not yet considered.

Furthermore, Uranus is known to have a strong connection with groups, social organizations, and humanitarian causes. Therefore, its position in a horary chart could shed light on the querent's relationship with their community, participation in social activism, or collaboration with like-minded individuals.

Neptune

Existing at the furthest reaches of the solar system, Neptune is revered as the supreme ruler of dreams, intuition, imagination, art, and spiritual enlightenment. It represents mysterious forces and the elusive realm of the subconscious, often leading to profound insights and hidden truths. In this context, the meaning and interpretation of Neptune in horary astrology elucidate its notable impact on the outcome of inquiries and the lives of individuals.

Neptune represents spiritual wisdom and creative abilities.
https://pixabay.com/es/photos/neptuno-planeta-sistema-solar-67537/

Meaning and Interpretation of Neptune in Horary Astrology

Neptune can be an enriching and challenging presence in an astrological chart, depending on its placement and the aspects it forms with other planets. When Neptune occupies a prominent position, it bestows individuals with heightened intuition, creative abilities, and spiritual wisdom. These people are often deeply connected with mysticism and the arts and are considered artistically and spiritually gifted. So, Neptune stands out as a powerful force for inspiration, artistic expression, and spiritual enlightenment.

However, Neptune has the potential to challenge and bewilder, as its placement in a chart may indicate deception, confusion, or illusion. Negatively, it can lead an individual to experience uncertainty and disorientation in dealing with reality. It may manifest as fantasies, delusions, or even escapism in its bearer. The ethereal nature of Neptune signifies a vulnerability to addictive behavior, substance abuse, and other ungrounded pursuits.

For instance, inquiring about a querent's future in a horary chart, if Neptune is positioned in the Third House, which symbolizes communication, intellect, and the immediate environment, it could imply a period of confusion, misunderstandings, or false information. On the other hand, this placement may grant them exceptional creative thinking or a surge of inspiration in their intellectual and communicative endeavors.

The interpretation of Neptune in a horary chart depends on the question and the sign and house it occupies. For example, if a querent asks about their romantic prospects and Neptune is present in the Seventh House, representing partnerships, it could suggest their future relationships may be filled with illusions, dreams, and idealization. Understanding the varied aspects of Neptune in a horary chart ultimately allows the astrologer to discern the role Neptune plays, shaping the reading and guiding the individual accordingly.

Pluto

Pluto represents transformation, power, renewal, and deep, hidden secrets in horary astrology. As a ruling planet in horary charts, Pluto is a harbinger of profound revelations or radical changes that may take place in the native's life, depending on its position and aspects with other planetary bodies. As the furthest-known celestial body in the solar system, Pluto's influence is considered mysterious and enigmatic, often revealing truths lying beneath the surface or shedding light on the darker aspects of an individual's subconscious.

Pluto represents transformation.
https://pixabay.com/es/photos/plut%c3%b3n-planeta-espacio-astronom%c3%ada-6595130/

Meaning and Interpretation of Pluto in Horary Astrology

Pluto's placement in horary astrology adds a significant layer of depth and meaning to a horary question. Interpreting a horary chart, an astrologer will scrutinize Pluto's location within the zodiac sign, house, and the aspects with other planets to unveil its potential influence on the querent's life circumstances.

When Pluto is prominently featured in a horary chart, it might indicate the question requires truth-seeking, transformation, or confronting and overcoming something deeply buried within the querent. Essentially, Pluto's presence in the astrological chart points toward a deep-seated issue or challenge the individual must confront and surmount to embark on a new path toward spiritual growth and personal evolution.

For instance, if Pluto is situated in the third house of the horary chart, which corresponds to communication, intellectual pursuits, and the local environment, an astrologer may deduce that the question involves a significant change or challenges related to these areas. The querent may be in a situation where they must express their thoughts or engage in difficult conversations to bring about the necessary transformations.

The aspects formed by Pluto in a horary chart shed light on the potential outcomes and challenges faced by the querent. Notably, Pluto's aspects with powerful planets like Saturn can suggest the person may have to navigate through obstacles or restrictions to reach their desired goal.

Similarly, a harmonious aspect between Pluto and Venus might hint that a transformative experience in the realms of love, relationships, or personal values could profoundly impact the querent's life. On the other hand, if Pluto has challenging aspects, it could indicate potential disruptions, upheavals, or events that test the individual's strength and resilience.

Chapter 6: Planetary Dignities and Joys

Have you heard of horary astrology and wondered what it is all about? One of the initial steps in understanding horary charts is comprehending the concept of the dignities and joys of planets. This critical concept recognizes the power, authority, or dignity of a planet to the chart being studied. When applying this principle, the analysis focuses on the traditional rulership qualities associated with each planet, deciphering Ptolemy's chart and calculating the same signs of dignity or strength that exist. This magnification of each planet's ability allows an astrologer to gauge an individual's joys and their respective growth position within the chart. This analysis can suggest areas where an individual succeeds or struggles, giving insight into their true potential for success. Understanding the planet's dignities and joys can be one of the most complex aspects of horary astrology - but it can prove highly rewarding for those pursuing this path.

What Are Dignities?

In horary astrology, dignities refer to the specific positions of a celestial body in the sky. In particular, they determine how well a planet is placed in a sign. Dignities factor into many aspects of horary astrology, like the strength of an individual's character or destiny and their place in the world. The term "dignity" comes from the Latin *dignus*, meaning "possessing worth."

There are five traditional dignities in horary astrology: domicile (the sign a planet is most powerful in), exaltation (the sign where it is second-most strong), detriment (the weakest position for a planet), fall (the second weakest), and triplicity (to do with elements). Knowing each planet's dignities is important because it helps create a clear picture of how each function within the chart and their influence on the outcome. For example, suppose a planet is in its domicile or exaltation. In that case, it will be stronger than in its detriment or fall.

Knowing these dignities allows for interpreting different planetary combinations more accurately. For example, when two planets are conjunct in a chart, you can determine which is more likely to take precedence by looking at their respective dignities. If one has strong dignity and the other weak, the stronger one will likely dominate the weaker one. It helps distinguish between positive and negative outcomes for certain questions or situations.

What Are Joys?

The term "joys" in astrology refers to the specific houses associated with each of the seven traditional planets. Each planet is assigned to a particular house. A planet is said to be "rejoicing" when it is in its "joys," as explained below.

In other words, the planet is at its strongest influence when placed in the corresponding house.

Knowing the planet's joys in horary astrology can be helpful because they provide insight into how different planetary energies manifest within a chart. For example, if Jupiter were placed in the 11th house, luck and good fortune would likely come your way, as Jupiter's joy lies in this house. Conversely, Saturn would bring feelings of restriction or limitation if placed in its joy (the 12th house). Therefore, understanding the joys allows an astrologer to quickly identify which energies will likely be dominant at any given time and interpret their influence on an individual's life.

The Joys of Planets

Planet	Joys
Sun	9th House
Moon	3rd House
Mercury	1st House
Venus	5th House
Mars	6th House
Jupiter	11th House
Saturn	12th House

Ptolemy's Chart on Essential Dignities

Ptolemy, a renowned astronomer, mathematician, and astrologer in the 2nd century CE, developed a chart illustrating the dignities and rulership of the celestial bodies. This chart represents the complex dynamics and correspondences between the planets, zodiac signs, and astrology houses, enabling astrologers to make sense of the myriad influences in the cosmos.

A Table of the Essential Dignities of the PLANETS according to Ptolemy

Sign	Houses of the Planets	Exaltation	Triplicity of Planets D	Triplicity of Planets N	The Terms of the Planets					The Faces of the Planets			Detriment	Fall
♈	♂ D	☉ 19	☉	♃	♃ 6	♀ 14	☿ 21	♂ 26	♄ 30	♂ 10	☉ 20	♀ 30	♀	♄
♉	♀ N	☽ 3	♀	☽	♀ 8	☿ 15	♃ 22	♄ 26	♂ 30	☿ 10	☽ 20	♄ 30	♂	
♊	☿ D	☊ 3	♄	☿	☿ 7	♃ 14	♀ 21	♄ 25	♂ 30	♃ 10	♂ 20	☉ 30	♃	
♋	☽ D/N	♃ 15	♂	♂	♂ 6	♃ 13	☿ 20	♀ 27	♄ 30	♀ 10	☿ 20	☽ 30	♄	♂
♌	☉ D/N		☉	♃	♄ 6	☿ 13	♀ 19	♃ 25	♂ 30	♄ 10	♃ 20	♂ 30	♄	
♍	☿ N	☿ 15	♀	☽	☿ 7	♀ 13	♃ 18	♄ 24	♂ 30	☉ 10	♀ 20	☿ 30	♃	♀
♎	♀ D	♄ 21	♄	☿	♄ 6	♀ 11	♃ 19	☿ 24	♂ 30	☽ 10	♄ 20	♃ 30	♂	☉
♏	♂ N		♂	♂	♂ 6	♃ 14	♀ 21	☿ 27	♄ 30	♂ 10	☉ 20	♀ 30	♀	☽
♐	♃ D	☋ 3	☉	♃	♃ 8	♀ 14	☿ 19	♄ 25	♂ 30	☿ 10	☽ 20	♄ 30	☿	
♑	♄ N	♂ 28	♀	☽	♀ 6	☿ 12	♃ 19	♂ 25	♄ 30	♃ 10	♂ 20	☉ 30	☽	♃
♒	♄ D		♄	☿	♄ 6	☿ 12	♀ 20	♃ 25	♂ 30	♀ 10	☿ 20	☽ 30	☉	
♓	♃ N	♀ 27	♂	♂	♀ 8	♃ 14	☿ 20	♂ 26	♄ 30	♄ 10	♃ 20	♂ 30	☿	☿

https://astrology8.livejournal.com/1513.html

The rows in Ptolemy's Chart of Dignities display a comprehensive understanding of each planet's roles and influences over the zodiac signs. This chart is based on the ancient astrological system of dignities and debilities. It presents a hierarchical order of planetary influences on each zodiac sign, determining their strength, weakness, or level of affinity with other celestial bodies.

The first column of Ptolemy's Chart of Dignities enumerates the twelve zodiac signs, starting with Aries and ending with Pisces. Each sign has unique characteristics, qualities, and symbolic meanings that directly influence the lives and personalities of those born under them.

The second column of the chart, known as the rulers of the signs, lists the traditional planetary rulers associated with each zodiac sign. These rulers are considered the planets with natural "houses" or "homes" within the signs they rule. For example, Mars rules Aries and Scorpio, making these signs its natural domain. A planet within its own sign has a strong influence, resulting in its qualities flourishing.

The third column reveals where each planet is considered exalted and the specific degree of exaltation. Exaltation is a powerful and fortunate position for a planet, signifying its highest potential of expression and influence within the sign, often bringing prosperity and success. For instance, the Sun is exalted in Aries at the 19th degree. This degree is particularly potent, but generally, the entire sign confers a heightened dignity to the exalted planet.

The planetary rulership of triplicities - the groups of three signs sharing the same basic nature – fire, earth, air, and water- are represented in the fourth column. Here, you can observe how the fire triplicity of Aries, Leo, and Sagittarius repeats itself. Each triplicity ruler bestows its elemental qualities on the corresponding signs, further empowering and shaping them.

The fifth column unveils the specific degrees where rulership by term, known as bound rulership, occurs. This scheme divides each sign into five unequal segments, with each planet ruling a specific degree range. For example, Jupiter rules the first six degrees of Aries, signifying that Jupiter has some influence within this degree range.

The sixth column of Ptolemy's chart represents the rulership by face, known as decanates. It breaks down each zodiac sign into three distinct 10-degree segments, each ruled by a specific planet. For instance, in Aries, Mars rules the first 10 degrees (0°00' - 9°59'), the Sun rules the next 10 degrees (10°00' - 19°59'), and a different planet governs the third 10 degrees. This adds depth to understanding how planets influence zodiac signs within specific degree ranges. It helps astrologers interpret specific degrees in a chart, providing a more detailed analysis of an individual's planetary placements.

The seventh column focuses on the detriment concept, occurring when a planet is in a sign opposite the one it rules. This placement is considered unfavorable because the planet is at a disadvantage, far from its natural home. Consequently, the characteristics associated with the planet are often weakened or obstructed. Each planet in Ptolemy's chart, except for the Sun and Moon, has two signs of detriment, one to the opposite of each of its two ruling signs.

The eighth column describes a planet's fall, a situation where a planet is located opposite to the sign of its exaltation. When a planet is in exaltation, it is at its highest period of expression and power. It is in a weakened state when it is in the opposing sign or fall. In these scenarios, the positive qualities of the planet are diminished, and astrologers could interpret it as a challenging or unfavorable influence in a chart. Like the concept of exaltation, each planet has only one sign for exaltation and fall.

Planets and Their Dignities and Joy

Sun

The Sun's dignities and joys, as derived from Ptolemy's chart, hold significant importance in understanding the influence of celestial bodies on our personalities and lives in astrology. The chart meticulously analyzes the Sun's influence in various astrological signs and houses, indicating specific qualities it possesses and the respective strengths in different placements. Exploring each facet of these complex concepts is crucial to deeply grasping what the Sun's dignities and joys convey.

The Sun's dignities reflect its inherent power, prestige, and influence in different astrological signs. It refers to the relationship between the Sun and certain signs enhancing or diminishing its potency. There are four hierarchical levels of dignities: domiciles or rulership, exaltation, triplicity, and term or bounds. Each level signifies a particular degree of authority the Sun possesses in different placements.

The Sun is the dominant and natural ruler of the zodiac sign of Leo. It asserts a direct and tremendous influence on the qualities of this fiery sign. Leos, in turn, are governed by energizing, warm, and confident characteristics associated with the Sun.

Aries is the exaltation sign for the Sun, considered in its highest potency. In this placement, the Sun demonstrates a powerful and jubilant expression of its traits, rendering Aries individuals determined, enthusiastic, and charismatic.

The Sun rules the fire triplicity, including Aries, Leo, and Sagittarius. Consequently, individuals born under these signs exhibit pronounced characteristics of ambition, passion, and self-motivation that the Sun embodies.

In Ptolemy's chart, there are specific degrees within astrological signs wherein the Sun is considered to have mild authority. Although not remarkably influential, these placements reflect minute control over the person's characteristics and life events.

In addition to dignities, the Sun's joy is in a specific house of the astrological chart - the 9th House. This house represents philosophy, religion, higher education, foreign travel, and broader perceptions. Since the Sun is universally acknowledged as the celestial symbol of vitality, consciousness, and self-expression, its association with the 9th house reflects the joy of expanding intellectual horizons, discovering new experiences, and seeking the truth.

Moon

The Moon, one of the seven classical planets in traditional astrology, has its dignities and joy giving deeper insights into its impact on an individual's life.

In the Ptolemy chart, the Moon's dignities are categorized into different levels; essential and accidental. Essential dignity refers to the positions where the Moon can express itself most powerfully without being hindered by other astrological factors. These positions are known as Rulership, where a planet is considered most at home to express itself most effectively. For the Moon, this position is in the zodiac sign of Cancer, where it is the natural ruler. The Moon can fully express its nurturing, intuitive, and emotional side, bringing strong comfort, security, and sensitivity to the individual's life.

In the Ptolemy chart, the Moon is exalted in the sign of Taurus, allowing the individual to tap into its supportive, grounding, and productive qualities. With the Moon in this position, people can use its steady, dependable energy to lay the grounds for solid relationships and living foundations.

On the other hand, accidental dignity refers to the contextual factors helping improve the Moon's influence, like its placement in specific houses within a person's birth chart. A planet's Joy indicates the position where it performs best, and for the Moon, this is the third house of communication, siblings, and the local environment. This association with the third house is interesting, as the third house corresponds to a person's life strategy and highlights the Moon's connection with the emotional aspects of communication and relationships with the local community.

Mercury

In Ptolemy's chart, the essential dignities of Mercury are highlighted to showcase the planetary characteristics and strengths, depending on the various positions within the zodiac signs. Ptolemy's chart reveals the detailed dignities and the joy of Mercury to understand its overall astrological significance better. Mercury's essential dignities are classified into five categories: domicile, exaltation, triplicity, term, and face (or decan).

Mercury's domicile is in the mutable air signs of Gemini and Virgo. Mercury displays its full potential when residing in these zodiac signs enabling individuals to manifest better communication skills, curiosity, adaptability, and analytical thinking. Mercury is at ease in its domicile, and people with this placement can effectively utilize its energies.

Mercury is exalted in the sign of Virgo, meaning Mercury has an especially powerful expression in Virgo than in other positions. In Virgo, Mercury enjoys the benefits of its domicile and gets an extra boost in strength. It enhances intellectual abilities, better use of logical reasoning, and a more practical and organized approach to life.

The term "triplicity" describes the classical division of the twelve zodiac signs into three groups of the four elements of fire, earth, air, and water. This classification considers Mercury, the ruler of the air triplicity, including the air signs of Gemini, Libra, and Aquarius. Mercury's communicative, social, and intellectual traits are emphasized in these signs. They manifest as the ability to adapt to various social settings swiftly, driving individuals with this placement to become more influential in their environment.

As per Ptolemy's chart, Mercury has rulership in specific terms across all twelve signs, allowing enhanced expression of its energies during certain degrees of each sign. Depending on their birth chart, these specific degrees can modify how Mercury's influence is felt individually.

Next is Face or Decan. The signs are divided into three decans or faces, each consisting of 10 degrees. Mercury is the ruler of the first decan of Gemini and Virgo to heighten its influence and abilities in these signs. Those born with Mercury in these decans could find stronger analytical, perceptive, and communicative talents, resulting in more significant expression of Mercury's energies in their lives.

Mercury joy is in the first house – a position known as the "helm" or "ascendant." Mercury's residence in the first house reinforces personal identity and expression, allowing individuals to adeptly demonstrate their intellectual and communicative abilities. Those with Mercury in the first house can have a natural ease when interacting with others, exchanging ideas, and asserting their perspective.

Venus

Venus's dignities are primarily based on the planet's position within specific zodiac signs, ruling over two signs: Taurus and Libra. Venus is considered in its domicile when placed in these signs, meaning its natural characteristics are enhanced and strengthened. In Taurus, Venus influences sensual and material desires, cultivating a love of beauty, comfort, and stability. In Libra, Venus's signature focuses more on partnership, balance, and fairness, encouraging diplomacy and harmonious relationships.

Besides its domicile, Venus has a significant relationship with another astrological configuration: exaltation. It occurs when Venus is in Pisces, elevating its natural characteristics to their highest potential. In this placement, the planet's energies reflect an unconditional, spiritual love and compassion, transcending the material realm and fostering deeper empathy and understanding.

Conversely, Venus experiences detriment when positioned in Mars-ruled signs, Aries and Scorpio. In these placements, the planet's natural disposition is weakened, resulting in a more challenging expression of love, beauty, and harmony. Individuals with Venus in Aries or Scorpio might find it harder to express tenderness and placidity, leading to potential tensions in relationships, emotional volatility, or problems with self-worth.

Furthermore, Venus experiences its fall in Virgo, revealing the planet's weakest expression. In this meticulous earth sign, Virgo's analytical and critical nature dampens Venus's natural affinity for love, beauty, and harmony. As a result, individuals with Venus in Virgo might struggle to accept and express love in its purest form, often becoming overly critical of themselves and others.

Beyond dignities, Ptolemy's astrology describes the concept of Venus's joy, which occurs when Venus is placed in the fifth house of the birth chart. Here, Venus's association with love, beauty, creativity, and pleasure is allowed to fully manifest and flourish, leading to a natural inclination toward artistic expression, romantic relationships, and personal enjoyment. This placement is considered auspicious, as Venus's energies align harmoniously with the fifth house's emphasis on self-expression and joyful experiences.

Mars

According to Ptolemy's chart, Mars, known as the red planet and the fourth planet from the Sun, holds significant astrological importance. Mars has particular dignities, which determine its power and effectiveness in the astrological chart. The primary dignity of Mars is its rulership and exaltation in the signs of Aries, Scorpio, and Capricorn. Mars is most potent and influential when it is in Aries or Scorpio, while Mars in Capricorn is at its peak effectiveness. In these positions, Mars expresses its natural qualities of assertiveness, courage, aggression, and competitiveness with greater ease, positively impacting individuals born under these signs.

On the other hand, Mars has its detriments and falls in the signs of Libra and Cancer. Mars is considered weaker and less effective during these placements, as its natural attributes are challenged, negatively impacting individuals born under these signs or with less intensity.

The concept of *joys* refers to the special connection between certain planets and specific houses in the horoscope, according to Ptolemy's chart. Mars is associated with the joy in the 6th House, primarily linked to work, service, health, and daily routines. Mars' connection to this house signifies a proactive approach, discipline, and strategic thinking when dealing with work and health matters. It can indicate a strong sense of duty and responsibility in these areas.

In symbolic terms, Mars' dignities and joys in Ptolemy's chart depict the energy and influence it has on individuals in different positions in the zodiac. Mars governs drive, determination, assertiveness, and passion, making it a decisive force in defining an individual's mannerisms, motivations, and ambitions, especially during interactions with work, service, and health.

Jupiter

Jupiter's dignities and joy in Ptolemy's Chart provide a detailed understanding of the planet's astrological significance, its influence on human life, and the various areas it governs.

Jupiter, often called the *king of the gods* in Roman mythology, is the largest planet in the solar system and represents abundance, growth, and optimism in astrology. Its dignities in Ptolemy's Chart are closely tied to the zodiac signs it rules and its various relationships. The dignities give different levels of power to the planet based on the zodiac sign it is in. Jupiter's major dignities are as follows:

Jupiter rules over the signs of Sagittarius and Pisces. When it is in these signs, it is in its domicile, and its positive qualities are displayed most effectively in individuals born under these signs. Individuals with a strong Jupiter influence could exhibit benevolence, generosity, wisdom, and a strong desire to pursue knowledge.

Jupiter is exalted in the sign of Cancer, signifying that its beneficial influences are amplified when positioned in it. People with Jupiter in Cancer enjoy great emotional wealth, nurturing instincts, and an affinity for home and family life.

In triplicity in Ptolemy's chart, Jupiter governs the water signs – Cancer, Scorpio, and Pisces – indicating the planet's expression of natural affinity for those individuals born under these signs. As a result, their lives may be enhanced with heightened creativity, intuition, and emotional depth.

Ptolemy assigned specific degree ranges within each zodiac sign where a celestial body exhibits particular influence or affinity. Jupiter's "terms" are within portions of each zodiac sign where these traits are most operative.

The face dignity, known as decan, divides each zodiac sign into three equal segments of 10 degrees, ruled by three different planets. Jupiter rules specific faces in different signs, bestowing its nobility and good fortune to those born under these placements.

Regarding its joy, Jupiter is most favorably placed in the eleventh house of the astrological chart, defined as the house of good fortune or the house of friends. This placement emphasizes the auspiciousness associated with friendships, aspirations, and achievements. In the 11th house, Jupiter's ability to bring about growth, expansion, and celebration is heightened, allowing individuals with this position to benefit from strong social networks, philanthropy, and long-term goals realizations.

Understanding Jupiter's dignities and joy in Ptolemy's Chart provides crucial insights into the planet's astrological significance and influence on human life. It sheds light on Jupiter's relationships with the zodiac signs and how its energy manifests in people's lives. As the planet is associated with abundance, growth, and optimism, Jupiter's dignities and placements reveal the path to good fortune and success in various spheres of life.

Saturn

Saturn is the planet of structure, responsibility, and authority in horary astrology. Saturn's energy reflects a deep sense of duty, commitment, and determination to complete tasks excellently. It can reflect a person's psychological state, security, and stability. Through Ptolemy's wheel chart in horary astrology, insight is gained into how Saturn's influence manifests in each sign.

Saturn, the 6th planet from the Sun, is prominent in astrology and Ptolemy's chart of dignities and joys. Ptolemy's chart reveals Saturn's various strengths and weaknesses, depending on its position in the zodiac and its relationship with other celestial bodies. Saturn's dignities include its sign of rulership, exaltation, and triplicity, which determine its level of power and influence over an individual's life and character.

In Ptolemy's chart, Saturn has its sign of rulership in Capricorn and Aquarius. Therefore, Saturn is the most potent and effective in these signs, leading to increased discipline, structure, and ambitions for people with Saturn strongly placed in Capricorn or Aquarius. Saturn's exaltation is in Libra, signifying its next most powerful position. Saturn brings balance, justice, and strong critical thinking skills when well-aspect in a natal chart.

Triplicity rulership is another aspect of dignity, shared among three planets for the four elements (fire, earth, air, and water). Saturn has triplicity rulership in the air signs - Gemini, Libra, and Aquarius - further emphasizing its affinity with intellectual pursuits and communication.

The joys refer to the specific connection between the traditional planets and the twelve houses in astrology. Saturn's joy is in the 12th house – the house of introspection and self-undoing. This placement allows Saturn's inherent wisdom and introspective nature to reflect upon past actions and facilitate spiritual growth.

Chapter 7: Major Planetary Aspects

One of astrology's most fascinating elements is its planetary aspects. It is the concept of the solar system's planets influencing the lives of humans through their movements and alignment. Understanding astrology requires learning about its five main planetary aspects: oppositions, trines, squares, sextiles, and conjunctions. Each aspect is significant when interpreting a person's horoscope. This chapter takes you on a journey through these aspects to uncover deeper astrology secrets.

Horary Charts and the Five Planetary Aspects

One of the biggest benefits of studying planetary aspects is they can help you make better life decisions. Understanding the planet's dynamics and interactions lets you know which decisions will likely lead to positive or negative results. You can use planetary aspects to predict the future to help determine how to proceed – and they also provide insight into relationships. Understanding how the planets influence each other and the energies they create, you get a better sense of how relationships will likely work out, improving communication with others and the dynamics of relationships. Studying planetary aspects offers a deeper understanding of yourself and your place in the universe. Learning the energies the planets create – and how they interact – provides a better understanding of individual energy and how it is used in harmony with the universe. It can be a powerful tool for personal growth and development.

Major aspects are the angles between the planets and describe their relationship. Usually formed when two planets are a certain number of degrees apart, this number of degrees is known as the "orb." Aspect patterns form when several planets are connected in a certain way, known as a "configuration," essential for understanding and interpreting the birth chart. Astrologers rely on this specific mix of planetary energies to interpret the planetary forces in the birth chart and analyze how they affect the native's life. Aspects have different meanings depending on which planets are involved and their position in the chart. The most basic aspects are:

- The Conjunction
- The Sextile
- The Square
- The Trine
- The Opposition

Each has a different meaning and influence on the planets. It determines the current positions of the planets in the sky and analyzes the aspects between them. For example:

- **A conjunction** occurs when two planets are in the same degree of the zodiac and is considered a very close relationship between them. This aspect indicates a deep union between two people or a powerful connection between two events.
- **A sextile** occurs when two planets are in the same sign but at a 60-degree angle from each other. This aspect indicates a strong connection between two people or a strong energy between two events
- **A square** occurs when two planets are in the same sign but at a 90-degree angle from each other. This aspect indicates a challenging relationship between two people or a struggle between two events
- **A trine** takes place when two planets are in the same sign but at a bigger angle from each other, or about 120 degrees. This aspect indicates a harmonious relationship between two people or an easy flow of energy between two events
- **An opposition** occurs when two planets are in the same sign but at a 180-degree angle from each other. This aspect indicates an intense relationship (similar to a square but less extreme)

between two people or a struggle between two events.

Understanding these five planetary aspects is essential to interpret a birth chart and understanding the native's energies and influences. Let's explore each one further.

The Conjunction

Conjunctions are an interesting phenomenon, adding an extra layer of meaning to an answer. They are two or more planets together in close proximity in the zodiac. Essentially, they are the relationship between two planets or points in a horoscope, like the Ascendant, the Midheaven, or a particular house cusp. This relationship is established when the two planets or points are placed within a certain angular separation from each other, usually from 0° to 8°. The conjunction's orb creates an energetic connection between the planets with positive and negative effects. For instance, when two planets are in conjunction, they amplify each other's energy, creating a powerful effect.

On the other hand, if the planets are in opposition, they create tension and conflict. The effect's strength depends on the degree of the conjunction, the planets involved, and the sign where the conjunction takes place. The closer the two points are, the stronger the influence of the conjunction. For example, two planets *in the same sign or house indicate* a strong bond, like friendship or partnership. In contrast, two planets in *opposing signs* or houses mean a struggle or conflict between them.

The Conjunction refers to the energies of two planets combined. When two planets are in the same sign or house, the combined energies of the planets will be more powerful than the individual planet's energies. For example, suppose two planets are in the sign of Aries. In that case, the combined energy might be interpreted as strong, passionate, and courageous energy.

How Conjunction Work in the Charts

Conjunctions bring out the special relationship between the planets involved, amplifying their influence and intensifying their energies. Every conjunction has a specific energy. For example, the conjunction of:

- Jupiter and Saturn signify a period of great success and accomplishment
- Mars and Neptune bring out creativity and self-expression
- Mars and Venus in the chart indicate a passionate relationship

- Saturn and the Sun indicate a period of struggle and difficulty

Conjunctions can identify the planets' or points' impact on each other. For example, a conjunction between the Moon and Jupiter indicates the Moon is influencing Jupiter's energy. A conjunction between the Sun and Saturn indicates the Sun is suppressing Saturn's ability to bring about positive results.

Conjunctions provide insight into the relationship between planets and points in the chart. For example, a conjunction between Mercury and Jupiter indicates Mercury influencing Jupiter's ability to manifest its goals and ambitions, while one between the Moon and Mars indicates the Moon is affecting Mars' ability to achieve desired outcomes.

The Sextile

The Sextile is an aspect of astrology describing the relationship between two planets 60 degrees apart. It is considered a "soft" aspect, which is less intense than the conjunction, trine, or square aspects. This harmonious angle between two planets acts as a bridge connecting two energies together. Since a sextile is quite auspicious and an indication of good things to come, it symbolizes a "meeting of the minds" and the formation of a strong and lasting connection between two planets. It signifies balance and stability and often manifests as creative energy, productive partnerships, and successful collaborations. The Sextile aspect is considered a "lucky" aspect because it can open the door to possibilities. For example:

- It indicates where you can find success and the areas where the most progress can be made.
- It indicates where natural talents and abilities lie and can point people in the right direction.

The sextile aspect can be used to understand relationships with others. For example:

- It shows how to work together with partners, family members, and friends.
- It identifies potential conflicts between two people or situations.

The Sextile shows signs of growth and development to promote self-discovery and advancement in life goals. It can be benefit answering questions about achieving ambitions.

How Sextile Work in the Charts

Let's look at how the sextile aspect works with more prominent celestial bodies to understand better how it works with different planets.

- When the Moon and the Sun are sextile, it indicates a strong connection to emotions.
- When Mercury and Venus are sextile, it shows the ability to express yourselves more easily and take risks without fear of failure.
- When Mars and Jupiter are sextile, it indicates optimism and motivation.
- When Saturn and the Moon are sextile, self-awareness and groundedness indicate a time for self-reflection.

Overall, the sextile aspect is a powerful tool that can help connect to emotions and push toward growth. Understanding how the sextile aspect works with the different planets can be advantageous.

The Square

Astrology is a field filled with complex and intricate concepts. One concept is the square aspect. It's easy to feel overwhelmed trying to understand what it means. It's called a square because this angle is 90°, making it look like a square when viewed on a chart. The planets or points in the square aspect are in two different signs and are usually a source of tension in the chart because the two planets' energies are at odds with each other.

The square is a sign of inner conflict between two opposite energies, and it can manifest in different ways. For instance:

- It manifests as a fear of failure, an inability to make decisions, or a fear of rejection.
- It manifests signs of being stuck and unable to move forward.

Balancing the two sides of the chart during a reading can be difficult. The astrologer must find a way to bring the two sides of the chart together to deal with this tension. It is necessary because, despite the problematic features of the square, it is a source of potential growth and transformation.

How The Square Work in the Charts

It is often said that when the square is present in the horoscope, it indicates a person's ability to face challenges and change their life. When paired with the different planets, squares interact differently. For example:

- When the Moon is in square aspect to the Sun, it signifies inner turmoil and difficulty balancing the need for attention and time for oneself.
- Venus and Jupiter show confusion between material matters and spiritual matters.
- Saturn and Mercury indicate fear of the unknown and a lack of confidence in deciding.
- Mercury and Venus reflect difficulty communicating and expressing feelings.
- Mars and Jupiter represent a person pushing themselves too hard and unable to control their ambitions.

The Trine

Astrology uses the trine to analyze a person's character and potential. It is shaped like a triangle and formed when two planets in a birth chart are approximately 120 degrees apart. When two planets are aligned this way, they often create favorable energy. The trine aspect is often compared to the square. While the square represents difficulty and struggle, the trine shows the opposite; luck and ease. This aspect can determine if a relationship will likely succeed in the long run. Trines provide insight into:

- The individual's actions and reactions to different situations.
- The individual's strengths and weaknesses and how they can best use them to their advantage.
- How the individual can best use their energies to create positive and beneficial changes in their life.

One of the most powerful effects of the trine is its ability to unlock hidden potential, enabling success in various fields.

How The Trine Work in the Charts

The trine aspect works differently for each planet, creating different effects in the chart.

- When the Moon is involved in a trine aspect, it shows emotional sensitivity and intuition. It indicates someone is more empathetic and open to others. With a trine aspect between the Sun and Moon, a person is more likely to find success and fulfillment in their life.

- When Mercury is involved in a trine aspect, it facilitates the ability to think clearly and logically. It indicates someone is articulate and communicative. With a trine aspect between Mercury and Venus, a person is more likely to find success in relationships and social engagements.
- When Venus is involved in a trine aspect, it shows an increased ability to express love and compassion. With a trine aspect between Venus and Mars, a person is more likely to find success in their creative endeavors.
- When Mars is involved in a trine aspect, it shows someone energetic and assertive. With a trine aspect between Mars and Jupiter, a person is more likely to find success in their career and business ventures.
- When Saturn is involved in a trine aspect, it indicates someone responsible and focused. With a trine aspect between Saturn and the Moon, a person is more likely to find success and stability in their life.

The Opposition

The opposition is an important aspect in horary charts as it reveals the tension between two entities. For instance, it can measure the relationship between two people or predict the outcome of a specific event. It can analyze the motives of both parties in a situation. The opposition formation occurs when two planets are just a 180 degrees angle apart. It creates tension between them that can be interpreted to gain insight into the situation.

The opposition is considered a major planetary aspect because it reveals the tension between two entities. It indicates conflict but can also indicate a coming together of forces. For instance, it can reveal the current state of a relationship between two people or the expected outcome of a certain event. It is possible to use the opposition to discover the hidden motives of the parties in a situation.

The opposition is a powerful tool for gaining insight into the energies in a particular situation. It can help identify areas of conflict and potential collaboration. By analyzing the opposition, you better understand the forces influencing a situation, make informed decisions, and avoid potential pitfalls.

The opposition is an aspect of tension and conflict in astrology because when two planets oppose each other, they are in disagreement and clash energetically. It creates tension and difficulty in the areas of life represented by the planets. For example, if the Moon and Mars were in opposition, it could indicate difficulty in relationships and emotions. However, the opposition has a positive side, bringing balance and harmony to the areas of life it affects. The opposing planets represent two sides of the same coin and bring out the best and worst in each other, essentially showing how balance can be achieved by understanding both sides of a situation. Oppositions profoundly impact life, as they indicate how to interact with the people and situations people encounter. It can also:

- Provide insight into relationships, as it can show how to interact with others and how interactions affect lives.
- To understand strengths and weaknesses and how to use them advantageously.

How the Opposition Work in the Charts

Opposition works differently with each planet and represents a tension between two points of view. For example, the Moon is the most sensitive planet, and its opposition acts as a buffer against the powerful, dominating energy of the sun. Other examples include:

- The opposition between Mercury and Venus creates a dynamic between reason and feeling.
- The opposition between Mars and Jupiter highlights the tension between power and growth.
- The opposition of Saturn and the Sun creates a balance between the conscious and unconscious.
- The opposition of Uranus and Neptune highlights the tension between the material and spiritual worlds.

Each opposition works differently, creating different tension levels and enabling an understanding of how these planets work together and affect life. Ultimately, the opposition between the planets creates a push and pull between two forces, enabling people to create balanced, healthy lives.

Depending on the planets involved, the opposition can bring positive and negative qualities during a reading. For example:

- When the Moon is in opposition to the sun, it can evoke sensitivity or insecurity.
- When Mercury is in opposition to Venus, it reveals differences in communication styles. Mercury is more analytical, and Venus is more emotive, so this opposition creates an imbalanced energy between the two.
- When Mars is in opposition to Jupiter, it induces a competitive spirit. Jupiter is the planet of luck and abundance, while Mars is the planet of action and drive. When these two planets are in opposition, they create a spirit of rivalry as they push each other to be more ambitious.
- When Saturn is in opposition to another planet, it can induce fear and caution. Saturn is a planet of restrictions and limitations, and when in opposition to another, it causes a person to be overly cautious or pessimistic.

One of the most important aspects of astrology is learning how the major planetary aspects work. These planetary aspects are the links between the planets in the solar system and the energies produced by them. Understanding these aspects gives a better understanding of the energies in people's lives and how they can affect circumstances and experiences.

Chapter 8: Minor Planetary Aspects

As a complex field of study, astrology uses different categories of planetary aspects to interpret the movements of the planets and stars and their effects on people. Astrology is divided into major and minor aspects; each provides extra insight into chart analysis. Major aspects explored in chapter 7 are the main planetary configurations for interpreting a birth chart, while minor aspects add flair to prediction. This chapter explores the minor aspects of astrology and how to use them to gain an even deeper insight into the answers you seek.

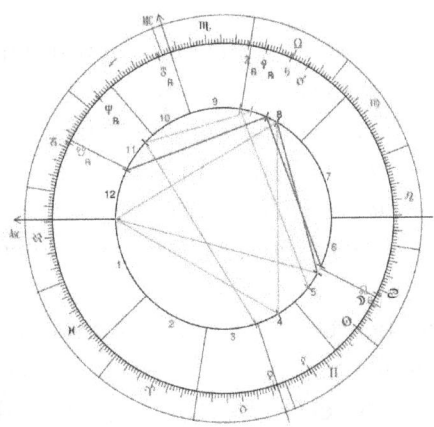

Planetary aspects on a birth chart.
Mom, CC BY-SA 3.0 <https://creativecommons.org/licenses/by-sa/3.0>, via Wikimedia Commons
https://upload.wikimedia.org/wikipedia/commons/4/43/Natal_Chart_-_Adam.svg

Minor Astrological Aspects

Astrologers use various methods to interpret the positions of the stars, including using minor aspects. Minor aspects are the angular distances between planets less than 150 degrees, like 45 degrees, 60 degrees, and 72 degrees. They are less commonly used than the major aspects but are still vital to understanding the influence of the planets in a birth chart or reading. Astrologers use different minor aspects, but some of the most commonly used are sextiles, semi-squares, sesquiquadrates, quintiles, and quincunxes.

- The sextile is formed when two planets are 60 degrees apart and is often a harmonious aspect foreshadowing luck and opportunity.
- The semi-square is formed when two planets are 45 degrees apart and is a challenging aspect of predicting tension and conflict.
- The sesquiquadrate is formed when two planets are 135 degrees apart and is a difficult aspect showing stress and discord.
- The quintile is formed when two planets are 72 degrees apart and is an opportunity to create something new and unique.
- The quincunx is created when two planets are 150 degrees apart, and it represents complicated and surprising changes.

When astrologers use minor aspects, they look at the subtle influences between planets and how they influence different areas of life. For example:

- A minor aspect between Venus and Saturn indicates a person's relationship with authority.
- A minor aspect between the Sun and Mars indicates a person's ability to take action and be assertive.

Moreover, looking at the interconnections between planets, astrologists use minor aspects to determine how these planets affect an individual's life. For example:

- A minor aspect between Mars and the Sun indicates a person's drive and ambition.
- A minor aspect between Venus and Neptune indicates a person's ability to be creative and imaginative.

The minor aspects are often combined with other astrological techniques, such as transits, progressions, and midpoints, to form a more comprehensive understanding of how the planets influence someone. Overall, astrologers use minor aspects to look at the subtle connections between planets and gain insight into a person's character, strengths, and weaknesses. It helps them make more accurate readings and give better advice.

The Semi-Sextile

The semi-sextile planetary is created when two planets are apart by a 30-degree angle. It is an aspect of adjustment, meaning it helps people adjust to the energy of the planets involved and accept the changes they bring. For example:

- Encourages taking action and learning from mistakes.
- Draws connections between different areas of life.
- Compromises between two conflicting forces.

It is one of the so-called minor aspects of astrology, but it has a powerful influence on chart reading. During a reading, astrologers report the semi-sextile to:

- Signifies restlessness and dissatisfaction. It shows a sense of wanting more but not having the necessary motivation to take steps to get what they want. It is particularly helpful for those who feel stuck in a rut and unable to move forward.
- Predict uncertainty and confusion. It shows how someone questions their decisions and feels overwhelmed by their choices. It identifies someone with difficulty deciding and lacking confidence in their judgment.

Astrologers believe the energies associated with the semi-sextile can bring about positive and negative results.

- On the one hand, it inspires creativity and new ideas.
- On the other hand, it causes doubt and confusion.

These discrepancies occur because celestial energies are unique to each individual, depending on other aspects in their chart. Overall, the semi-sextile is an aspect that should not be overlooked. It can predict powerful and unique energies to unlock potential and provide insight into a person's personality and life path. However, its effects are limited. It cannot be used to signify drastic elements. Instead, it should be used to balance two conflicting forces.

How Semi-Sextile Work in the Charts

When the planets in a chart form a semi-sextile aspect, they can have a very subtle but powerful influence on a person's life. Essentially, they are in a state of tension and disagreement. They don't necessarily have to conflict with each other, but they can. This tension manifests in different ways, depending on the other aspects and positions in the horoscope. It has the potential to bring out the best in each planet, but you must approach it with an open mind and learn to work with it. For example:

- If the Sun and Venus are in a semi-sextile aspect, it means the person will have difficulty finding balance in their relationships. They can struggle to accept love and express their emotions and will constantly feel on edge.
- On the other hand, if the Moon and Jupiter are in a semi-sextile aspect, it can mean the person is creative and optimistic. They may have an easier time expressing their emotions and be more willing to take risks and try new things.
- If the Sun is semi-sextile to the Moon, it shows a blend of compassion and assertiveness in the individual. This observation makes it easier for the astrologer to find a balance between their ambitions and emotions during a reading.
- If Venus is semi-sextile to Jupiter, it signifies how astrologers should encourage their clients to seek beauty and joy while staying grounded in reality.
- When Saturn is semi-sextile to Mercury, it helps astrologists apply a practical approach to communication.
- When Mars is semi-sextile to the Moon, it signifies a blend of aggression and receptiveness, allowing the expression of needs without being too pushy or aggressive.

The Quincunx

As a sign of growth or transformation, the quincunx aspect is considered an aspect of adjustment. Formed when two planets are 150 degrees apart (five signs apart) in the zodiac wheel, this oddly angled aspect is not found in any other aspect, so considered quite unique. Quincunxes can symbolize challenges or difficulties that must be overcome to progress in life. It is often a sign that some adjustment or transformation must happen to reach a certain goal. Depending on the planets involved, it could be a mental, emotional, physical, or spiritual adjustment. The quincunx is often:

- A sign of growth and evolution.
- A sign that a person is ready to move on to the next level but must make certain changes.
- A sign that a person is undergoing transformation and they must make adjustments to navigate the process successfully.

How Quincunx Work in the Charts

The quincunx aspect can show where to find balance and harmony. It can give insight into how to overcome difficulties and helps understand where people struggle.

- The Sun is the source of all life and energy, so a quincunx aspect can indicate a struggle to find balance or harmony in life.
- The Moon is associated with emotions and feelings, so a quincunx aspect can indicate difficulty expressing feelings or finding emotional balance.
- Venus is the planet of love and relationships, so a quincunx aspect can indicate a lack of harmony in relationships.
- Jupiter is the planet of expansion and good fortune, so a quincunx aspect can indicate a struggle to find success or abundance.
- Saturn is the planet of limitation and restriction, so a quincunx aspect can indicate difficulty in achieving goals or finding stability.
- Mercury is the planet of communication, so a quincunx aspect can indicate a struggle with communication or expressing yourself.
- Mars is the planet of action and energy, so a quincunx aspect can indicate difficulty in taking action or finding motivation.

The Quintile

The quintile aspect is created when two planets are separated by 72 degrees. This angle creates energy between the two planets, which can be positive and negative. Astrologers believe it to be especially beneficial for creative and intuitive endeavors. It signifies a strong connection between the planets, allowing a greater understanding of each individual and a more powerful creative force. The energies associated with the quintile

help attain success and achieve ambitions.
- It emphasizes taking advantage of opportunities, as it encourages being open to new experiences and taking risks.
- It notifies positive energy, and astrologers often recommend it to their clients as a way to move forward in life. They will suggest the client meditate on the energies associated with the quintile and use them to create positive change and success.
- Besides bringing luck, it can open up new opportunities, so astrologers might suggest their clients take advantage of these opportunities.

How Quintile Work in the Charts

When the five planets in a quintile are in their respective positions, they form a pentagram. Each point of the pentagram is connected to a different planet. The Sun is connected to the base point, the Moon to the top point, Venus to the left point, Jupiter to the right point, and Saturn to the upper middle point. This pentagram influences the energies of each planet. Together the planets of a quintile are acknowledged as a spiritual aspect. They serve as a bridge between the physical and the spiritual worlds. For example:

- The Sun is the most affected by the quintile aspect, bringing an intense focus, energy, and ambition to the person's life.
- The Moon is associated with emotional intensity, a deeper understanding of relationships, and increased intuition.
- Venus promotes joy and pleasure, a greater appreciation of beauty, and increased charisma.
- Jupiter symbolizes luck, wealth, and increased optimism.
- Saturn is associated with greater responsibility, discipline, and practicality.

The Bi-Quintile

The bi-quintile is a relatively lesser-known planetary aspect in astrology. The 144-degree aspect with unique associated energy can manifest creative and innovative solutions to problems. The bi-quintile is considered one of the most creative aspects of astrology because it brings out the best in a person and helps them manifest their dreams and aspirations. The bi-quintile can also:

- Promote thinking outside the box and creating creative solutions to problems.
- Help a person find a unique approach to a situation.
- Manifest positive changes in a person's life.

The bi-quintile has spiritual energy associated with it. This aspect allows a person to tap into the spiritual realm and receive guidance and insight into matters related to their spiritual path. Besides helping a person connect to their higher self, it can give them clarity and insight into their lives.

How Bi-Quintile Work in the Charts

The bi-quintile aspect is a relatively rare astrological aspect, often overlooked in favor of more traditional aspects, like the conjunction, trine, and square. This harmonious aspect is usually associated with two planets in a supportive relationship.

The Sun, Moon, Mercury, Mars, Venus, Saturn, and Jupiter create the bi-quintile aspect. The Sun and Moon are the most important planets in this aspect. When the Sun and Moon form a bi-quintile, it is a favorable time for making important decisions and finding harmony and balance.

- Venus and Jupiter, in a bi-quintile aspect, bring the potential for great luck and abundance. It is an ideal time for taking risks with investments, starting a new business, or expanding creative endeavors.
- Saturn and Mercury, in a bi-quintile aspect, are beneficial for business transactions and negotiations. These two planets can potentially push learning new skills or gaining knowledge.
- In a bi-quintile aspect, Mars and Venus can help find balance in relationships. It indicates the suggestion to make compromises, find a middle ground, and take the right path.

The Semi-Square

The semi-square is a very subtle aspect and can be quite challenging to handle because it is rarely used in traditional astrology. Formed at a 45-degree angle between two planets, representing tension, conflict, and discord, astrologers can still use this aspect to help understand a person's challenges, blocks, and obstacles. The person might be prone to conflict and misunderstandings in relationships. When astrologers consider the semi-square aspect, they look at the planets it affects. The planets provide

insight into what conflicts and obstacles the individual is facing. For example:
- If the semi-square aspect affects the planet of relationships, then it can indicate the person is struggling in their relationships.
- If the semi-square aspect affects the planet of career, then it indicates the person experiences difficulty in their career.

Astrologers must also consider the planets' sign to gain a deeper understanding of the semi-square aspect. For example:

If the planets are in an often difficult or challenging sign, then the semi-square aspect will be even more pronounced.

How Semi-Square Work in the Charts

The semi-square aspect is one of the most potent astrological configurations and can strongly influence how planets interact. It creates a powerful connection between the planets and in the horoscope as a ray of energy connecting them. The Sun, Moon, Venus, Jupiter, Saturn, Mercury, and Mars all have the potential to be connected by a semi-square aspect. When two of these planets form a semi-square, the energy between them is quite intense, and the effects can be felt in the individuals' lives.

- The Sun is the source of all power in astrology, and when connected by a semi-square, it can bring a strong personal power.
- When a semi-square connects with the Moon, it can trigger powerful emotions and cause the individual to be more sensitive to external influences.
- Venus is the planet of love and relationships, and when connected by a semi-square, it can create strong attraction and desire.
- Jupiter is the planet of luck and fortune, and when connected by a semi-square, it can produce positive changes and unexpected opportunities.
- Saturn is the planet of limitations, and when connected by a semi-square, it can bring restriction and blockage.
- Mercury is the planet of communication and intellect, and when connected by a semi-square, it can facilitate a better understanding of ideas and concepts.
- Mars is the planet of aggression and action, and when connected by a semi-square, it can evoke impatience and a need for quick

action.

The Sesquiquadrate (Sesquisquare)

Astrologers use the sesquiquadrate aspect to identify potential areas of tension and friction in a person's life. A sesquiquadrate aspect is formed on the birth chart when two planets are separated by a 135-degree angle. The sesquiquadrate aspect is a relatively minor influence in a birth chart but can still have a significant impact. It indicates a conflict between the two planets and a need for adjustment to bring the two energies into harmony. Essentially, it is a warning sign of potential problems and challenges. For example, it indicates the reconciliation of different parts of yourselves or resolving conflicts between your internal and external worlds.

Often described as a "crisis of transformation," it can force people to confront difficult issues and make difficult decisions. It brings inner conflict and can make it difficult for the person to decide, leading to anxiety, fear, and worry.

How Sesquisquare Work in the Charts

The sesquisquare aspect can be formed between the Sun, Moon, Venus, Jupiter, Saturn, Mercury, and Mars, although it commonly involves the Sun and Moon.

As the most important planet in the solar system, the Sun gives each individual a purpose and identity. The Sun's sesquisquare aspect can bring intense development in the individual's life because it is associated with life-giving energy.

- The sesquisquare aspect of the Moon signifies a period of inner exploration and reflection. There might be a need to examine a person's inner psyche and look within. It can be a time of great healing and transformation as the individual works through their emotional blocks.
- The sesquisquare aspect of Venus indicates a period of romantic and creative exploration. A person might want to connect with others and express themself meaningfully. It can create a heightened appreciation for beauty and the finer things in life.
- The sesquisquare aspect of Jupiter suggests a period of growth and opportunity. As a result, there could be a need to take risks and trust in life's process. Jupiter is known as the planet of luck

and fortune, so it can show a period of luck and opportunity.
- The sesquisquare aspect of Saturn signifies a period of hard work and dedication. It can be a time when the individual is challenged to face their fears and take responsibility for their actions. Individuals might have to be honest with themselves and stay disciplined during this time.

Astrologers use minor aspects to add further depth to a horoscope. These planetary aspects are subtle but can give greater insight into the individual's character. Minor aspects uncover hidden traits, tendencies, and potentials not as apparent when looking at the major aspects alone. While the major aspects focus on the more straightforward and obvious elements, the minor aspects provide a more nuanced understanding. For example, suppose the minor aspects reveal a person to be more emotionally sensitive than previously thought. In that case, the astrologer can suggest ways to help the individual cope with their sensitivity. Minor aspects are invaluable for astrologers as they provide invaluable insights into their clients' lives.

Chapter 9: Planetary Transits

As you know by now, horary astrology deals with answering specific questions by interpreting the positions of the planets and stars at the moment a question is asked. How a planet moves can paint a clearer picture of the answer sought by the horary astrologer. One of the critical factors in understanding these movements is the concept of planetary transits. Planetary transits are crucial in horary astrology, as they help the astrologer interpret the current state of affairs and predict what will likely occur. By understanding planetary transits, the astrologer can predict the movement of the planets in the future and, therefore, anticipate the possible events that could occur.

Understanding the significance of planetary transits is imperative if you are a student of horary astrology. It is not enough to merely read a chart and interpret its meaning without considering the movements of the planets. Planetary transits provide valuable information to help you interpret horary readings accurately and gain insight into the future. This chapter explores the concept of planetary transits in more detail. By the end of this chapter, you'll have a comprehensive understanding of planetary transits and their significance in horary astrology. You can apply this knowledge to your readings and gain a deeper insight into current affairs and possible future events.

Planetary Transits vs. Aspects

In horary astrology, the concept of planetary transits is particularly important. Horary astrology deals with interpreting the planet's and star's positions at the moment a specific question is asked, aiming to provide answers and insights into the situation. Planetary transits in horary astrology refer to the current movement of the planets through the zodiac and their relationship to the planets and houses in the horary chart. Each planet's transit through a particular sign and house provides valuable information about the current state of affairs and the possible future outcome of the situation being questioned.

For example, if a person asks a horary question about their financial situation. The astrologer may look at Jupiter's current position, the planet associated with wealth and abundance, and its transit through the houses and signs of the chart to gain insight into the person's financial prospects. Unlike aspects, which focus on the relationship between two planets at a specific moment, planetary transits provide a broader context for understanding the planet's movement and influence. By looking at the broader patterns and movements of the planets, astrologers can gain a deeper understanding of the energies and influences shaping the situation.

While both planetary transits and aspects are important concepts in astrology, they have distinct differences in their focus and interpretation. Planetary transits focus on the planets' current movement through the zodiac and their relationship to the houses and signs of the chart. This movement occurs over a longer period, days, weeks, or even months, depending on the planet and its orbit's length. Aspects provide a snapshot of the current planetary relationships, whereas planetary transits provide a broader context for understanding the planets' movement and influence. Transits can indicate major themes or changes likely to occur in a person's life, while aspects provide more specific information about the energies and influences in a particular situation.

Another difference between planetary transits and aspects is the frequency of their occurrence. Aspects occur relatively frequently, sometimes several times a day, while planetary transits are rarer and occur over a longer period. So, while aspects can provide information about shorter-term influences and energies, planetary transits can offer insight into more significant long-term trends and themes. Overall, both planetary transits and aspects are important tools in the astrologer's toolkit and can be used together to gain a more comprehensive understanding of a person's life and the energies and influences. Astrologers can provide more accurate and insightful readings for their clients by understanding these differences.

Mutual Reception

Mutual reception is an astrological term referring to a unique relationship between two planets in each other's signs of rulership. This occurs when two planets are in signs ruled by the other planet, creating a connection between them that can enhance their energies. For example, Venus is in Scorpio, and Mars is in Libra. In this case, Venus is in Mars's sign of rulership (because Mars rules Scorpio), while Mars is in Venus's sign of rulership (because Venus rules Libra). This creates a mutual reception between the two planets, indicating a harmonious connection and the potential for increased energy and productivity.

The astrological process of mutual reception occurs when two planets are in each other's signs of rulership. This creates a unique energy that can amplify both planets' influence and produce positive results. In the example above, Venus in Scorpio and Mars in Libra would be in mutual reception, as they are in each other's signs of rulership. When planets are in mutual reception, they can work together more integrated and powerfully, leading to increased energy, productivity, and harmony in the areas of life ruled by those planets. For example, suppose Venus and Mars were in mutual reception. It could indicate a positive and productive time for relationships and partnerships, as Venus rules love and relationships while Mars rules action and energy.

Mutual reception is a relatively rare occurrence in astrology, as it requires two planets to be in each other's signs of rulership. However, it can be a powerful and positive influence when it does occur. When each planet goes through this process can vary depending on the planets' specific positions and the signs they are in. However, astrologers can use software or ephemerides to calculate the exact dates and times when mutual reception occurs based on the planet's movements through the zodiac. Overall, mutual reception is a valuable tool for astrologers to interpret horary charts and gain insights into the planets' unique relationships.

Other examples of mutual reception can include:

1. Venus in Scorpio and Mars in Libra

In this case, Venus is in Scorpio, ruled by Mars, and Mars is in Libra, ruled by Venus. This is a commonly occurring example of mutual reception. When these particular planets are in mutual reception, they can be found in each other's specific home sign. It allows them to work together harmoniously and express their energies more effectively.

In this case, Venus in Scorpio can access the powerful and transformative energy of Mars, helping Venus express its desire for intimacy and emotional depth more effectively. On the other hand, Mars in Libra can benefit from Venus's diplomatic and harmonizing energy, helping Mars express its assertiveness and take action more effectively. This placement might suggest a relationship where both partners understand and appreciate each other's needs and desires.

2. Mercury in Pisces and Neptune in Gemini

When Mercury and Neptune are in mutual reception, it means each planet is in the sign ruled by the other planet. In this case, Mercury is in Pisces (which Neptune rules), and Neptune is in Pisces (which Neptune *also rules*). This placement can profoundly impact your mental state and perception of reality. Mercury governs communication, learning, and logical thinking, while Neptune represents intuition, spirituality, and the subconscious. When the two planets are in mutual reception, their energies can work together, creating a period of heightened intuition and sensitivity.

People are more in tune with their inner voice and the world around them during this time. Their dreams and inner visions might be more vivid, and they might be drawn to creative pursuits, such as writing, art, or music. Simultaneously, this placement can make them more prone to escapism and daydreaming, so they must be mindful of staying grounded and in reality.

3. Jupiter in Aries and Mars in Sagittarius

Jupiter and Mars in mutual reception means Jupiter is in Aries (the sign ruled by Mars), while Mars is in the sign ruled by Jupiter (Sagittarius). This mutual reception creates a positive and harmonious energy between these two planets and has several implications. Firstly, Jupiter is the planet of expansion, growth, and optimism, while Mars is the planet of action, passion, and drive. When these two planets are in mutual reception, it can indicate a period of increased energy and enthusiasm, especially in pursuing goals and taking risks. People may feel more confident and willing to take on challenges and try new things during this time.

Secondly, this placement can indicate when a person feels confident to make decisions and take action. Jupiter's influence can bring a sense of faith and trust in a person's abilities, while Mars' influence can provide the drive and motivation to act on those beliefs. It can be a favorable time to start new projects, take on leadership roles, and pursue passions. Overall, Jupiter and Mars, in mutual reception, can bring harmony and balance between expansion and action, faith and drive, leading to a productive and fulfilling period.

Planets in Retrograde

Retrograde motion in astrology refers to the apparent backward motion of a planet observed from Earth. This occurs due to differences in the orbital speed and distance of the planets and the Earth's orbital motion. If a planet is in retrograde, it will appear to move in a backward direction through the zodiac. However, this is just an illusion caused when the Earth passes a slower-moving planet in its orbit. During this period, the planet's energy is thought to turn inward, causing people to reflect on the themes associated with that planet. Each planet goes through this process at different times and for different durations. Mercury, Venus, Mars, Jupiter, and Saturn experience retrograde periods.

1. Mercury Retrograde

Mercury retrograde is perhaps the most well-known retrograde period in astrology. This event occurs approximately three times yearly and lasts about three weeks. As with any retrograde event, the planet, in this case, Mercury, appears to move backward through the zodiac. Mercury is associated with communication, technology, transportation, and travel. Therefore, these areas can be affected when it goes retrograde, and challenges can arise. Common experiences during Mercury retrograde include communication breakdowns, technical glitches, delays, and misunderstandings.

Mercury retrograde can affect specific areas; communication is perhaps the most significant. It can be when misunderstandings and miscommunications are more likely to occur, leading to problems in personal and professional relationships and delays in getting things done. Technology and transportation can be affected during Mercury retrograde. It is not uncommon for computers to crash, phones to break, and cars to break down during this period. Therefore, it might be best to back up important files and avoid making major technology purchases or scheduling important trips during this time.

2. Venus Retrograde

Venus retrograde is considered to be comparatively rare and only occurs every 19 months, lasting about 6 weeks. During this period, Venus appears to move backward through the zodiac, impacting various aspects of life, like love, relationships, beauty, art, and values. Therefore, when it goes into retrograde, these areas can be affected, and challenges can arise. You may experience a range of emotions related to personal relationships. It can be a time when old flames return or past relationships resurface. However, remember these might not necessarily be opportunities for reconciliation or rekindling a relationship.

Venus retrograde is a time for introspection and reflection on your values and self-worth. It is a good time to question your beliefs about love and beauty and reevaluate whether they serve you. For creative endeavors, Venus retrograde can be a time to revisit past projects or reevaluate your artistic vision. It is a time to review what you have created and assess whether it aligns with your current creative goals.

3. Mars Retrograde

Mars retrograde takes place every two years, during which the planet Mars seems to move backward in its orbit. During Mars retrograde, the planet's energy is intensified and can significantly impact astrological readings and interpretations. Mars is associated with drive, ambition, and assertiveness. So, when it goes retrograde, many feel frustrated or blocked in their efforts to pursue their goals, leading to restlessness, impatience, lashing out, or impulsiveness.

On the positive side, Mars retrograde can be a time for introspection and self-reflection. It can be an opportunity to slow down, re-evaluate priorities, and reflect on actions and decisions. It could be a time for resolving conflicts and working on communication skills. Those with Aries or Scorpio in their birth chart might be particularly affected by Mars retrograde, as Mars is the ruling planet of both signs. These signs may experience heightened emotions, conflicts, and challenges during this time.

4. Saturn Retrograde

Saturn retrograde happens approximately once every year and lasts for around four and a half months. When Saturn goes into retrograde, you may feel pressure, particularly where you have been neglecting your responsibilities or where you need to take more accountability. Saturn retrograde can be a time for self-reflection and reevaluating your long-term goals and plans.

Those with Capricorn or Aquarius in their birth chart may be particularly affected by Saturn retrograde, as these signs are ruled by

Saturn. During this time, these signs may experience greater responsibility and pressure in their professional and personal lives.

5. Jupiter Retrograde

Jupiter retrograde occurs yearly for a comparatively longer period than other retrograde events, lasting about four months. Jupiter is associated with expansion, growth, and abundance. When Jupiter goes into retrograde, people feel contraction – particularly where they have been over-indulging or overextending themselves. Those with Sagittarius or Pisces in their birth chart may be particularly affected by Jupiter retrograde, as they are ruled by Jupiter. During this time, these signs could experience greater introspection and inner growth and a focus on their spiritual and philosophical development.

Overall, retrograde periods are considered times for reflection, review, and reassessment rather than for initiating new projects or making major changes. Being mindful of the energy of the retrograde planet during these periods and using the time wisely for personal growth and introspection is important.

When Planets Combust

In horary astrology, the *combustion of a planet* occurs when a planet is within 8.5 degrees of the Sun and is considered a significant condition affecting the interpretation of a horary chart. When a planet is in combustion, its significators become weakened. The heat and light of the Sun can overpower the qualities and attributes of the planet, making it harder for the planet to function effectively. The planets most commonly affected by combustion are Mercury and Venus, as they are the closest planets to the Sun. However, all planets can go through a combustion period, depending on their distance from the Sun and their position in the zodiac.

When a planet is in combustion, it is "under the beams" of the Sun. As the planet moves closer to the Sun, it becomes increasingly weakened and might not deliver its results. The effects of combustion can last for different periods, depending on the planet and its position in the zodiac. The planet's significators might not manifest as strongly as usual. There could be delays, obstacles, or challenges with the planet's significators. The planet's position in the horary chart, its aspect to other planets, and the house it rules should be considered to understand its impact on the chart.

When Mercury is in combustion, it can affect communication, intelligence, and logical thinking. Mercury represents communication, learning, and exchange of information, and when it is in combustion, it leads to misunderstandings, delays in communication, and difficulty in comprehending information. It affects technology, transportation, and travel, as Mercury rules these areas. During this period, it is advisable to be extra careful in communication and avoid making important decisions requiring a clear understanding of information.

When Venus is in combustion, it can affect relationships, love, and creativity. Venus represents social relationships, romantic connections, and artistic expression. When Venus is in combustion, there could be challenges in these areas, like misunderstandings, disagreements, or delays. It may affect matters of finance, luxury items, and beauty. During this period, it is advisable to be cautious in relationships and avoid making important financial decisions or big purchases of luxury items.

Planetary transits in horary astrology are like cosmic traffic signals, providing valuable information about the universe's energetic flow and how it influences people's lives. Like a skilled driver, a skilled astrologer can use this information to navigate the twists and turns of life, avoiding roadblocks and finding the smoothest path to their destination. Whether you seek clarity on a specific question or merely deepen your understanding of the cosmic dance, planetary transits offer a fascinating and illuminating lens through which to view the mysteries of the universe.

Chapter 10: How to Read Any Horary Chart

You've reached the final chapter of your exploration into the world of horary astrology. It's time to put your learned knowledge and skills to the test. You've learned about the symbols and meanings of the planets, houses, aspects, and planetary transits. Now, it's time to take the next step and learn to read a horary chart to find the answers you seek. Horary astrology is a unique form of divination requiring a specific moment and a clear question to work effectively. It's like tuning into a specific frequency on a radio - you need the right time and place to access the information you seek. However, unlike other forms of divination, horary astrology is not about changing the outcome to fit your desires. It's about gaining insight and understanding into a situation and discovering the best path forward.

Interpreting a horary chart can be challenging and complex, but with practice and patience, it can be a powerful tool for gaining clarity and decision-making. It requires a keen eye for detail, an open mind, and trust in the symbols and signs. By learning to read a horary chart, you can access a pearl of deeper wisdom and guidance available at the moment. This chapter highlights the key concepts and techniques for interpreting a horary chart, providing step-by-step instructions and plenty of examples to help you get started. So, start exploring the mysteries of the universe and discover what the stars have in store for you.

Creating a Horary Chart

Creating a Horary Chart requires noting the exact time, location, and question being asked. To create a horary chart, follow these steps:

1. Determine the exact time, location, and question being asked. Ensure the time is noted as accurately as possible, including the seconds, and it is the local time of the person asking the question. The location of the person asking the question is important as it provides information for determining the ascendant and the houses of the chart. Additionally, the question should be clear and specific to allow precise chart interpretation.
2. Use an ephemeris to determine the positions of the planets and luminaries (Sun and Moon) at the exact time and location of the question. An ephemeris is a table or book listing the celestial bodies' positions at different times. You can find an ephemeris online or in a book.
3. Determine the ascendant by using the location and time of the question. It is the sign rising on the eastern horizon when the question is asked. You can use an online calculator or refer to an ephemeris to determine the ascendant.
4. Draw a chart with the ascendant on the left and the other signs in the same order as they appear in the zodiac. The chart should have 12 houses, with the first house starting at the ascendant and proceeding in a counterclockwise direction.
5. Place the planets and luminaries in the appropriate houses of the chart based on their positions when the question is asked. The planets' positions are indicated in the ephemeris. For example, if Mars were in the sign of Taurus at the time of the question, it would be placed in the second house of the chart (corresponding to Taurus).
6. Consider the planetary aspects (angles) and their meanings. Aspects are formed when planets are certain degrees apart and indicate positive or negative interactions between planets. You can use an online calculator or an ephemeris to determine the aspects between planets. You've already studied the planetary aspects in previous chapters, and examples can include oppositions, conjunctions, or trines.

7. Interpret the chart based on traditional horary astrology principles, including the meanings of the houses, planets, and aspects. The chart interpretation is a complex process requiring knowledge of astrological symbolism and traditional principles of interpretation. You should seek guidance from an experienced astrologer if you are unfamiliar with these principles.

Alternatively, online horary chart calculators and software can create a chart based on input information. These can be helpful for beginners not familiar with astrological symbolism. However, the chart's accuracy generated by software or calculators can vary, depending on the program quality and the data's accuracy.

Example 1:

Let's use an example to better explain the creation of a horary chart. For this example, a person asks whether they will get a job offer for the specific position they applied for. Here are the steps to follow:

1. Determine the exact time, location, and question: You asked the question on February 22, 2023, at 3:45 pm in Los Angeles, California. The asked question is, "Will I be able to get the position I applied for?"
2. Use an ephemeris to determine the positions of the planets and luminaries at the exact time and location of the question: Consulting an ephemeris at 3:45 pm in Los Angeles on February 22, 2023, the positions of the planets and luminaries are as follows:

    o Sun: 4 degrees Pisces

    o Moon: 18 degrees Virgo

    o Mercury: 11 degrees Aquarius

    o Venus: 2 degrees Pisces

    o Mars: 16 degrees Capricorn

    o Jupiter: 11 degrees Pisces

    o Saturn: 9 degrees Aquarius

    o Uranus: 9 degrees Taurus

3. Determine the ascendant: To determine the ascendant, you must know the exact time and location of the question. Using an online calculator or an ephemeris, the ascendant at 3:45 pm

in Los Angeles on February 22, 2023, is 14 degrees Scorpio.
4. Draw the chart: you can use software or draw the chart by hand. The chart should have the ascendant on the left, and the signs must be in the same order as they appear in the zodiac. The chart will have 12 houses, with the first house starting at the ascendant and proceeding counterclockwise. The exact position of each house in this chart is:
   o First House (ascendant): Scorpio
   o Second House: Sagittarius
   o Third House: Capricorn
   o Fourth House: Aquarius
   o Fifth House: Pisces
   o Sixth House: Aries
   o Seventh House: Taurus
   o Eighth House: Gemini
   o Ninth House: Cancer
   o Tenth House: Leo
   o Eleventh House: Virgo
   o Twelfth House: Libra
5. Place the planets and luminaries in the appropriate houses of the chart: Place them in the appropriate houses of the chart using the planets' and luminaries' positions. For example, the Moon is in the sixth house, Venus is in the first house, and Mars is in the ninth house.
6. Consider the planetary aspects. You can use an online calculator or an ephemeris to determine the planetary aspects. For example, Mars may be forming a sextile aspect (60 degrees) with Jupiter, which is in the eleventh house.
7. Interpret the chart: Interpreting the chart requires knowledge of traditional principles of horary astrology, including the meanings of the houses, planets, and aspects you've learned from this book.

Example 2:

A person asks whether they should buy a particular car they've been eyeing. Here are the steps to follow:

1. Determine the exact time, location, and question: The person asked the question on March 10, 2023, at 10:30 am in Miami, Florida. The question is, "Should I buy the blue Toyota Camry I saw at the dealership yesterday?"
2. Use an ephemeris to determine the planets' and luminaries' positions at the exact time and location of the question: Consulting an ephemeris at 10:30 am in Miami on March 10, 2023, the positions of the planets and luminaries are as follows:

    o Sun: 19 degrees Pisces

    o Moon: 5 degrees Capricorn

    o Mercury: 27 degrees Aquarius

    o Venus: 28 degrees Aquarius

    o Mars: 16 degrees Taurus

    o Jupiter: 16 degrees Pisces

    o Saturn: 8 degrees Aquarius

    o Uranus: 14 degrees Taurus

3. Determine the ascendant: To determine the ascendant, you must know the exact time and location of the question. Using an online calculator or an ephemeris, the ascendant at 10:30 am in Miami on March 10, 2023, is 22 degrees Cancer.
4. Draw the chart: You can use software or draw the chart by hand. The chart should have the ascendant on the left, and the signs must be in the same order as they appear in the zodiac. The chart has 12 houses, with the first house starting at the ascendant and proceeding counterclockwise. The exact position of each house in this chart is:

    o First House (ascendant): Cancer

    o Second House: Leo

    o Third House: Virgo

    o Fourth House: Libra

    o Fifth House: Scorpio

    o Sixth House: Sagittarius

    o Seventh House: Capricorn

    o Eighth House: Aquarius

- Ninth House: Pisces
- Tenth House: Aries
- Eleventh House: Taurus
- Twelfth House: Gemini

5. Place the planets and luminaries in the appropriate houses of the chart: Place them in the appropriate houses of the chart using the planets' and luminaries' positions. For example, the Moon is in the third house, Venus is in the third house, and Mars is in the ninth house.
6. Consider the planetary aspects: You can use an online calculator or an ephemeris to determine the planetary aspects. For example, Mars may be forming a trine aspect (120 degrees) with Uranus, which is in the ninth house.
7. Interpret the chart: Interpreting the chart requires knowledge of traditional principles of horary astrology, including the meanings of the houses, planets, and aspects you've learned from this book.

The next section discusses the interpretation of a horary chart in more detail.

Interpreting a Horary Chart

Interpreting a horary chart is a complex and nuanced process requiring a deep understanding of astrology principles and an ability to synthesize information from different areas of the chart. The horary chart is a snapshot of the moment the question was asked and provides insight into the querent's motivations, the situation, and its potential outcome. When you want to interpret a horary chart in detail, you must consider the position of the planets, the signs and houses they occupy, and even their relationship to one another. Each placement and aspect provide a piece of the puzzle. So, viewing the chart as a whole is essential for a meaningful and helpful interpretation. With careful analysis and interpretation, a horary chart can provide valuable insight and guidance to the querent. Here are detailed steps for interpreting a horary chart:

1. **Identify the primary significator:** The primary significator is the planet ruling the house representing the question. For example, if the question concerns a job, the tenth house would represent the question, and its ruling planet, Saturn, would be

the primary significator.

2. **Look for the secondary significators:** The secondary significators are the planets with a special connection to the question or querent. For example, the Moon represents the querent, and planets in the same sign or house as the Moon would be secondary significators.

3. **Consider the position and aspects of the primary *significator*:** The position and aspects of the primary significator provide essential information about the question's answer. For example, if Saturn is in a favorable aspect with Venus, this could indicate a positive outcome about the job.

4. **Look for interceptions and void, of course, planets:** Interceptions occur when a sign is intercepted within a house. They can indicate hidden or delayed outcomes about the question. Void-of-course planets do not make any major aspects before they are supposed to leave their occupied sign. They can indicate delays or lack of progress on the question.

5. **Consider the position and aspects of the Moon:** The position and aspects of the Moon provide information about the querent's emotional state and involvement in the situation. For example, if the Moon is in a favorable aspect with the primary significator, this could indicate the querent is in an excellent position to achieve the desired outcome.

6. **Look for accidental dignities:** Accidental dignities are factors influencing the strength or weakness of a planet in a chart. For example, if a planet is in its own sign, in a favorable aspect with a benefic planet, or in the same sign as the ascendant, it could be considered strong.

7. **Look for the final dispositor:** A final dispositor is the planet with the most power in a chart due to being in charge of other planets through various house placements. For example, if Mars is the final dispositor of the chart, its influence would be heightened.

8. **Consider the chart as a whole:** It is essential to view the chart as a whole and consider all the factors discussed above when interpreting a horary chart. An experienced astrologer can provide more in-depth and nuanced analysis.

Overall, interpreting a horary chart can be a complex process requiring a good understanding of astrology principles and an ability to synthesize information from different areas of the chart. Anyone seeking to interpret a horary chart consulting an experienced astrologer is recommended.

An interpretation of the first example chart discussed above will look like this:

1. **Identify the primary significator**: The primary significator can be identified by considering a few factors. The tenth house represents the job, and its ruling planet is Jupiter, so Jupiter is the primary significator.

2. **Look for the secondary significators**: The Moon represents the querent, so it is a secondary significator. In this chart, the Moon is in the same sign as Jupiter, indicating a strong connection between the querent and the job.

3. **Consider the position and aspects of the primary significator**: Jupiter is in the sign of Capricorn and, in the eleventh house, a favorable position for job-related matters. Jupiter is in close conjunction with Venus, which represents harmony and positive outcomes. These factors suggest a positive outcome for the querent about the job.

4. **Look for interceptions and void-of-course planets**: This chart has no interceptions or void-of-course planets.

5. **Consider the position and aspects of the Moon**: The Moon is in the sign of Capricorn, which is the same sign as Jupiter, indicating a strong connection between the querent and the job. The Moon is in a favorable aspect with Jupiter and Venus, which further indicates a positive outcome about the job.

6. **Look for accidental dignities**: Jupiter is in its own sign, a strong accidental dignity, and is in a favorable aspect with Venus, another benefic planet, further strengthening Jupiter's position in the chart.

7. **Look for the final dispositor**: Jupiter is the final dispositor of the chart, as it is the ruler of the ascendant and the house representing the job. It indicates that Jupiter has a strong influence and power over the chart.

8. **Consider the chart as a whole**: Overall, the chart suggests a positive outcome for the querent about the job. Jupiter, the

primary significator, is in a strong and favorable position, and the Moon, representing the querent, is well-aspect. No significant negative factors are present in the chart, which further supports a positive outcome. However, astrology is not deterministic, so there could be other factors that cannot be fully captured in the chart.

An interpretation for the second example (a person inquiring whether they should purchase a car) would have these steps:

1. **Identify the primary significator**: The question pertains to purchasing a car, which falls under the domain of the second house. The ruling planet of the second house is Venus, so Venus is the primary significator.
2. **Look for the secondary significators**: The Moon represents the querent, and planets in the same sign or house as the Moon would be secondary significators.
3. **Consider the position and aspects of the primary significator**: Venus is in Aries in the ninth house, which suggests the person is enthusiastic and eager about the idea of buying the car. Venus is in a square aspect with Mars in Capricorn, indicating potential obstacles or conflicts about the purchase.
4. **Look for interceptions and void-of-course planets**: This chart has no interceptions or void-of-course planets.
5. **Consider the position and aspects of the Moon**: The Moon is in Gemini in the fourth house, suggesting the querent is curious and seeking information about the car. The Moon is in a square aspect, with Neptune in Pisces in the third house, indicating confusion or deception around the purchase.
6. **Look for accidental dignities**: Venus is in its own sign of Aries, a positive factor indicating strength and potency.
7. **Look for the final dispositor**: Jupiter is the final dispositor in this chart, as it rules the Moon in Gemini and Venus in Aries.
8. **Consider the chart as a whole**: The chart suggests that while the person is excited about the prospect of buying the car, there could be some conflicts that must be addressed before the purchase is finalized. The Moon's aspect with Neptune suggests confusion or deception around the purchase. Therefore, the person should gather more information before

deciding.

Creating and interpreting a horary chart can be a complex process. Still, with the knowledge and techniques you've learned in this chapter, you are well on your way to becoming an adept practitioner of horary astrology. Remember, take time to carefully consider the question, consult an ephemeris, and draw the chart accurately. As you interpret the chart, pay attention to the relationships between the planets, houses, and aspects. Always refer to previous chapters and the glossary to quickly identify various glyphs and symbols in the chart. You can become proficient in this ancient and powerful divinatory art with practice and dedication.

Glossary of Terms and Glyphs

Zodiacs

Aries (♈) - Aries is the first sign in the zodiac and represents self-initiative, energy, courage, and leadership. It is symbolized by the Ram, a creature that charges forward aggressively, representing its assertive nature.

Taurus (♉) - Taurus is an earth sign focusing on material gain and stability. The Bull glyph associated with this sign reflects its stubbornness and patience while pursuing what it desires.

Gemini (♊) - Gemini is an air sign represented by two figures of twins connected at the head. This connection symbolizes communication and duality, which are characteristic qualities of a Gemini individual.

Cancer (♋) - Cancer is a water sign, and its glyph is the Crab which symbolizes instinctive reactions, protectiveness, and sensitivity. This sign rules the home and emotions making it very nurturing in nature.

Leo (♌) - Leo is a fire sign represented by the Lion, a creature that exhibits strength, courage, loyalty, and wisdom. It is an extroverted sign focusing on playfulness and creativity.

Virgo (♍) - Virgo is an earth sign represented by the Virgin, who symbolizes purity of heart and mind. This sign has analytical tendencies and focuses on details, especially when it comes to problem-solving tasks.

Libra (♎) - Libra is an air sign represented by the Scales, which symbolizes balance and justice. This sign is diplomatic in nature, always striving to reach harmony in any situation.

Scorpio (♏) - Scorpio is a water sign, and its glyph is the Scorpion which symbolizes strength of character and an ability to survive and overcome obstacles. It has a mysterious aura around it as it is considered one of the most intense signs in the zodiac.

Sagittarius (♐) - Sagittarius is a fire sign represented by an Archer that symbolizes courage, optimism, a freedom-loving spirit, and enthusiasm for life. A Sagittarian individual loves adventures and exploring new places.

Capricorn (♑) - Capricorn is an earth sign represented by the Goat, which symbolizes ambition, discipline, and hard work. This sign is practical in nature and takes a methodical approach to achieve its goals.

Aquarius (♒) - Aquarius is an air sign represented by the Water Bearer, which symbolizes knowledge, intelligence, and humanitarianism. An Aquarian individual loves to be around people but also needs plenty of alone time for introspection.

Pisces (♓) - Pisces is a water sign represented by two Fish swimming in opposite directions, one representing the spiritual world and the other representing the material world. A Piscean individual has sensitivity, imagination, and creativity as its main traits.

Alchemical Three Primes

Cardinal: This prime represents action, start, and movement. It is associated with the zodiac signs Aries, Cancer, Libra, and Capricorn and typically appears as an inverted triangle or arrowhead symbol in a horary chart. It reflects our ability to take the initiative and make decisions in order to achieve our goals.

Mutable: This prime signifies changeability and adaptability. It is associated with the zodiac signs Gemini, Virgo, Sagittarius, and Pisces and typically appears as a wave symbol in a horary chart. It reflects our ability to adjust to changing circumstances and adapt quickly to new situations.

Fixed: This prime represents stability and consistency. It is associated with the zodiac signs Taurus, Leo, Scorpio, and Aquarius and typically appears as a cross symbol in a horary chart. It reflects our ability to stay focused on our goals despite the potential for disruption or distraction.

Planets

Sun ☉: The Sun represents the conscious self, offering clarity on matters involving identity and purpose. It symbolizes vitality, creativity, and ambition. Its presence suggests taking action to manifest your desires and pursue new endeavors. The Sun's glyph looks like a circle with a dot in the center, representing its strong focus on goal achievement and creative expression.

Moon ☽: The Moon symbolizes the subconscious, providing insight into your unconscious motivations and emotions. This planet is associated with intuition, emotions, instinct, and unconscious desires. Its presence suggests exploring your inner depths and gaining a better understanding of you as a person. The Moon's glyph is shaped like a crescent moon, representing its connection to your emotional needs.

Mercury ☿: Mercury represents intellect and communication, helping make sense of the world through analysis and reason. It encourages curiosity, exploration, and learning new things. Its presence suggests paying closer attention to your thoughts and ideas to better understand yourself and the people around you. The Mercury glyph looks like a circle with a cross inside, symbolizing its ability to bring order out of chaos.

Venus ♀: Venus symbolizes love, beauty, and harmony. It encourages you to seek pleasure and comfort in your lives and appreciate the beauty around you. Its presence suggests enjoying life's luxuries and finding joy in simple pleasures. The Venus glyph looks like a circle with an arrow pointing up, symbolizing its connection to our capacity for love and appreciation.

Mars ♂: Mars represents energy, passion, and aggression. It helps you take action toward achieving your goals and overcoming obstacles. Its presence suggests taking decisive steps toward success instead of waiting passively for things to happen. The Mars glyph is shaped like an arrow pointing forward, representing its willingness to push ahead despite any challenges it may face.

Jupiter ♃: Jupiter symbolizes expansion and abundance, helping you grow and succeed in your endeavors. It encourages you to take risks, aim high and reach for the stars. Its presence suggests making the most out of opportunities that come your way. The Jupiter glyph looks like a four-pointed star, representing its ability to bring luck and success into our lives.

Saturn ♄: Saturn represents structure, discipline, and responsibility. It helps to create order in your life by setting boundaries and taking control of your environment. Its presence suggests creating rules and regulations in order to get things done effectively and efficiently. The Saturn glyph is shaped like a cross inside a circle, symbolizing its capacity to bring order out of chaos.

Uranus ⛢: Uranus symbolizes rebellion and disruption, helping to break free from oppressive environments and stand up for what you believe in. Its presence suggests taking bold actions to achieve your goals without being afraid of the consequences. The Uranus glyph looks like an inverted cross inside a circle, representing its capacity to overturn the status quo.

Neptune ♆: Neptune symbolizes intuition and spirituality, providing insight into unseen forces at work in our lives. It encourages us to explore our spiritual side and connect with higher powers. Its presence suggests trusting your instincts when making decisions. The Neptune glyph looks like two crescents overlapping each other, representing its ability to open us up to unseen realms of understanding.

Pluto ♇: Pluto represents transformation and rebirth, helping you confront your fears and make dramatic changes. Its presence suggests taking a hard look at yourselves and finding the courage to let go of old patterns that are no longer serving you. The Pluto glyph looks like an oval with a cross inside, symbolizing its capacity to help us break free from outdated ways of thinking.

Planetary Aspects

1. **Conjunction (☌):** This aspect occurs when two planets are in close proximity to each other, and their energies converge. It is usually interpreted as representing a union between both parties or an intensification of either one's energy, depending on the context.

2. **Opposition (☍):** This aspect occurs when two planets are 180 degrees apart from each other in relation to the Earth's position. This usually suggests tension between two forces, conflict, and possibly even conflicting opinions or values.

3. **Square (□):** This aspect occurs when two planets are 90 degrees apart from each other in relation to the Earth's position. It is generally interpreted as representing obstacles or challenges that must be overcome for a successful outcome.
4. **Trine (♃):** This aspect occurs when two planets are 120 degrees apart from each other in relation to the Earth's position. It usually symbolizes harmony, balance, mutual understanding between two forces, and an opportunity for growth and development.
5. **Sextile (∗):** This aspect occurs when two planets are 60 degrees apart from each other in relation to the Earth's position. It often indicates potential opportunities or favorable conditions that may arise if one makes use of them.
6. **Quintile (●):** This aspect occurs when two planets are 72 degrees apart from each other in relation to the Earth's position. It is usually interpreted as a hint or a clue that can lead one to uncover hidden potentials or latent abilities that may be beneficial if tapped into.
7. **Semisextile (△):** This aspect occurs when two planets are 30 degrees apart from each other in relation to the Earth's position. It often symbolizes subtle yet important changes or developments that could have far-reaching implications depending on how they are handled.
8. **Semisquare (△):** This aspect occurs when two planets are 45 degrees apart from each other in relation to the Earth's position. It usually suggests that one should take caution when making decisions or entering into agreements, as doing so may lead to complications.
9. **Sesquiquadrate (△):** This aspect occurs when two planets are 135 degrees apart from each other in relation to the Earth's position. Interpreted negatively, it can suggest blocked energy or difficulty in solving conflicts. However, looked at positively, it can indicate a need for greater effort and focus on a task or project for successful outcomes.
10. **Quincunx (⚻):** This aspect occurs when two planets are 150 degrees apart from each other in relation to the Earth's position. It typically symbolizes a need to compromise or adjust one's mindset in order to move forward. It can also indicate a potential solution if

looked at from the right perspective.

11. **Parallel (| |):** This aspect occurs when two planets are aligned with each other but not in exact conjunction. It usually suggests two forces working together towards common goals or objectives and the possibility of gaining insight on how best to reach those outcomes.

Angles

Ascendant A^{sc}: The Ascendant or Rising sign is the sign that was rising on the horizon at the exact moment of birth. It forms the eastern point in an astrological chart and can be thought of as a lens through which all energies travel, framing your behavior and attitude toward life. The glyph for this angle is a stylized figure of an arrow pointing up.

Midheaven M^c: This angle represents our ambition, career objectives, and public reputation. Its placement in a chart reveals how we may express ourselves to others, what kind of work suits us best, and how we will achieve success in life. The glyph for this angle looks like two inverted V's, one inside the other.

Vertex Vx: This angle is a kind of "fateful point," representing destiny, luck, and the power of fate. It often appears to be a coincidence or chance meeting that occurs at just the right time. The symbol for this angle looks like an inverted triangle with four lines coming out of it. Each line represents one side of the square that contains your lifetime journey. The vertex helps you make sense of these directions by understanding how they all interconnect and form a larger whole.

Conclusion

As you journey through the rich landscape of horary astrology, you discover that this ancient practice is as much an art as it is a science. The rules and guidelines provide a helpful framework, but your intuition, experience, and connection to the universe's energy ultimately guide you in interpreting the chart. You may tap into a pearl of deeper wisdom transcending astrology by learning this art.

By paying attention to the subtle signals and messages arising within and around you, you'll develop a heightened awareness and intuition to serve you well in all areas of your life. Whether you seek guidance on a particular issue or simply explore the vast expanse of astrological knowledge, the more you put into the practice, the more you'll get out of it.

At times, horary astrology might challenge you to confront difficult truths or make tough decisions. But with each reading, you'll gain a deeper understanding of yourself and the world around you and develop a greater appreciation for the complexity and beauty of life. As you practice horary astrology, approach each chart with reverence and respect. Remember, you are working with forces beyond your control; your role is to listen, observe, and respond with humility and grace.

This book has revealed the intricate dance between the planets and the zodiac and how these patterns offer insight into the questions weighing on your mind. But perhaps the greatest gift of horary astrology is not in the answers it provides but in the questions it inspires. By encouraging you to pause, reflect, and tune in to the universe's rhythms, horary astrology offers a powerful reminder of the interconnectedness of all things.

Always remember that horary astrology is a tool for growth and discovery, not a means of control or prediction. The chart offers valuable insight into a particular question or situation, but it is up to you to use the information to make choices aligning with your values and goals. Remember, horary astrology is only one tool in your toolbox. It offers valuable insight and guidance, but it is ultimately up to you to take ownership of your life and chart your path forward.

So, as you journey through the fascinating world of horary astrology, may you be guided by the star's wisdom, your intuition's power, and the universe's endless possibilities. Be inspired, motivated, and encouraged to live your best life using horary astrology as your ultimate guide.

Part 2: Solar Returns

The Ultimate Guide to the Sun Returning, Predictive Astrology for Beginners, the Twelve Houses, Planets in Transits, and Astrological Chart Interpretation

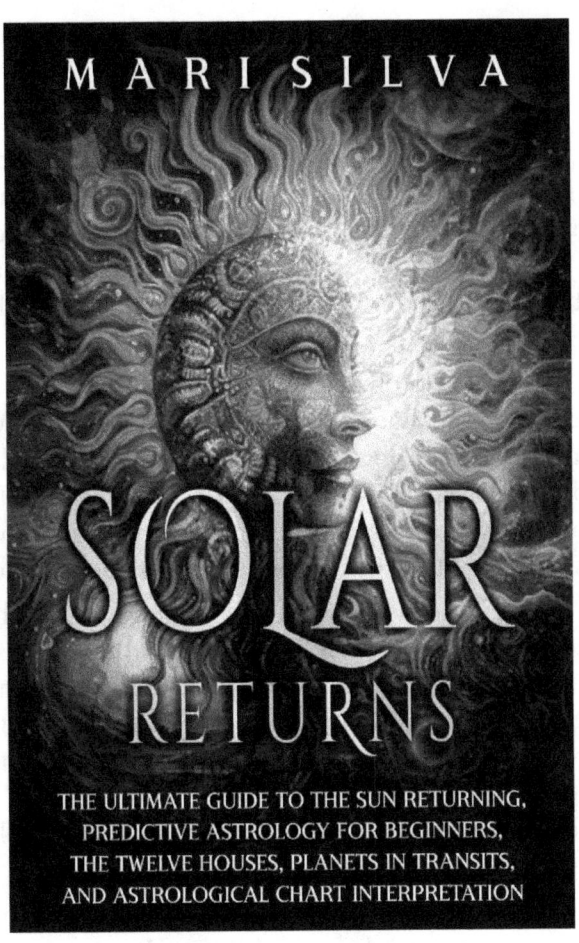

Introduction

Do you ever feel like you're floating aimlessly through life without any clear direction? Do you ever wonder why some years seem filled with constant struggle while others seem to flow easily? If so, perhaps you're searching for a deeper understanding of your life's path and purpose. Look no further than "Solar Returns - The Ultimate Guide to the Sun Returning."

This book is a comprehensive guide to predictive astrology for beginners, offering a clear and concise introduction to the twelve houses, planets in transit, and astrological chart interpretation. Whether you're new to astrology or have been exploring it for some time, this book will provide the tools to unlock the mysteries of your birth chart and gain a deeper understanding of the cosmic forces at work in your life.

What sets "Solar Returns" apart from other astrology books on the market is its user-friendly approach to what may otherwise be considered a very complex subject. This book is specifically designed with beginners in mind, offering easy-to-follow instructions and hands-on methods to help you interpret your birth chart and gain insight into your future. With its clear explanations and step-by-step guidance, "Solar Returns" will help you build a solid foundation of astrological knowledge and develop your own unique astrological style.

But this book is more than just a beginner's guide to astrology. "Solar Returns" focuses on the annual event of the sun's return to its exact birth position, known as the solar return chart. This chart provides insight into the themes and challenges you'll face in the coming year and can help you navigate the twists and turns of life with greater ease and clarity. By understanding the significance of your solar return chart, you can harness the power of the planets and stars to make conscious choices aligning with your higher purpose.

If you're ready to deepen your understanding of astrology and unlock the secrets of your birth chart, then "Solar Returns - The Ultimate Guide to the Sun Returning" is the book for you. With its clear, concise language and practical, hands-on approach, this book will empower you to take charge of your life and navigate the cosmic forces with greater ease and grace. So why wait? Take the first step on your astrological journey today and discover the transformative power of the stars.

Chapter 1: Understanding Solar Returns

What on Earth Is a Solar Return?

A solar return is not some strange dance move or a funky new cocktail recipe, though it's pretty easy to see how the phrase may sound a bit peculiar to the uninitiated. No, in astrology, a solar return is a significant event that occurs when the sun returns to the exact position it held in the zodiac at the moment of your birth. This cosmic occurrence marks the beginning of a new astrological year for you. Many astrologers believe we can glean the energy and themes of the year ahead by analyzing the position of the planets and stars at the moment of your solar return.

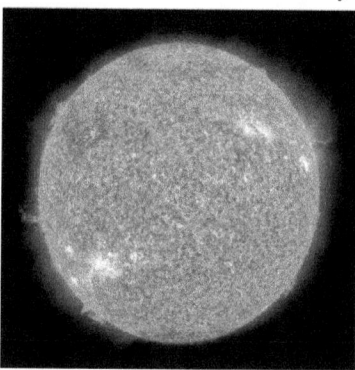

A solar return is a significant event that occurs when the sun returns to the exact position it held in the zodiac at the moment of your birth.
https://www.pexels.com/photo/sun-fire-hot-research-87611/

It's a bit like celebrating a personal New Year's Day — a time to reflect on the past and set intentions for the future. Some people choose to mark the occasion with rituals or ceremonies, while others simply take note of the date and use it as a point of reference throughout the year. Of course, as with all things astrological, there are differing opinions on the significance of solar returns, and not everyone buys into the idea of using astrology as a tool for personal growth and understanding. But for those who do, a solar return can be a powerful time to connect with the universe's rhythms and gain insight into your life's journey.

The Connection between Astrology and Solar Returns

Predictive astrology is a specific branch that focuses on making predictions about future events and trends based on the movement of the planets and stars. Unlike other forms of astrology that may focus more on understanding a person's character or inner psychology, predictive astrology is primarily concerned with what is to come.

While all forms of astrology are based on the same fundamental principles, predictive astrology relies on different techniques and approaches to interpreting astrological charts. For example, a predictive astrologer may use transits (the current position of the planets) to make predictions about upcoming events or analyze the progressions (the movement of the natal chart over time) to gain insight into the major themes of a person's life.

This form of astrology can be a powerful tool to gain insight into the future and prepare for what is to come, but it is important to remember that astrology is not a crystal ball. While astrology can provide valuable guidance and support, ultimately, it is up to each individual to make their own choices and decisions in life. Whether you choose to engage with predictive astrology or other forms of astrology is a deeply personal choice, and there is no one right way to practice this ancient art. Ultimately, what matters most is that you use astrology as a tool for self-reflection, growth, and transformation and allow the wisdom of the stars to guide you on your journey.

The concept of a solar return has been a part of astrological practice (including predictive astrology) for centuries, with ancient astrologers using the movement of the sun and stars to track the passage of time and gain insight into the human experience. In modern astrology, the solar return chart is created by looking at the position of the planets and stars at the precise moment the sun returns to its natal position. This chart provides a snapshot of the energies and themes that will be present in the year ahead, allowing the individual to prepare and make the most of the opportunities and challenges that may arise.

Interestingly, some astrologers believe the solar return chart can be more accurate in predicting events than the birth chart. This is because the solar return chart is specific to each year, whereas the birth chart remains the same throughout a person's life. It's also worth noting that the solar return is just one of many astrological techniques used to gain insight into the human experience. From the movement of the planets and stars to the study of astrological houses and aspects, astrology offers a rich and complex system for understanding the mysteries of the universe and our place within it. In the end, you can't deny that the solar return can be a valuable tool for self-reflection, growth, and transformation for those drawn to the stars and the wisdom they offer.

Historical and Cultural Background

The use of astrology and the study of the stars have been woven into the fabric of human culture for millennia. The ancient Babylonians, for example, were known for their advanced astronomical observations and calculations. They used their knowledge of the stars to develop a complex system of astrology tied to the moon's cycles and the planets' movement.

The Egyptians, too, were fascinated by the stars and their movements, and they developed a complex system of astrology based on the concept of cosmic harmony. They believed that the movement of the stars and planets was intimately connected to the fate of individuals and nations. They used their knowledge of astrology to predict the outcome of battles and other important events.

The Greeks, who are often credited with laying the foundation for modern Western astrology, also believed in the power of the stars and their influence on human affairs. The philosopher Pythagoras, for example, is said to have used astrology to predict the outcome of the Olympic Games, while the poet Hesiod wrote about the astrological influences on the seasons and the cycles of the Earth.

In each of these cultures and many others throughout history, the study of the stars was seen as a way to gain insight into the mysteries of the universe and the human experience. The solar return and the creation of a solar return chart are just one of many techniques used to harness the power of the stars and gain a deeper understanding of yourself and the world around you. The solar return and the creation of a solar return chart are ancient practices used for centuries to mark the passage of time and gain insight into the human experience. From the ancient Babylonians to the Egyptians, Greeks, and beyond, studying the stars and their movements has been a central part of human culture and belief systems for thousands of years.

In many cultures, the sun was seen as a symbol of life and vitality, and the sun's return to its natal position was celebrated as a time of renewal and rebirth. For example, the ancient Romans celebrated the winter solstice (the longest night of the year) with the festival of Saturnalia. During that time, they honored the Sun God Sol Invictus and exchanged gifts and feasts.

In the realm of astrology, the solar return chart is said to offer valuable insights into the year ahead and can help individuals prepare for the challenges and opportunities which may arise. By looking at the position of the planets and stars at the moment of the sun's return to its natal position, astrologers can glimpse the energies and themes that will be present in the year ahead. But the solar return is not just about predicting the future — it is also about honoring life cycles and the natural rhythms of the universe. By tuning into the wisdom of the stars and their movements, you can deepen your connection to yourself, others, and the world around you.

So, as you explore the world of astrology and the mysteries of the solar return, remember that you are part of a long and rich tradition that spans the ages. Whether you use astrology as a tool for self-reflection, prediction, or simply to connect to the beauty and wonder of the universe, know that you are part of a grand tapestry woven by the stars themselves.

Benefits of Working with Your Solar Return

By working with a solar return chart, you can gain valuable insight into the major themes and trends that will likely arise in your life over the coming year. This can include various factors, such as changes in your career or relationships, opportunities for personal growth and development, and challenges you may need to overcome. The solar return chart can provide a roadmap for navigating these different experiences and challenges, helping you stay grounded and centered even during times of uncertainty and change. By gaining a deeper understanding of the energy and themes that will be present in your life over the coming year, you can prepare yourself to meet these challenges head-on and take advantage of the opportunities that arise.

This can be especially valuable if you are going through a period of transition or uncertainty in your life, such as starting a new job, ending a relationship, or embarking on a major personal project. With the solar return chart, you can better prepare yourself to navigate these challenges gracefully and emerge stronger and more resilient on the other side.

In addition, the chart can help you better understand your personal growth and development over the course of the year. You may discover areas in which you need to improve and grow, and with this knowledge, you can take intentional steps to cultivate personal growth and become the best version of yourself.

Another one of the benefits of using a solar return chart is that it can guide how to utilize your time and energy best in the coming year. The chart can help you identify areas of your life where you may be putting in too much energy or not enough and where you may need to make adjustments to achieve your goals and fulfill your purpose. For example, suppose your chart shows that you will face challenges in your career. In that case, it may be wise to focus your energy on developing new skills or seeking new opportunities that align with your passions and strengths. On the other hand, if your chart indicates that you will experience growth in your personal relationships, you may want to prioritize spending more time with loved ones and cultivating meaningful connections.

Feeling Doubtful?

The idea of astrology and using a solar return chart may seem far-fetched or even superstitious to some. It is understandable to have reservations about something not based on empirical evidence or scientific method. However, you should keep an open mind and consider the benefits you stand to gain from exploring this ancient practice, which can help you cultivate a greater sense of mindfulness and intentionality in your daily life.

Understandably, some may still doubt the validity of astrology and the use of a solar return chart. However, it is important to remember that astrology does not replace critical thinking or personal responsibility. Rather, it is a complementary practice that can offer additional information and guidance as you navigate life's challenges and opportunities. If you are a skeptic or doubter, don't be so quick to dismiss solar return charts. Approach astrology with an open mind and a willingness to learn. Find a reputable astrologer who can provide accurate and insightful information about your birth and solar return charts. Ask questions, engage in dialogue, and keep an open mind as you explore this ancient practice.

Ultimately, whether or not you choose to explore astrology and use a solar return chart is a personal decision. However, there is great value to be found in this practice for those willing to give it a chance. By gaining insight into your life, cultivating self-awareness, and approaching challenges with intentionality and mindfulness, you may find that astrology can be a powerful tool for personal growth and transformation.

So, in what ways do you think your solar return chart may be able to improve your life? Are you curious to find out all the nuts and bolts of the process of crafting and reading a chart? Move on to the next chapter to learn about the relevance of planets, cardinal points, and other important stuff you need to know about before working with your chart.

Chapter 2: Planets, Cardinal Points, and More

Now, it's time to look at the most fundamental astrological factors you must consider on any chart, whether a solar return chart or something else, beginning with the cardinal points.

The Cardinal Points

The four cardinal points on an astrological chart are the Ascendant, the Descendant, the Midheaven (also known as the Medium Coeli), and the Imum Coeli. These points mark the beginning of the four cardinal signs of the zodiac (Aries, Cancer, Libra, and Capricorn) and are significant in determining the overall themes and energies present in a person's chart. Together, the four cardinal points on an astrological chart form a fundamental framework for understanding a person's personality, relationships, career path, and overall life direction. By examining these points, along with the positions of the planets and other factors in the chart, astrologers can gain a deeper understanding of a person's unique strengths, challenges, and potential for growth.

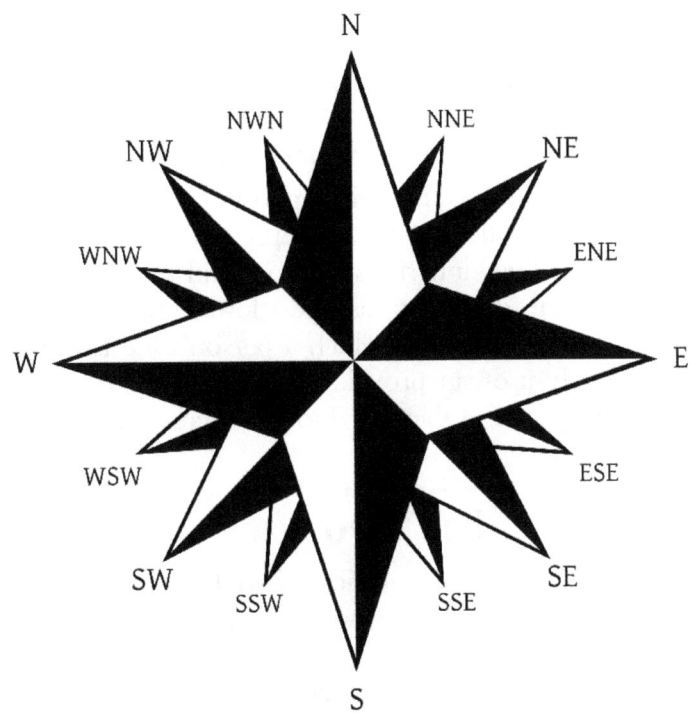

The cardinal points.
CC BY-SA 3.0 DEED <https://creativecommons.org/licenses/by-sa/3.0/deed.en> via Wikimedia Commons https://commons.wikimedia.org/wiki/File:Cardinal_directions.svg

The Ascendant, also known as the rising sign, is the point at which the eastern horizon intersects with the ecliptic. It represents how an individual presents themselves to the world, as well as their physical appearance and overall demeanor. The Ascendant is often described as the mask that a person wears in public and can indicate how they approach new situations and people. You'll learn much more about this in a later chapter.

On the other hand, the Descendant is the point opposite the Ascendant, at which the western horizon intersects with the ecliptic. It represents how an individual relates to others and the qualities they look for in a partner or close relationship. The Descendant is often described as the "other half" of the chart, representing the traits a person may be drawn to in others and the qualities they seek to cultivate within themselves through their relationships.

The Midheaven, or Medium Coeli, is the point at which the ecliptic intersects with the meridian at the top of the chart. It represents a person's career, public reputation, and overall life direction. The Midheaven is often described as the "highest point" in the chart, representing the pinnacle of a person's achievements and ambitions. The sign and planets in this house can provide insight into the type of career a person may be suited for and their overall goals and aspirations.

Finally, the Imum Coeli is the point opposite the Midheaven, at which the nadir intersects with the ecliptic. It represents a person's home and family life, as well as their innermost feelings and emotional needs. The Imum Coeli is often described as the "lowest point" in the chart, representing the foundation upon which a person's life is built. The sign and planets in this house can provide insight into a person's upbringing and the type of environment they need to feel secure and fulfilled in their personal life.

The Two Axes

The cardinal points of any astrological chart form two axes. The axis formed by the Ascendant and Descendant points is often called the relationship axis. This axis, also called the *life axis*, can give insights into an individual's approach to social situations, communication style, and relationship needs. The axis formed by the Midheaven and Imum Coeli points can give insights into how an individual balances their personal and professional lives, what motivates them in their careers, and what they value in their personal lives.

The Role of the Planets in Astrology

Planets in astrology represent different aspects of human beings, with their own unique characteristics and tendencies. Planetary movements and alignments can influence everything from moods to major life events. Astrologers use this knowledge to gain insight into the underlying forces shaping our lives, examining the positions and movements of the planets to gain a deeper understanding of the individual and collective human experience.

The Sun

Energy and effect: The Sun is a powerful planet in astrology, representing your sense of self, identity, and willpower. Its placement in a solar return chart can indicate areas of growth and success for the upcoming year, while a weak or afflicted Sun can bring challenges to your confidence and a sense of purpose. It also governs the masculine energy, the father figure, and authority.

Glyph: The glyph of the Sun is a circle with a dot at its center, representing the core of our identity and sense of self. The Sun is the center of our solar system, and its glyph reflects its central role in your astrological chart. The glyph can be seen as a representation of the Sun's radiating energy, which affects all living beings on Earth.

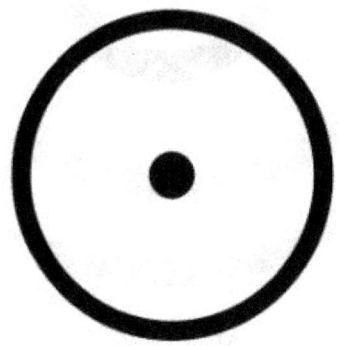

Glyph of the Sun.
https://freesvg.org/sun-and-fish-ancient-symbol

Keywords: Vitality, creativity, ego, confidence, individuality, leadership, and self-expression.

Planet event-related correspondences: The Sun is associated with the color gold, and its day of the week is Sunday. The Sun is also associated with the summer season and the sign of Leo, which it rules. People born under the sign of Leo tend to have strong, dynamic personalities and a natural sense of leadership. They are creative and confident and excel in areas that allow them to express themselves.

The Moon

Energy and effect: The Moon symbolizes emotions, instincts, and the subconscious mind in astrology. It represents the inner self and affects people's moods and behaviors. During a solar return, the Moon's placement and aspects indicate emotional expression, personal changes, and receptivity to new experiences.

Glyph: The Moon's glyph represents the crescent shape of the Moon, which reflects its cyclical nature and phases. The Moon's glyph looks like a circle on top of a half-circle, which is said to symbolize the mind's receptivity to different stimuli.

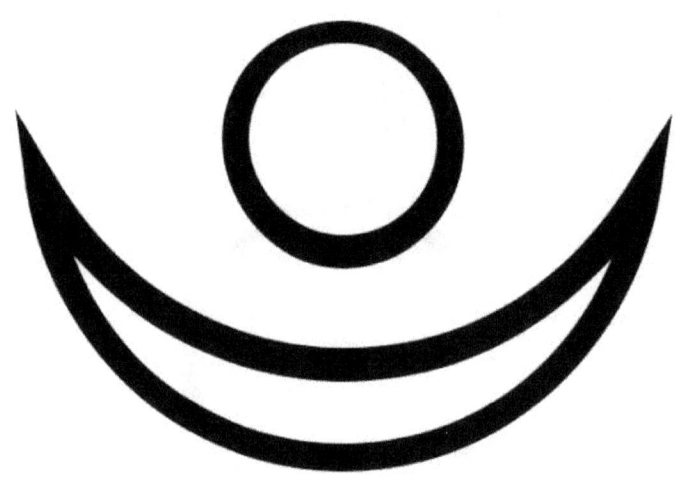

Moon Glyph.
https://freesvg.org/holy-egyptian-sign-of-crescent-and-sun

Keywords: Emotions, instincts, intuition, inner self, receptivity, sensitivity, changeability, nurturing, security.

Planet event-related correspondences: The Moon is associated with the night, Mondays, and white and silver colors. The lunar phases correspond to the seasons, with the full Moon associated with summer and the new Moon associated with winter. It is important to note that the Moon has two nodes; The South Lunar Node and the North Lunar Node.

The South Lunar Node

Energy and effect: The South Lunar Node's energy is about releasing and letting go of the past, whether that be past habits, beliefs, relationships, or experiences. It urges you to break free from old patterns that hold you back and keep you stuck. This can be challenging as it requires confronting your fears and stepping outside your comfort zone. However, the South Lunar Node's energy can also be liberating and bring a sense of lightness and clarity to your life.

Glyph: The glyph for the South Lunar Node is represented by an inverted horseshoe shape with two tails pointing in opposite directions. The shape is reminiscent of a dragon's tail, symbolizing the south lunar node's connection to the karmic past and the journey toward spiritual growth.

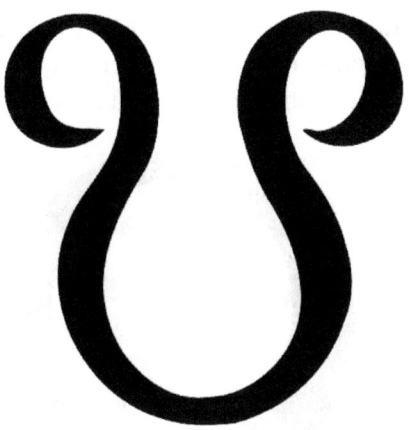

South Lunar Node.
Lucis, CC BY-SA 3.0 <https://creativecommons.org/licenses/by-sa/3.0>, via Wikimedia Commons https://commons.wikimedia.org/wiki/File:Southnode-symbol.svg

Keywords: Past life experiences, karma, soul lessons, unconscious patterns, familiar habits, comfort zone, repetitive behavior, old wounds to heal, letting go, releasing attachments, moving away from the familiar, breaking free from limitations, confronting fears, accepting change, spiritual growth, liberation, surrendering to destiny.

Planet event-related correspondences: The South Lunar Node is associated with the color black, Saturdays, the winter season, and the zodiac sign Capricorn. Its energy is also linked to the planet Saturn, which represents responsibility, structure, and authority. During a solar return, the South Lunar Node's placement can indicate the areas of your life where you need to release old patterns or beliefs to move forward toward growth and evolution.

The North Lunar Node

Energy and effect: Also known as the True Node, this is a significant point in astrology that represents the path that an individual is meant to follow in their lifetime. It is associated with the future, growth, and development. It indicates what energies and experiences are needed to develop to achieve growth and success. During the solar return, the North Lunar Node can bring opportunities for growth and expansion and may bring people, events, or situations into your life that will aid in personal development.

Glyph: The glyph for the North Lunar Node looks like a horseshoe shape with two curved lines connected to a straight line in the middle. Unlike the South node, it forms a shape like the letter "n," not "u." The horseshoe shape represents a container open toward the future, while the straight line represents the path one is meant to follow.

North Lunar Node.
Lucis, CC BY-SA 3.0 <https://creativecommons.org/licenses/by-sa/3.0>, via Wikimedia Commons https://upload.wikimedia.org/wikipedia/commons/e/e8/Northnode-symbol.svg

Keywords: Future-oriented, growth and development, destiny, purpose, moving forward, exploration, novelty, unfamiliar territory.

Planet event-related correspondences: White, silver, and pale blue are often used to represent its energy. These represent the night, the reflection of light, and the mysterious and mystical qualities associated with the Moon. They can be used to enhance meditation and spiritual practices connected to the Moon's energy. The day of the week associated with this node is Monday, which is considered good for introspection, emotional healing, and connecting with one's inner self. It is associated with the winter season, characterized by darkness, introspection, and quiet.

Mercury

Energy and effect: Mercury in astrology governs communication, intelligence, and technology. Its symbol merges spirit, receptivity, and matter. Mercury represents agility, curiosity, and adaptability. During the solar return, its placement affects thinking, communication, and learning abilities, indicating a time of increased mental activity and flexibility in thinking and communication.

Glyph: The glyph for Mercury is made up of the circle of spirit, indicating the power of thought, and the crescent of receptivity, suggesting openness to new ideas. It also features a cross on top of the circle, representing the merging of spirit and matter.

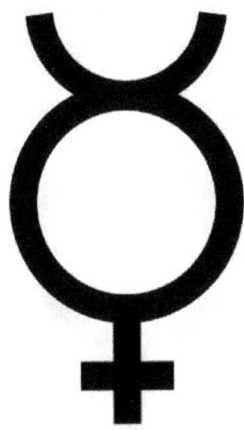

Mercury Glyph.
https://www.needpix.com/photo/download/30682/planet-symbols-mercury-astronomical-planetary-astrological-astrology-free-vector-graphics-free-pictures

Keywords: Communication, thinking, writing, learning, adaptability, flexibility, curiosity, information.

Planet event-related correspondences: Mercury's planet event-related correspondences include yellow and orange, representing its energetic and stimulating nature. Wednesday is associated with Mercury, perfect for engaging in Mercurial activities like studying, networking, and business deals. The spring and fall seasons, zodiacal seasons for Gemini and Virgo, are ideal for embracing change, exploring new ideas, and tapping into one's intellectual curiosity. Mercury's energy during these seasons is potent and can help people express themselves clearly, generate new ideas and adapt to changes.

Venus

Energy and effect: Venus is the planet in astrology that governs love, beauty, and pleasure. It is associated with the Roman goddess Venus, who embodied love, beauty, and fertility. In astrology, Venus represents our capacity for love, aesthetic tastes, and ability to find pleasure in life. Venusian energy is all about creating harmony, balance, and beauty in our lives, whether through relationships, art, or our environment. During the solar return, the placement of Venus can influence our relationships, aesthetic tastes, and overall enjoyment of life. It can indicate a time of increased social activity, creativity, and sensuality.

Glyph: The glyph for Venus is a circle on top of a cross, representing the spirit and matter coming together. It is also said to represent the hand mirror of Venus, as beauty and reflection are closely tied to the planet.

Venus Glyph.
Sebastian Lönnlöv, CC BY-SA 4.0 <https://creativecommons.org/licenses/by-sa/4.0>, via Wikimedia Commons https://commons.wikimedia.org/wiki/File:Venus_symbol_(painted).jpg

Keywords: Love, beauty, harmony, balance, creativity, sensuality, pleasure, attraction.

Planet event-related correspondences: Venus's planet event-related correspondences include the colors green and pink, which represent growth, harmony, and love. Friday is the day associated with Venus, perfect for engaging in Venusian activities like beautifying oneself or one's environment, spending time with loved ones, or indulging in pleasurable experiences. The spring and fall seasons, zodiacal seasons for Taurus and Libra, are ideal for embracing Venusian energy and creating beauty and balance in your life.

Mars

Energy and effect: Mars is the planet of action, drive, and determination in astrology. It represents our physical energy, ambition, motivation, and ability to take risks and assert ourselves. Mars' energy is dynamic, assertive, and passionate, encouraging you to pursue your goals with strength and conviction. In solar return charts, the placement of Mars can indicate a time of increased physical energy, a need for action and assertiveness, and a desire to pursue your passions and goals with greater determination.

Glyph: The glyph for Mars is a circle with an arrow pointing outwards, representing the planet's energy and assertiveness. It is also said to symbolize the shield and spear of the Roman god Mars, the god of war and agriculture.

Mars Glyph.

IZN1TEN, CC BY-SA 4.0 <https://creativecommons.org/licenses/by-sa/4.0>, via Wikimedia Commons https://commons.wikimedia.org/wiki/File:Mars_symbol.jpg

Keywords: Action, aggression, passion, courage, strength, competition, assertion, willpower.

Planet event-related correspondences: Mars' planet event-related correspondences include red and black, representing its intense and forceful nature. Tuesday is the day associated with Mars, ideal for engaging in activities requiring strength, courage, and determination. The seasonal periods associated with Mars are summer and early fall, and these are the zodiac seasons for the signs Aries and Scorpio, which Mars rules. These seasons are ideal for pursuing new projects, taking risks, and asserting yourself with greater conviction. Metals like iron and steel are associated with Mars, and gemstones like ruby and garnet.

Jupiter

Energy and effect: Jupiter is the largest planet in our solar system and represents growth, expansion, and abundance in astrology. Its energy is optimistic, confident, and generous, encouraging us to seek opportunities for growth and abundance. Jupiter is connected to higher learning, philosophy, and spirituality, and during a solar return, its placement can indicate a year of expansion, growth, and abundance. It can also suggest pursuing higher learning, spiritual journeys, and seeking personal and professional advancement opportunities.

Glyph: The glyph for Jupiter resembles the number 4, with a cross or crescent above a half-circle. The crescent represents receptivity, while the cross or horizontal line represents matter. The half-circle or semicircle is associated with the physical realm, and the vertical line represents spirit. Together, these symbols suggest the expansive, generous, and philosophical nature of Jupiter.

Jupiter Glyph.
Thyj, CC0, via Wikimedia Commons https://commons.wikimedia.org/wiki/File:Rma_-_lh.svg

Keywords: Expansion, growth, abundance, generosity, optimism, faith, wisdom, higher learning, spirituality.

Planet event-related correspondences: The colors associated with Jupiter are royal blue and purple, reflecting its regal and expansive energy. Thursday is the day associated with Jupiter, making it ideal for spiritual pursuits, higher learning, and seeking out growth opportunities. Jupiter's energy is at its most potent during the winter, the zodiac season for Sagittarius, which Jupiter rules. This time is ideal for expanding one's horizons, seeking new experiences, and embracing a sense of adventure.

Saturn

Energy and effect: Saturn is the planet in astrology that governs structure, responsibility, limitations, and discipline. It is associated with the Roman god Saturn, the god of agriculture and time, often depicted holding a scythe. In astrology, Saturn represents the areas in your life where you need to take responsibility, work hard, and learn lessons through challenges and limitations. Its energy is grounded, patient, and enduring. It encourages you to be responsible and disciplined in your approach to life. When it comes to solar return, the placement of Saturn can indicate a year of hard work, challenges, and the need for self-discipline and perseverance. It can also indicate a time to learn important life lessons and take on greater responsibilities.

Glyph: The glyph for Saturn resembles a cross with a half-moon on top. The cross represents the material world, while the half-moon symbolizes the soul or spirit. It suggests a need for balance and integration between the physical and spiritual realms.

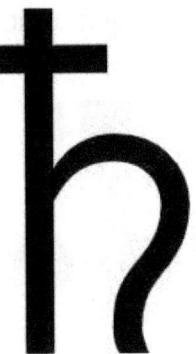

Saturn Glyph.
https://upload.wikimedia.org/wikipedia/commons/archive/7/74/20061003140009%21Saturn_symbol.svg

Keywords: Responsibility, discipline, structure, limitations, challenges, perseverance, hard work.

Planet event-related correspondences: Saturn's planet event-related correspondences include black and dark blue, representing its serious and grounding energy. Saturday is associated with Saturn, a day for introspection, hard work, and discipline. Winter is the season associated with Saturn, a time for reflection, inner work, and taking responsibility for your life.

Uranus

Energy and effect: Uranus is the planet in astrology that governs innovation, change, and rebellion. It is associated with the Roman god of the sky, Uranus, who represents freedom and limitless potential. Uranus represents your need for independence, individuality, and originality in astrology. It is also connected to your ability to break free from traditional structures and embrace new and unconventional ideas. Uranus's energy is electric, unpredictable, and revolutionary. It encourages innovation, experimentation, and a desire to be true to oneself. When it comes to solar return, the placement of Uranus can indicate a time of sudden changes, breakthroughs, and a need to break free from old patterns and embrace new possibilities.

Glyph: The glyph for Uranus features a circle that represents the boundless nature of the universe and a cross on top of it that symbolizes matter and limitation. The crescents on both sides of the glyph suggest receptivity and openness, while the horizontal line in the middle represents a bridge between matter and spirit.

Uranus Glyph.

Keywords: Innovation, change, revolution, individuality, independence, experimentation, originality.

Planet event-related correspondences: Uranus is associated with the colors blue and green and the day Saturday. It is linked to the Aquarius zodiac sign, making winter an ideal time to embrace change and explore new possibilities. Uranian energy during this time can help you to break free from old structures, embrace individuality, and experiment with new ideas.

Neptune

Energy and effect: Neptune governs imagination, intuition, and spirituality in astrology and is associated with the Roman god of the sea. It represents how we connect with the divine and our capacity for self-transcendence. Neptune's energy encourages us to let go of our rational minds and connect with our intuition and deepest emotions. Its placement during a solar return can indicate a time of heightened sensitivity, artistic inspiration, and spiritual growth, but it can also suggest confusion or delusion if not handled well.

Glyph: The glyph for Neptune is made up of the trident of Poseidon, the Roman god of the sea, and the crescent of receptivity, which suggests openness to inspiration and intuition. The trident represents Neptune's power to transform, dissolve boundaries, and create new realities.

Neptune Glyph.
https://www.needpix.com/photo/30817/neptune-planet-symbols-zodiac-western-astrology

Keywords: Imagination, intuition, creativity, spirituality, dreams, illusion, delusion, confusion.

Planet event-related correspondences: Neptune's planet event-related correspondences include blue and purple, representing its dreamy and mystical nature. Thursday is associated with Neptune, ideal for engaging in Neptunian activities like meditation, prayer, and artistic expression.

Winter is the zodiac season for Pisces, the sign ruled by Neptune, and it is an ideal time to connect with one's intuition, explore the realm of dreams, and engage in spiritual practices. The energy of Neptune during this season is potent and can help you to dissolve boundaries, open the heart, and access the realm of the divine.

Pluto

Energy and effect: Pluto is a planet that governs transformation and regeneration in astrology. Its energy is intense, powerful, and transformative. Pluto is associated with the Roman god of the underworld and represents the shadowy, hidden aspects of life. In astrology, Pluto's energy is connected to power, control, obsession, and transformation issues. It is the planet of endings, new beginnings, death, and rebirth. When Pluto is prominent in a birth chart or during solar return, it can indicate a time of profound transformation, letting go of old patterns and embracing new possibilities.

Glyph: The glyph for Pluto is a circle representing the spirit or soul, with a crescent underneath, symbolizing the receptivity of the soul. Above the crescent is a cross, representing the intersection of spirit and matter. Attached to the cross is a transverse line representing the energy of transformation.

Pluto Glyph.
https://creazilla.com/nodes/2000075-pluto-clipart

Keywords: Transformation, power, intensity, rebirth, regeneration, depth, obsession.

Planet event-related correspondences: Pluto's planet event-related correspondences include black, representing the planet's intense and transformative energy. Tuesday is the day associated with Pluto, ideal for delving deep into one's shadow and exploring hidden aspects of the self. The season associated with Pluto is winter, when the days are the shortest and the night is the longest, representing a time of darkness, introspection, and inner transformation.

Beyond the Planets

Other celestial bodies are important in astrology and worth a look at when it comes to analyzing your solar return chart. Among them are Chiron, Ceres, and Black Moon Lilith

Chiron

Energy and effect: Chiron is a minor planet in astrology that has gained increasing attention in recent years. In mythology, Chiron was a wise centaur known for his healing abilities and knowledge of medicine, astrology, and the arts. In astrology, Chiron represents our deepest wounds and the potential for healing and transformation that arises from facing and integrating them. It highlights areas where you feel wounded, inadequate, or unhealed and encourages you to confront and work through these issues. Chiron's energy is therefore associated with the process of healing and spiritual growth, as well as the ability to transcend personal limitations and turn pain into wisdom.

Glyph: Chiron's glyph features a key-like shape with a circle on top, representing the opening of doors and unlocking hidden knowledge. The glyph is also said to resemble a keyhole, suggesting the potential for unlocking hidden or repressed parts of the self.

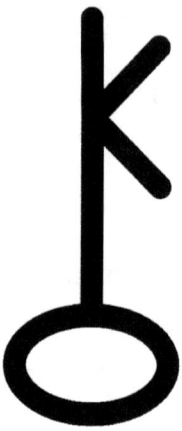

Chiron Glyph.
https://commons.wikimedia.org/wiki/File:Chiron_symbol_%28fixed_width%29.svg

Keywords: Wounding, healing, transformation, spiritual growth, wisdom, integration, pain, trauma, mentorship.

Planet event-related correspondences: Chiron is not traditionally associated with specific planet event-related correspondences such as colors or days of the week. However, its themes of healing and transformation make it a relevant energy to work with during times of personal crisis or transformation, such as during a solar return or during significant life transitions. Chiron's energy encourages you to confront and work through your deepest wounds and limitations, ultimately leading to growth, healing, and wisdom. Working with Chiron's energy through meditation, therapy, journaling, or other forms of self-reflection and healing work can be helpful.

Ceres

Energy and effect: Ceres is an asteroid in astrology that symbolizes nurturing, nourishment, and the cycles of life and death. Its energy is compassionate and protective, encouraging us to care for ourselves and others, recognize growth and cycles, and honor the earth and its rhythms. Ceres' placement in a birth chart can indicate your nurturing style and relationship with food and nature. Conversely, in a solar return chart, it can suggest a year of heightened nurturing and growth and a need for self-care and a deeper connection with the earth.

Glyph: Ceres is represented in astrology by the glyph of a scythe or sickle, symbolizing the harvest and the nurturing of life.

Ceres Glyph.
https://upload.wikimedia.org/wikipedia/commons/c/ca/AstrologicalGlyphs-AsteroidsChaldean.jpg

Keywords: Nurturing, nourishment, motherhood, growth, agriculture, cycles of life and death.

Planet event-related correspondences: Ceres' planet event-related correspondences include green and brown, representing this asteroid's earthy, nurturing energy. There is no specific day of the week or season associated with Ceres in astrology, but it is often connected with the harvest season in fall, when people celebrate the abundance of the Earth's harvest and give thanks for its bounty. Ceres is also associated with the zodiac sign of Virgo, which is known for its practicality, attention to detail, and nurturing qualities.

Black Moon Lilith

Energy and effect: Black Moon Lilith, also known as the "Dark Moon," is not a planet. It is a mathematical point in astrology that represents the Moon's apogee, or the point in the Moon's orbit farthest from Earth. In astrology, Black Moon Lilith represents your deepest desires, fears, and hidden aspects of yourself that you may try to suppress or reject. It is associated with the archetype of the "wild woman" or "dark feminine," representing the power and wisdom that can be found in embracing your shadow self and connecting with your primal instincts.

Glyph: The glyph for Black Moon Lilith is a crescent moon on top of a cross, representing the primal, wild, and instinctual energy of Lilith merging with the material world. The crescent moon symbolizes the cyclical and mysterious nature of femininity, while the cross suggests a point of intersection between matter and spirit. This glyph represents Lilith's power as a transformative force, urging individuals to embrace their primal nature and break free from societal norms and constraints.

Keywords: Shadow self, primal instincts, raw emotion, taboo desires, inner darkness, embracing the wild, feminine power.

Planet event-related correspondences: Black Moon Lilith is not a planet and does not have established planet event-related correspondences, but some astrologers associate it with the colors black and dark red. Its placement in a birth chart is believed to indicate areas where a person may struggle with their shadow selves or repressed desires and where they may need to confront and embrace these aspects of themselves to find healing and wholeness.

Chapter 3: When Planets Move in Retrograde

When a planet goes retrograde, it's like a celestial dance in which the planet appears to be moving backward in the sky. It's as if the planet is taking a step back from its usual forward motion, and this can have some interesting effects down here on Earth. Now, you may be wondering why a planet would bother to do this retrograde dance in the first place. Well, it's because of how the planets move around the sun. You see, sometimes, when the planet Earth is passing by another planet in its orbit around the sun, it can make that planet appear to be moving backward for a while. Mind you, this is just an optical illusion, but it can have some very real effects on everyone's lives.

The planets' placements and movements around the sun define their retrograde.

Horse power(H.P), CC BY-SA 4.0 <https://creativecommons.org/licenses/by-sa/4.0>, via Wikimedia Commons https://commons.wikimedia.org/wiki/File:Planets2013.svg_and_the_sun.png

Mercury in Retrograde

During your solar return, Mercury's placement can impact your thinking, communication, and learning abilities for the upcoming year. Suppose Mercury is retrograde during your solar return. In that case, it may indicate a time of increased mental activity and a need to stay informed and flexible in thinking and communication. You may find yourself revisiting past projects or relationships, and it can be a good time for introspection and reflection. It is important to be patient and cautious in communication and travel during this time and to double-check important details to avoid misunderstandings and mistakes. On the other hand, if Mercury is direct during your solar return, it may signify a time of forward progress and clarity in communication and learning. You may be more focused and productive in your work, and new opportunities for growth and expansion may arise. Overall, the placement of Mercury during your solar return can provide valuable insights into how to best navigate the upcoming year. Expect this retrograde to come three to four times a year.

Venus in Retrograde

During your solar return, Venus in retrograde can significantly impact your relationships, finances, and creative expression for the upcoming year. It can be a time of introspection, reflection, and reevaluation of your values and desires in these areas. Regarding relationships, Venus in retrograde during your solar return may bring up past issues or unresolved feelings with romantic partners or friends. It can also lead to reassessments of what you want in relationships and whether certain connections serve your highest good.

Financially, Venus in retrograde during your solar return may bring unexpected expenses or changes in income. It is a time to be cautious with investments and to reassess your financial goals and priorities. Creatively, Venus in retrograde during your solar return may lead to blocks or delays in artistic projects. It can also be a time to reflect on your creative passions and whether they align with your values and purpose. This retrograde happens once every 18 to 19 months.

Mars in Retrograde

During Mars retrograde, you may feel a bit of a slowdown or blockage in your ability to take action or assert yourself. This can be frustrating, but it's important to remember that it's only temporary. This period can be a good time for introspection and reflection, as you may be forced to examine your motivations and desires more closely.

Suppose Mars is retrograde in your solar return chart. In that case, it may indicate that the coming year will be a time of reflection and reassessment regarding your goals and desires. You may question whether you're on the right path or feeling frustrated by delays or obstacles. However, this can also be a time of deep insight and growth as you delve into the inner workings of your own psyche. Mars retrogrades once every couple of years.

Jupiter in Retrograde

When Jupiter is in retrograde, its energy is turned inward, which can lead to a time to review your beliefs, values, and philosophy of life and to make any necessary adjustments. It can also be a time to focus on personal growth and development, as you may feel the need to explore new ideas or experiences. If Jupiter is in retrograde in your solar return chart, it may indicate a period of inner growth and transformation. You may question your beliefs or seek a deeper understanding of the world around you. This can be a time of great expansion and learning as long as you're willing to be open to new ideas and experiences.

However, Jupiter retrograde can also bring some challenges. You may feel like your luck has run out or your goals and dreams are out of reach. It's important to remember that this is only temporary and that Jupiter's retrograde motion is ultimately designed to help you grow and evolve. Jupiter retrogrades once a year.

Saturn in Retrograde

Saturn is a mighty planet known for its serious, structured energy, so things can get a bit intense when it goes into retrograde. It happens once every year, lasting four and a half months, and when it does, Saturn's energy is turned inward, which can lead to some introspection and reflection. This is a time to review your responsibilities, commitments, and achievements and make necessary adjustments. It can also be a time to focus on your personal boundaries, as you may feel the need to set clearer limits and expectations for yourself and others.

If this planet is in retrograde on your solar return, it may indicate a period of hard work and discipline. You may feel like you have a lot of responsibilities or obligations to meet and that the road ahead is long and challenging. However, this can also be a time of great achievement and growth as long as you're willing to put in the effort and stay focused on your goals.

Uranus in Retrograde

First off, it's important to understand what Uranus represents in astrology. This planet is known as the "Great Awakener" because its energy is associated with sudden change, innovation, and disruption. When Uranus is in retrograde (once a year, lasting five months), this energy may be turned inward and may bring up deep-seated questions and doubts about your path in life. You may feel restless and uncertain about your current situation and may be tempted to make sudden changes or take risks.

Uranus is associated with sudden change and disruption, so you may experience unexpected events or surprises during this time. This could manifest as a sudden change in your job, a relationship ending, or an unexpected opportunity. This could also be a time of heightened intuition and creativity. You may find you have sudden insights or breakthroughs in your work or personal life or feel more connected to your creative side.

Neptune in Retrograde

Neptune is a planet often associated with creativity, spirituality, and intuition. And when it goes into retrograde, it can create a shift in the way we experience these energies. Neptune is known as the "Planet of Dreams" because its energy is associated with imagination, intuition, and spiritual awareness. When Neptune is in retrograde, you reflect on your inner world and the deeper meanings behind your experiences. It's a time for spiritual growth, so you may be drawn to creative and spiritual pursuits, such as art, meditation, or yoga. This could be a good time to explore your inner world and connect with your deeper self.

When Neptune goes into retrograde, its energy shifts inward, causing us to reflect on our inner selves and our connection to the universe. This can be a time of heightened creativity, imagination, and spiritual and intuitive insights. You may find you are more in tune with your inner voice and more sensitive to the energy around you. Neptune retrogrades annually, and this period lasts 6 months.

Pluto in Retrograde

At this time, you may experience an intense desire to explore the unknown or hidden aspects of yourself or your life or a need to confront deep-seated fears and insecurities. During your solar return, Pluto in retrograde can be a particularly potent time for self-discovery and growth. This may involve confronting old patterns or beliefs holding you back and finding the strength and courage to let go of them. You may also find yourself drawn to experiences that push you out of your comfort zone, whether traveling to a new place, taking on a new challenge, or exploring your spirituality.

This can be a challenging time, but it can also be incredibly empowering. As you confront your fears and insecurities, you may discover hidden strengths and resources within yourself that you never knew existed. You may also find that you are more capable than you ever thought possible of achieving your goals and pursuing your dreams. Pluto retrogrades annually and remains that way for about 6 months.

Chiron in Retrograde

Chiron in retrograde is an astrological event that can profoundly affect your life, particularly during your solar return. Chiron is often called the "wounded healer" and represents the healing of emotional and spiritual wounds. When Chiron is in retrograde, its energy is turned inward, causing you to reflect on your own emotional and spiritual wounds. Your solar return may signify a time of healing and self-discovery. You may feel drawn to activities or experiences that help you explore your inner world and understand your emotional and spiritual wounds more deeply.

For example, you may feel compelled to explore past traumas or revisit relationships or situations that trigger emotional pain. You may find yourself drawn to therapy, meditation, or other spiritual practices that help you connect with your inner self and process difficult emotions. You may also find that you are more sensitive to the emotions of others and feel a greater sense of empathy and compassion for those struggling. This can be a challenging time, as it requires you to confront difficult emotions and experiences from your past. However, it can also be a time of great personal growth and transformation as you work through these issues and emerge stronger and more self-aware on the other side. Chiron goes into retrograde once a year, typically for around five months at a time.

Ceres in Retrograde

When it's your solar return, Ceres's retrograde energy may signify a time of reflection on your relationship with nurturing, self-care, and self-love. You may find yourself drawn to activities or experiences that help you connect with your inner child and tap into your nurturing instincts, such as spending time in nature, practicing mindfulness, or engaging in creative pursuits. This can be a time to focus on self-care and nurturing yourself on a deeper level. You may be inspired to explore new ways of taking care of your physical and emotional needs, such as adopting a healthier lifestyle, seeking support from loved ones, or prioritizing time for rest and relaxation.

You may also find that you are more in tune with the cycles of growth and transformation and feel a greater sense of connection to the natural world around you. This can be a powerful time for personal growth and transformation as you tap into the energy of Ceres in retrograde and use it to nurture and support your inner growth. It's important to approach this process with self-compassion and kindness, as nurturing oneself is not always easy, especially if you have neglected your needs for some time. However, with the energy of Ceres in retrograde on your solar return, you can deepen your connection with yourself and the world around you and emerge stronger, more resilient, and more in tune with your own needs and desires. Ceres goes into retrograde once a year, typically for around three and a half months at a time.

Black Moon Lilith in Retrograde

During your solar return, the energy of Black Moon Lilith in retrograde may signify a time of introspection and reflection on the more primal aspects of yourself, such as your deepest desires and fears. You may find yourself drawn to activities or experiences that help you explore these aspects of yourself, such as engaging in shadow work, exploring your sexuality or primal urges, or connecting with the natural world. This can be a time to embrace your inner wildness and reconnect with the parts of yourself that you may have suppressed or ignored in the past. You may find that you are more in touch with your instincts and intuition and can tap into a deeper sense of personal power and confidence.

However, with the energy of Black Moon Lilith in retrograde, it's important to approach this process with caution and self-awareness, as the primal aspects of the self can be intense and powerful. It's important to be mindful of your boundaries and to approach these energies with respect and reverence. With the energy of Black Moon Lilith in retrograde on your solar return, you can embrace your inner power and explore the darker, more primal aspects of yourself safely and constructively. This can be a time of deep personal growth and transformation as you tap into the energy of Lilith and use it to reclaim your power and connect with your truest, most authentic self.

The moon itself cannot go into retrograde, as it is always moving forward in its orbit around the Earth. However, some astrologers use the term "Black Moon Lilith" to refer to a hypothetical point in space representing the moon's farthest point from the Earth. This point can change in relation to the Earth and the other planets, and some astrologers believe that its movements can influence the human experience. The hypothetical point in space represented by Black Moon Lilith can be considered as being in retrograde motion relative to the Earth. However, this is a somewhat controversial concept in astrology, and not all astrologers use or agree with the use of Black Moon Lilith in their interpretations.

Chapter 4: Houses and Zodiac Signs 101

What Are Zodiac Signs?

Zodiac signs are the 12 astrological signs based on the division of the ecliptic into 12 equal parts, each named after a constellation positioned in that part of the sky during ancient times. The 12 signs are Aries, Taurus, Gemini, Cancer, Leo, Virgo, Libra, Scorpio, Sagittarius, Capricorn, Aquarius, and Pisces. Each sign has its own unique set of characteristics, personality traits, and symbolism associated with it. They are used in astrology to help you to understand individual personality traits and compatibility with others and to provide insight into different aspects of a person's life.

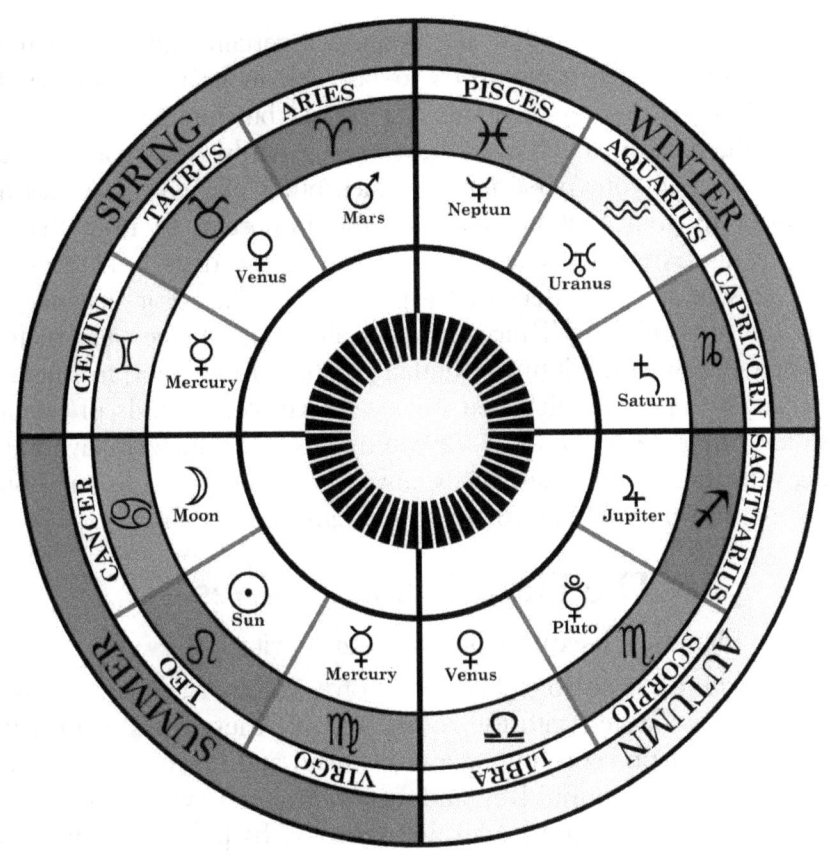

The houses of astrology.

What Are Houses?

In astrology, each of the 12 houses is associated with a particular sign of the zodiac, which governs its themes and energies. The houses start with the Ascendant or Rising sign, which is the sign that was on the horizon at the time of a person's birth.

The houses represent various aspects of a person's life, including personality, physical body, finances, home life, partnerships, career, spirituality, and more. By examining the placement of the planets within the houses of a birth chart, astrologers can gain insights into a person's life path, strengths and weaknesses, and potential challenges and opportunities. Each house has unique symbolism, themes, and correspondences, which can help illuminate different areas of a person's life and guide personal growth and development.

It is important to note that just because a certain sign rules a house doesn't mean the sign itself needs to be seen in its ruling house. For instance, Aries is in charge of the first house, but just because you are strongly influenced by this house does not necessarily mean you have a lot of Aries energy in your personality. In fact, other planetary energies may be stronger in your first house. It is also important to note that just because a sign is not in charge of a certain house does not necessarily mean that sign doesn't affect that aspect of your life. For instance, the second house is ruled by Taurus, and it's all about finances and material possessions. However, if it turns out that you had strong Scorpio Energy in your chart, it is possible that you will be drawn to the kinds of financial investments that are very intense, or you may have a transformative way of dealing with money. In other words, any sign can be found in any house. It all comes down to the placement of the signs on your chart.

The First House of Aries

Keywords: Identity, self-expression, appearance, vitality.

The first house in astrology is also known as the Ascendant or Rising sign, and it is associated with the zodiac sign of Aries. Aries is a cardinal fire sign with a glyph representing a ram's head and horns. As a fire sign, Aries is passionate, impulsive, and action-oriented, while its cardinal modality makes it a natural leader and initiator. Its polarity is masculine, which reflects its assertive, self-directed energy. The connection between Aries and the first house comes from the fact that the Ascendant is the sign on the eastern horizon at the time of a person's birth, and it represents their outward appearance and how they present themselves to the world. Aries, as the first sign of the zodiac, is associated with new beginnings, self-discovery, and taking action, which are all important themes for the first house.

The first house is an angular house, which means it is one of the chart's most powerful and significant houses. It represents the individual self, identity, personality, physical body, and overall health. The first house is also associated with the early years of life and the experiences and challenges that shape a person's sense of self. Having Aries as the ruler of the first house in your solar chart indicates that you are likely to have a strong sense of self and personal identity. You may be a natural leader or initiator who desires to take charge and make things happen. Your physical appearance and health may also be important, and you may have a strong drive to stay active and maintain a healthy lifestyle.

However, Aries can also be impulsive and quick to anger, so you may need to work on managing your emotions and impulses in a healthy way. The first house can also reveal information about your family background and any challenges or obstacles you may have faced early in life that have shaped your personality and sense of self. You can better understand yourself and your life path by exploring the themes and energies associated with the first house and Aries.

The Second House of Taurus

Keywords: Material possessions, values, self-worth, financial security.

The connection between Taurus and the second house is that both represent material possessions, resources, and self-worth. Taurus is an earth sign associated with practicality, stability, and security, which are relevant themes in the second house. The glyph of Taurus represents the head and horns of a bull, indicating the sign's tenacity, determination, and willingness to charge ahead in pursuit of what it wants. Taurus is a fixed sign, which means it is focused on stability and resistance to change. Its polarity is feminine (yin), which is receptive, nurturing, and introspective.

The second house represents your personal resources, including your possessions, finances, and self-worth. It is the house of material security and stability, as well as your values and priorities in life. It also indicates your ability to manage resources, both in terms of financial resources and your talents and abilities. Having a strong second house in your solar chart can indicate a focus on building and accumulating material possessions and developing a strong sense of self-worth and self-esteem. It can also indicate a focus on financial stability and management, and an appreciation for the beauty and pleasures of life. A weak or challenged second house can indicate difficulty in managing resources, issues with self-worth, or financial instability.

You may also be interested in developing your skills and talents to increase your earning potential. Alternatively, you may need to examine your relationship with money and possessions and develop a healthier sense of self-worth.

The Third House of Gemini

Keywords: Communication, learning, short trips, siblings.

The third house is connected to communication, learning, and the immediate environment. Gemini is an air sign with a mutable modality and a positive polarity, and its glyph represents the twins, signifying duality and versatility. The third house's energies reflect Gemini's intellectual curiosity, communication skills, and adaptability. This house deals with how you communicate, express yourself, and gather information. It also represents your immediate surroundings, such as siblings, neighbors, and daily routines.

The third house can provide insights into how you learn and process information, your communication style, and your relationship with siblings and neighbors. It also shows how you express yourself creatively through writing, speaking, or other means. Additionally, the third house is associated with short trips, transportation, and technology. A strong third house in a solar chart can indicate someone highly communicative, adaptable, and curious. They may excel in fields such as writing, teaching, journalism, or public speaking. However, a weak or afflicted third house may suggest difficulties with communication or learning or problems with siblings or neighbors.

The Fourth House of Cancer

Keywords: Home, family, roots, emotional security.

The fourth house is associated with the home, family, and emotional security, all important themes in Cancer's energy.

Cancer is a water sign, represented by the glyph of the crab. Water signs are known for their emotional depth, sensitivity, and intuition. Cancer is a cardinal sign, which means it is associated with taking the initiative, leadership, and action. It is also a feminine or yin sign, which means it is receptive and nurturing.

In astrology, the fourth house represents the foundation of one's physical and emotional life. It is associated with the home, family, and one's sense of security and roots. This house represents the past, particularly one's childhood and upbringing. It can provide insights into the influence of family dynamics and their role in shaping an individual's sense of identity and emotional needs.

The fourth house also governs one's private life, including the innermost aspects of the self that are not always visible to the public. This house is associated with one's emotional health, well-being, and sense of belonging and connection to others. It can also provide information on how an individual seeks comfort and security in life, both physically and emotionally.

During a solar return, the fourth house can indicate a focus on home and family matters and an increased need for emotional security and stability. It may also bring up issues related to one's past, particularly childhood experiences, and how they continue influencing one's emotional needs and sense of identity. A strong emphasis on the fourth house can suggest a need for introspection, inner work, and a focus on establishing a strong foundation for the future.

The Fifth House of Leo

Keywords: Creativity, self-expression, pleasure, children.

The fifth house is ruled by Leo, connected to this house because both relate to creativity, self-expression, and pleasure. Leo is a fixed fire sign, represented by the glyph of the lion, which signifies strength, courage, and leadership. Its element of fire symbolizes passion, enthusiasm, and creativity, while its fixed modality represents stability, determination, and persistence. Its polarity is yang, which means it is outgoing, active, and assertive.

The fifth house is commonly referred to as the House of Creativity, and it is associated with all forms of self-expression, including art, music, drama, and writing. It is also linked to romantic relationships, children, and leisure activities. This house represents how you express yourself creatively, seek pleasure and enjoyment, and relate to others in romantic and sexual relationships. In a solar chart, the fifth house can provide insight into your creative expression, hobbies and leisure activities, and your romantic relationships and attitude towards love. It can also reveal the type of people you are attracted to and the qualities you seek in a partner. Additionally, the fifth house can indicate your relationship with your children and those around you.

The Sixth House of Virgo

Keywords: Work, health, routine, service.

Virgo is an earth sign with the glyph of a maiden or virgin holding a bundle of wheat. It is a mutable sign, meaning it's adaptable and flexible, and it's also a feminine or receptive sign. The connection between the sixth house and Virgo lies in their focus on detail, organization, and practicality. Virgo is associated with the concept of service, and the sixth house is often linked with work and health, indicating a focus on helping others and taking care of oneself.

The sixth house governs how you take care of yourself and your responsibilities, and it's often linked to your relationship with coworkers and employees. A strong presence of planets in the sixth house during a solar return can suggest a time of increased focus on work and health matters. This may be a time for self-improvement and routine maintenance, whether establishing better habits for work productivity or focusing on physical health and self-care. It can also suggest a time of increased responsibility and attention to detail in daily life.

The Seventh House of Libra

Keywords: Relationships, partnerships, collaboration, marriage.

The connection between Libra, symbolized by the scales, and the seventh house is that both are related to relationships, balance, and harmony. Libra is an air sign associated with communication, ideas, and mental stimulation. It is a cardinal sign that is proactive, action-oriented, and focused on initiating new projects. Libra is also a masculine sign associated with assertiveness and outward expression.

The seventh house is often called the house of partnerships, marriage, and contracts. It represents your relationships with others, particularly your romantic and business partners. It is also associated with balance, harmony, diplomacy, negotiation, and compromise. The seventh house can give insights into the type of people you attract and your approach to relationships and partnerships. The seventh house can also reveal information about your shadow side, including the qualities and behaviors you may project onto your partners. It can also highlight any imbalances or issues within your relationships that must be addressed and resolved.

The Eighth House of Scorpio

Keywords: Transformation, shared resources, intimacy, power dynamics.

Scorpio is a fixed water sign. Its glyph is represented by a scorpion, which symbolizes the sign's deep emotional intensity and its ability to sting when threatened. The element of water represents emotions and intuition, while the modality of fixed means that Scorpio is stable and persistent in its pursuits. Scorpio is also a feminine sign and is associated with the polarity of yin.

The connection between Scorpio and the eighth house is rooted in their shared themes of transformation, regeneration, and intimacy. Scorpio is known for its intense desire for power and control, and the eighth house represents shared resources, such as finances, inheritances, and intimate partnerships. Both Scorpio and the eighth house deal with the darker aspects of life, including secrets, taboos, and death.

In a solar chart, the eighth house signifies deep psychological transformation, exploration, shared resources, and intimacy with others. This house can provide insight into one's attitudes toward sex, death, and other taboo subjects. The eighth house is also associated with inheritances, investments, and joint finances, making it an important area to examine for financial planning and decision-making. Additionally, the eighth house is related to the concept of rebirth and transformation, indicating that this house can provide insight into personal growth and evolution.

The Ninth House of Sagittarius

Keywords: Higher education, travel, philosophy, spirituality.

Sagittarius is a fire sign with the glyph of an archer shooting an arrow toward the sky. It's a mutable sign, indicating adaptability and flexibility, and its element is fire, representing inspiration, passion, and creativity. The polarity of Sagittarius is yang, which is associated with assertiveness, confidence, and action.

The connection between Sagittarius and the ninth house lies in their shared themes of exploration, expansion, and higher learning. Sagittarius is known for its love of adventure and exploration, and the ninth house reflects this through its association with higher education, travel, philosophy, and spirituality. Both Sagittarius and the ninth house seek to expand their horizons through physical or intellectual pursuits.

In terms of its significance in a solar chart, the ninth house reveals a person's attitudes toward higher education, philosophy, and spirituality. It indicates their desire to learn and explore the world around them, their ability to understand abstract concepts, and their willingness to seek truth and meaning. The ninth house also reflects a person's relationship with foreign cultures and their desire to travel and experience different ways of life. Additionally, the ninth house can reveal a person's attitude towards religion and their sense of purpose in life.

The Tenth House of Capricorn

Keywords: Career, reputation, public image, authority.

Capricorn is an earth sign with the glyph of the mountain goat. It is a cardinal sign, which means it is focused on taking action and initiating change. The element of Capricorn is earth, making it practical, grounded, and focused on material success. Its modality is also associated with structure and organization, making it a sign of authority and responsibility. Capricorn is a feminine yin sign, representing the receptive and reflective qualities of the universe.

The tenth house is traditionally known as the house of career, public image, and social status. It represents our aspirations, goals, and achievements in the outside world. The tenth house is the house of the father, authority figures, and government institutions. It also represents our sense of duty, responsibility, and reputation. This house is associated with your legacy and how society remembers you after you are gone.

The position of planets in the tenth house can provide insight into your career and professional pursuits. It shows your level of ambition, your drive for success, and the type of work you are best suited for. It can also reveal your relationship with authority figures, your need for recognition and approval, and your ability to handle responsibility. The condition of the ruler of the tenth house, Saturn, can indicate how you handle challenges and obstacles in your professional lives and the level of discipline and focus you bring to your work.

The Eleventh House of Aquarius

Keywords: Community, social groups, hopes and wishes, humanitarianism.

Aquarius is associated with the idea of community and social groups, and the eleventh house is associated with social connections and networks.

Aquarius is an air sign with the glyph of two wavy lines representing water or electricity. Its element is air, representing intellect, communication, and social connection. Aquarius is a fixed sign, indicating a stable and persistent nature, and its polarity is masculine, representing assertiveness and action.

The eleventh house is traditionally associated with hopes, dreams, aspirations, friendships, groups, and organizations. It represents the networks you form and the social circles you belong to. It is also associated with humanitarianism, philanthropy, and social causes.

In a solar chart, it can also indicate your aspirations and goals and your ability to work with others toward a common purpose. The sign ruling the eleventh house can also give insight into your approach to social connection and their attitudes towards community involvement.

The Twelfth House of Pisces

Keywords: Subconscious mind, spirituality, hidden influences, endings.

The twelfth house is associated with endings, spirituality, and hidden or subconscious influences. It is ruled by the zodiac sign Pisces, known for its dreamy and intuitive qualities. Pisces and the twelfth house represent the realm of the unconscious and the spiritual, both associated with surrender and release.

Pisces' glyph depicts two fish swimming in opposite directions, reflecting the dualistic nature of the sign. Pisces is a mutable sign, adaptable and flowing with changing circumstances. Neptune's ruling planet is associated with imagination, intuition, and spirituality. Pisces' element is water, emphasizing emotional depth and sensitivity, and its polarity is feminine, representing a passive, intuitive, and nurturing energy.

The twelfth house is associated with the subconscious mind, spirituality, and the ending of cycles. It represents the need for retreat and reflection and can be associated with hidden influences and secrets. Planets in this house can indicate where you may experience endings or the need for introspection in your life and provide insights into your relationship with spirituality and your ability to surrender and let go of control.

Chapter 5: Your Solar Return Ascendant

In astrology, the ascendant, also known as the rising sign, is the zodiac sign that was rising on the eastern horizon at the moment of one's birth. In a solar return chart, the ascendant represents the "mask" you wear during the year or how you present yourself to the world.

The ascendant in your solar return chart can indicate how your physical appearance may change or how you may project a different image to the world. Additionally, the ascendant can provide clues about the themes and areas of focus for the upcoming year, as it sets the tone for the entire chart.

The house placement of the ascendant in a solar return chart can also be significant, as it shows which area of life may be emphasized during the year. For example, suppose the solar return ascendant falls in the fourth house. In that case, there may be a focus on family, home, and emotional security during the year. If it falls in the tenth house, there may be a focus on career, public image, and achievement.

Ascendants in the Signs

Aries

When the solar return ascendant is in Aries, it can indicate a year of new beginnings and fresh starts. The individual may feel a renewed sense of vitality and energy and may be more eager to take on new projects and challenges. This placement can also suggest a need for independence and a desire to assert one's own will and identity.

Taurus
In a solar return chart, when the ascendant is in Taurus, it can indicate a year focused on stability, security, and material well-being. This may be a time for building foundations in one's life, such as purchasing a home or starting a long-term investment plan. Financial stability and security may also be a major focus, with opportunities for growth and expansion in this area.

Gemini
When the solar return ascendant is in Gemini, it suggests that the upcoming year will be a time of increased communication, networking, and learning. This may manifest as an increased social life, with opportunities to meet new people and engage in stimulating conversations. It may also indicate an increased interest in learning new things, taking courses, or pursuing higher education.

Cancer
The ascendant in Cancer indicates that the coming year will be a time of emotional growth and introspection. This placement suggests that the individual will be more in touch with their feelings and may have a greater need for emotional security and stability. They may feel more sensitive than usual and may need to take time for self-care and nurturing.

Leo
The themes of self-expression, creativity, and leadership are highlighted in Leo. You may find yourself in positions of authority or leadership during the coming year, and you are likely to feel comfortable and confident in these roles. Your creative energy is also likely high, and you may succeed in creative endeavors or artistic pursuits. This is a good time to showcase your talents and share your unique perspective with others.

Libra
The ascendant in Libra can indicate a year focused on relationships and creating harmony in your life. The Libra ascendant can bring a sense of balance and perspective to the year, helping to facilitate negotiations and compromise in difficult situations. This can be a year when relationships take center stage, and there may be opportunities to deepen existing connections or form new ones.

Scorpio

The Scorpio ascendant in the solar return chart can indicate a year of transformation and renewal. This may involve letting go of old patterns and beliefs and embracing a more authentic and powerful sense of self. There may also be a focus on deepening emotional connections with others, as Scorpio is a sign that is known for its ability to form intense bonds.

Sagittarius

The upcoming year will be a time of adventure, exploration, and growth. The individual may feel a strong desire to travel physically and mentally and may have opportunities to do so. They may also feel drawn to higher education or spiritual pursuits.

Capricorn

In Capricorn, you can expect a year focused on your career and achieving goals. This may be a time of increased responsibilities and a need for discipline and structure. It can also suggest a desire to establish or solidify one's reputation or status in a particular field. This may involve taking on new challenges or stepping up in leadership roles.

Aquarius

This placement can indicate a year of new ideas, unconventional approaches, and breaking free from societal norms. There may be a desire to stand out and be unique, which could be a good time to try new things and take risks. This placement can also indicate a focus on social justice and humanitarian causes, with opportunities to positively impact the world. It's important to keep an open mind and embrace change during this time, as Aquarius energy encourages innovation and forward-thinking.

Pisces

If the ascendant falls in Pisces, it suggests that the year ahead theme will strongly influence Piscean energy, which could mean a focus on spirituality, creativity, and emotional depth. You may find yourself drawn to artistic or humanitarian pursuits and may feel a stronger connection to your intuition and psychic abilities.

Ascendants in the Houses

Aries

House 1: This placement indicates a year of new beginnings, assertiveness, and independence, focusing on taking the initiative and being bold in one's actions.

House 2: Here, the individual may focus on personal resources, values, and financial matters during the year, with a potential for taking a more assertive and active approach to managing their resources.

House 3: Communication, learning, and short-distance travel may be emphasized during the upcoming year, focusing on independence and taking action on one's ideas.

House 4: With this placement, there is a focus on home, family, and emotional security during the year. There may also be a need to assert oneself in these areas, potentially leading to conflicts or challenges with family members or issues around independence and autonomy within the domestic sphere.

House 5: Expect to focus on creativity, self-expression, and taking risks in matters of the heart. This placement can also suggest a period of increased confidence and energy and a desire for fun and adventure.

House 6: Aries in the sixth house suggests a focus on work, health, and daily routines during the upcoming year. There may be an increased drive to take action and make changes in these areas and a need to balance assertiveness with cooperation in the workplace.

House 7: There's a focus on relationships, partnerships, and collaboration during the upcoming year, with potential themes of asserting oneself and taking the initiative in these areas.

House 8: Expect a year focused on transformation, intense experiences, and potentially encountering deep emotional or psychological issues.

House 9: In the ninth house, Aries suggests a focus on exploration, travel, education, and spiritual growth during the upcoming year.

House 10: Your attention will be on your career, public image, and status during the upcoming year.

House 11: The year will be about social networks, friendships, and group activities, with a potential for leadership or assertiveness in these areas.

House 12: In the upcoming year, there may be a need to face and confront subconscious patterns, emotions, and spiritual matters.

Taurus

House 1: A Taurus solar return ascendant in the first house indicates a focus on stability, security, and material comfort in the coming year, with a potential emphasis on personal values and self-worth.

House 2: This placement suggests a focus on financial stability, material possessions, and self-worth during the solar return year.

House 3: Here, there's a focus on practical communication and stable, comfortable relationships with siblings and neighbors.

House 4: Your attention should be on home and family life during the upcoming year, emphasizing creating a stable and secure foundation for yourself.

House 5: The Taurus solar return ascendant in the fifth house suggests a focus on creative self-expression, pleasure, and enjoyment, with a potential emphasis on romance and relationships.

House 6: A Taurus solar return ascendant in the sixth house suggests a focus on stability and routine in work and health matters during the upcoming year.

House 7: Having Taurus as the solar return ascendant in the seventh house suggests a year of potential stability and grounding in partnerships and relationships, focusing on the material and practical aspects of shared resources.

House 8: The Taurus solar return ascendant in the eighth house suggests a focus on financial stability, shared resources, and deep transformation during the solar return year.

House 9: Having Taurus as the solar return ascendant in the ninth house suggests a focus on practical matters related to higher education, travel, or spirituality during the coming year.

House 10: A Taurus solar return ascendant in the tenth house suggests a focus on career, stability, and material success in the coming year.

House 11: The Taurus solar return ascendant in the eleventh house suggests a focus on friendships, social groups, and personal goals, as well as a need for stability and practicality in these areas.

House 12: A Taurus solar return ascendant in the twelfth house suggests a year of introspection, retreat, and the need to examine and release old patterns and attachments.

Gemini

House 1: With a Gemini solar return ascendant in the first house, there may be a focus on communication, mental stimulation, and versatility in the coming year, with a potential emphasis on personal identity and self-expression.

House 2: This placement suggests focusing on information gathering to increase financial stability and material possessions during the solar return year.

House 3: Here, there may be a focus on communication with siblings and neighbors, as well as mental stimulation and education, during the upcoming year.

House 4: Your attention should be on home and family life – and communication within the family unit during the solar return year.

House 5: The Gemini solar return ascendant in the fifth house suggests a focus on communication and mental stimulation in creative self-expression and romantic relationships.

House 6: This placement suggests a focus on mental stimulation and communication in work and health matters, emphasizing versatility and adaptability.

House 7: With a Gemini solar return ascendant in the seventh house, there may be a focus on communication and mental stimulation in partnerships and relationships, with a potential emphasis on intellectual compatibility.

House 8: This placement suggests a focus on communication and information gathering to gain a deeper understanding and transformation in shared resources and intimate relationships.

House 9: With a Gemini solar return ascendant in the ninth house, there may be a focus on mental stimulation and travel in matters related to higher education, spirituality, or long-distance travel.

House 10: This placement suggests a focus on communication, networking, and career and public image versatility during the solar return year.

House 11: The Gemini solar return ascendant in the eleventh house suggests a focus on communication and mental stimulation in social groups and personal goals, with a potential emphasis on intellectual connections and networking.

House 12: This placement suggests a year of introspection and reflection on communication patterns and mental habits, as well as a need to release old patterns and attachments related to communication and mental stimulation.

Cancer

House 1: A Cancer solar return ascendant in the first house indicates a focus on emotional sensitivity and self-care, with potential emphasis on self-nurturing and personal growth.

House 2: This placement suggests a focus on financial security and emotional stability, potentially emphasizing creating a stable and secure foundation for yourself.

House 3: Here, there's a focus on communication and connection with siblings and neighbors, with a potential emphasis on emotional support and nurturing.

House 4: Your attention should be on home and family life, with a potential emphasis on emotional connection and nurturing in the domestic sphere.

House 5: The Cancer solar return ascendant in the fifth house suggests a focus on creative self-expression and emotional fulfillment, with potential emphasis on romantic relationships and personal passions.

House 6: A Cancer solar return ascendant in the sixth house suggests a focus on emotional well-being and self-care in work and health matters during the upcoming year.

House 7: Having Cancer as the solar return ascendant in the seventh house suggests a year of potential emotional connection and nurturing in partnerships and relationships, focusing on creating a safe and secure emotional foundation.

House 8: The Cancer solar return ascendant in the eighth house suggests a focus on emotional security and transformation in shared resources and intimate relationships during the solar return year.

House 9: Having Cancer as the solar return ascendant in the ninth house suggests a focus on emotional growth and nurturing in matters related to higher education, travel, or spirituality during the coming year.

House 10: A Cancer solar return ascendant in the tenth house suggests a focus on emotional fulfillment and nurturing in career and public life during the coming year.

House 11: The Cancer solar return ascendant in the eleventh house suggests a focus on emotional connection and support in friendships, social groups, and personal goals.

House 12: A Cancer solar return ascendant in the twelfth house suggests a year of emotional introspection, retreat, and the need to examine and release old emotional patterns and attachments.

Leo

House 1: A Leo solar return ascendant in the first house indicates a year of self-expression, personal power, and individuality, with an emphasis on creativity, passion, and confidence.

House 2: Having Leo as the solar return ascendant in the second house suggests a focus on financial stability and personal values, emphasizing investing in yourself and your passions.

House 3: A Leo solar return ascendant in the third house suggests a focus on self-expression, communication, and creativity in relationships with siblings and neighbors.

House 4: This placement suggests a focus on home and family life during the solar return year, emphasizing personal power, leadership, and creative self-expression in this area.

House 5: Having Leo as the solar return ascendant in the fifth house suggests a year of passionate self-expression, romance, and creativity, with a potential emphasis on children and fertility.

House 6: The Leo solar return ascendant in the sixth house suggests a focus on creativity and leadership in work and health matters during the upcoming year.

House 7: This placement suggests a focus on personal power and leadership in partnerships and relationships, with an emphasis on creativity, self-expression, and individuality.

House 8: Having Leo as the solar return ascendant in the eighth house suggests a focus on personal power, financial stability, and transformation during the solar return year.

House 9: A Leo solar return ascendant in the ninth house suggests a focus on creativity and self-expression in matters related to higher education, travel, or spirituality.

House 10: This placement suggests a focus on leadership and success in the public sphere, with an emphasis on creativity, self-expression, and individuality.

House 11: Having Leo as the solar return ascendant in the eleventh house suggests a year of leadership in friendships, social groups, and personal goals.

House 12: The Leo solar return ascendant in the twelfth house suggests a year of introspection and retreat, potentially emphasizing creative self-expression and healing.

Libra

House 1: A Libra solar return ascendant in the first house suggests a focus on balance, harmony, and aesthetics in the coming year, with a potential emphasis on personal relationships and partnerships.

House 2: Having Libra as the solar return ascendant in the second house suggests a focus on financial partnerships and shared resources and a desire for balance and harmony in material matters.

House 3: This placement suggests a focus on communication and relationships with siblings and neighbors, potentially emphasizing creating harmonious and peaceful connections.

House 4: A Libra solar return ascendant in the fourth house suggests a focus on home and family life during the upcoming year, emphasizing creating a peaceful and harmonious domestic environment.

House 5: This placement suggests a focus on creative self-expression and pleasure, potentially emphasizing artistic pursuits and romantic relationships.

House 6: A Libra solar return ascendant in the sixth house suggests a focus on balance and harmony in work and health matters, with an emphasis on creating a peaceful and harmonious work environment.

House 7: Having Libra as the solar return ascendant in the seventh house suggests a year of potential harmony, balance, and grounding in partnerships and relationships, with a focus on creating harmonious and equitable connections.

House 8: This placement suggests a focus on shared resources and deep transformation during the solar return year, with a potential emphasis on creating balance and harmony in these areas.

House 9: A Libra solar return ascendant in the ninth house suggests a focus on higher education, travel, or spirituality during the coming year, emphasizing creating a harmonious and balanced perspective in these areas.

House 10: This placement suggests a focus on career and public image, potentially emphasizing creating a balanced and harmonious reputation in the coming year.

House 11: Having Libra as the solar return ascendant in the eleventh house suggests a focus on friendships, social groups, and personal goals, with an emphasis on creating harmonious and equitable connections in these areas.

House 12: This placement suggests a year of introspection, retreat, and a need to examine and release old patterns and attachments to create a more balanced and harmonious spiritual perspective.

Scorpio

House 1: A Scorpio solar return ascendant in the first house suggests a year of personal transformation and empowerment, potentially emphasizing self-discovery and intensity.

House 2: The Scorpio solar return ascendant in the second house suggests a focus on financial transformation, deepening one's values, and the potential intensity in matters of self-worth.

House 3: Having Scorpio as the solar return ascendant in the third house suggests a focus on deep, transformative communication and relationships with siblings and neighbors.

House 4: The Scorpio solar return ascendant in the fourth house suggests a year of intense emotions and potential transformation related to home and family matters.

House 5: A Scorpio solar return ascendant in the fifth house suggests a year of deep emotional connection and intensity in creative self-expression and romantic relationships.

House 6: The Scorpio solar return ascendant in the sixth house suggests a focus on deep transformation and healing in work and health matters.

House 7: Having Scorpio as the solar return ascendant in the seventh house suggests a year of deep emotional connection and intensity in partnerships and relationships, with a potential need for transformation and empowerment in these areas.

House 8: The Scorpio solar return ascendant in the eighth house suggests a focus on deep transformation and empowerment related to shared resources and sexuality during the solar return year.

House 9: A Scorpio solar return ascendant in the ninth house suggests a year of deep transformation and intensity in higher education, travel, or spirituality matters.

House 10: Having Scorpio as the solar return ascendant in the tenth house suggests a focus on deep transformation and empowerment in career and public life during the upcoming year.

House 11: The Scorpio solar return ascendant in the eleventh house suggests a focus on deep, transformative friendships, social groups, and personal goals.

House 12: A Scorpio solar return ascendant in the twelfth house suggests a year of reflection, transformation, and a need to release the old.

Sagittarius

House 1: With a Sagittarius solar return ascendant in the first house, there may be a focus on personal growth, freedom, and adventure in the coming year, as well as a desire to expand one's horizons.

House 2: This placement suggests focusing on financial growth and stability and potentially emphasizing personal values and self-worth.

House 3: With Sagittarius as the solar return ascendant in the third house, there may be a focus on communication, learning, and travel during the upcoming year, with a potential emphasis on expanding one's knowledge and perspective.

House 4: This placement suggests a focus on home and family life and the need for freedom and independence within these areas.

House 5: A Sagittarius solar return ascendant in the fifth house suggests a focus on creative self-expression, pleasure, and enjoyment, with a potential emphasis on travel, adventure, and romance.

House 6: With Sagittarius as the solar return ascendant in the sixth house, there may be a focus on work, health, and service during the coming year, with a potential emphasis on growth and expansion in these areas.

House 7: This placement suggests a focus on partnerships and relationships, with a potential emphasis on growth, adventure, and shared experiences.

House 8: A Sagittarius solar return ascendant in the eighth house suggests a focus on deep transformation and growth and a potential emphasis on shared resources and financial stability.

House 9: With Sagittarius as the solar return ascendant in the ninth house, there may be a focus on higher education, travel, and spirituality during the upcoming year, with a potential emphasis on growth and expansion in these areas.

House 10: This placement suggests a focus on career, reputation, and public image, as well as a need for personal growth and expansion within these areas.

House 11: A Sagittarius solar return ascendant in the eleventh house suggests a focus on friendships, social groups, and personal goals, with a potential emphasis on growth, adventure, and shared experiences.

House 12: This placement suggests a year of introspection emphasizing personal growth and spiritual expansion.

Capricorn

House 1: The Capricorn solar return ascendant in the first house suggests a focus on personal responsibility, discipline, and achievement in the coming year, with an emphasis on practicality and hard work.

House 2: Having Capricorn as the solar return ascendant in the second house suggests a focus on financial stability, security, and material possessions during the upcoming year.

House 3: This placement suggests a focus on practical communication and stable relationships with siblings and neighbors, with a potential emphasis on career-related matters.

House 4: A Capricorn solar return ascendant in the fourth house suggests a focus on home and family life during the upcoming year, emphasizing creating a stable and secure foundation for oneself.

House 5: This placement suggests a focus on hard work, discipline, and practical creativity, with a potential emphasis on romantic relationships and pleasure.

House 6: The Capricorn solar return ascendant in the sixth house suggests a focus on responsibility and discipline in work and health matters during the upcoming year.

House 7: Having Capricorn as the solar return ascendant in the seventh house suggests a year of potential stability and grounding in partnerships and relationships, with a focus on practicality and material resources.

House 8: This placement suggests a focus on deep transformation and practicality in matters related to shared resources, finances, and intimacy.

House 9: A Capricorn solar return ascendant in the ninth house suggests a focus on practical matters related to higher education, travel, or spirituality during the coming year.

House 10: Having Capricorn as the solar return ascendant in the tenth house suggests a focus on career, status, and achievement in the coming year, with an emphasis on practicality and hard work.

House 11: This placement suggests a focus on friendships, social groups, and personal goals, as well as a need for practicality and discipline in these areas.

House 12: Capricorn in the 12th house indicates a reserved and serious nature towards exploring the subconscious mind and spirituality. You may struggle with expressing your emotions and may benefit from exploring your inner world and finding ways to connect with your feelings.

Aquarius

House 1: Having Aquarius as the solar return ascendant in the first house suggests a focus on individuality, innovation, and unconventional self-expression during the coming year.

House 2: This placement suggests a focus on financial stability, innovation, and self-worth through unique talents and resources during the solar return year.

House 3: Here, there's a focus on innovative communication, relationships with siblings and neighbors, and a potential emphasis on technology and networking.

House 4: Your attention should be on home and family life during the upcoming year, emphasizing creating a unique and unconventional living situation.

House 5: The Aquarius solar return ascendant in the fifth house suggests a focus on creative self-expression, individuality, and experimentation, with a potential emphasis on group or collective activities.

House 6: An Aquarius solar return ascendant in the sixth house suggests a focus on innovation and experimentation in work and health matters during the upcoming year.

House 7: Having Aquarius as the solar return ascendant in the seventh house suggests a year of potential experimentation and unconventional partnerships and relationships, with a focus on intellectual and social connections.

House 8: The Aquarius solar return ascendant in the eighth house suggests focusing on innovative financial and emotional partnerships and transformation and regeneration during the solar return year.

House 9: Having Aquarius as the solar return ascendant in the ninth house suggests a focus on unconventional higher education, travel, or spirituality during the coming year.

House 10: An Aquarius solar return ascendant in the tenth house suggests focusing on unique career goals and innovative public image in the coming year.

House 11: The Aquarius solar return ascendant in the eleventh house suggests a focus on friendships, social groups, and personal goals prioritizing innovation, experimentation, and intellectual connection.

House 12: Aquarius in the 12th house suggests a highly individualistic person with unconventional views regarding spirituality or the subconscious mind. This placement may also suggest a person who benefits from alone time and may have a deep interest in exploring their inner world through unconventional means.

Pisces

House 1: A Pisces solar return ascendant in the first house suggests a concentration on emotional sensitivity, creativity, and spiritual growth during the upcoming year.

House 2: This placement suggests a focus on self-worth, financial security, and material possessions during the solar return year.

House 3: Here, there's a focus on emotional communication, creativity, and spiritual growth in relationships with siblings and neighbors.

House 4: Your attention should be on emotional stability and security in the home and family life during the upcoming year, with a potential emphasis on nurturing and caring for loved ones.

House 5: The Pisces solar return ascendant in the fifth house suggests a focus on creative self-expression, spirituality, and emotional connections with others.

House 6: A Pisces solar return ascendant in the sixth house suggests a focus on emotional sensitivity and spiritual growth in work and health matters during the upcoming year.

House 7: Having Pisces as the solar return ascendant in the seventh house suggests a year of potential emotional depth and sensitivity in partnerships and relationships.

House 8: The Pisces solar return ascendant in the eighth house suggests a focus on emotional transformation, spirituality, and deep emotional connections during the solar return year.

House 9: Having Pisces as the solar return ascendant in the ninth house suggests a focus on spiritual growth, emotional sensitivity, and creativity related to higher education, travel, or philosophy during the coming year.

House 10: A Pisces solar return ascendant in the tenth house suggests a concentration on emotional sensitivity, spirituality, and creative self-expression in the coming year.

House 11: The Pisces solar return ascendant in the eleventh house suggests a focus on friendships, social groups, and personal goals that align with emotional sensitivity, creativity, and spirituality.

House 12: Pisces in the 12th house represents a placement where the individual may be highly intuitive and sensitive to the spiritual realm. You may struggle with boundaries and may need to find ways to ground yourself in the physical world.

Chapter 6: The Planets in the Houses

Now, it's time to talk about the planets once more. This chapter is very important because you'll have to return to it while reading your solar return chart.

The First House

Sun: When the Sun is found in the first house, you may experience a boost in confidence and self-esteem. You'll radiate with energy and feel more assertive than usual. You might also be more inclined to take on leadership roles and assert your authority.

Moon: When the Moon is in the first house, your emotions and instincts are heightened. You may feel more sensitive than usual and have a stronger intuition. You'll be more in tune with your emotions but may also be moodier and more unpredictable.

Mercury: When Mercury is in the first house, you'll be more communicative and talkative than usual. You'll be quick to express your thoughts and ideas and enjoy sharing your opinions. This placement also indicates a sharp mind and good communication skills.

Venus: When Venus is in the first house, you'll be more attractive and charming than usual. You'll be more concerned with your appearance and may be inclined to put more effort into your personal style. This placement also indicates a strong desire for love and affection.

Mars: When Mars is in the first house, you'll have a lot of energy and enthusiasm. You'll be more assertive and aggressive than usual and may be inclined to take risks. This placement also indicates a strong desire for physical activity and a competitive spirit.

Jupiter: When Jupiter is in the first house, you'll feel optimistic and enthusiastic about life. You'll have a sense of purpose and may feel like you're on a mission to achieve something important. This placement also indicates good luck and success.

Saturn: When Saturn is in the first house, you may feel restricted or limited in some way. You may be more cautious than usual and tend to hold back. This placement also indicates a need for discipline and structure in your life.

Uranus: You'll be more independent and unconventional than usual when Uranus is in the first house. You'll have a strong desire for freedom and may be inclined to rebel against authority. This placement also indicates a need for excitement and change.

Neptune: When Neptune is in the first house, you'll be more imaginative and intuitive than usual. You may be more inclined to daydream or lose yourself in your thoughts. This placement also indicates a strong desire for spiritual or creative pursuits.

Pluto: When Pluto is in the first house, you'll experience profound changes and transformations in your life. You may have a strong desire for power and control and may be inclined to confront challenges head-on. This placement also indicates a need for personal growth and self-discovery.

Chiron: When Chiron is in the first house, you may struggle with self-image issues or feelings of inadequacy. However, this placement also indicates a strong potential for self-discovery and personal growth as you work through your wounds and learn to embrace your true self.

Ceres: Ceres represents nurturing, motherhood, and the cycles of growth and decay. When Ceres is in the first house, you may have a strong desire to care for and nurture others, but you may also struggle with boundaries and putting yourself first. This placement also indicates a need for self-care, nourishment, and potential for new beginnings and personal growth.

Black Moon Lilith: When Black Moon Lilith is in the first house, you may have a rebellious or unconventional streak and may struggle with societal expectations or norms. However, this placement also indicates a strong potential for self-discovery and embracing your true desires and passions, even if they go against the status quo.

The Second House

The Sun: When the Sun is in the second house, you may feel a strong sense of self-worth and confidence in your ability to attract abundance and material possessions. This placement can also indicate a focus on building financial security and stability.

The Moon: When the Moon is in the second house, you may feel strongly connected to your possessions and material comforts. You may also be more attuned to your emotional needs and may prioritize self-care and nurturing practices.

Mercury: When Mercury is in the second house, you may be a skilled negotiator who can articulate your financial needs and desires. You may also be attracted to work that involves sales or financial management.

Venus: When Venus is in the second house, you may have a love for luxury and material possessions. You may also attract financial opportunities through your charm and social skills. This placement can also indicate a desire for harmonious relationships and a need to balance your material desires with your emotional needs.

Mars: When Mars is in the second house, you may be highly motivated to pursue financial success and take risks to achieve your goals. You may also be competitive in financial matters and may struggle with overspending or impulsive buying.

Jupiter: When Jupiter is in the second house, you may experience financial growth and opportunities for material success. This placement can also indicate a need to balance your desire for material possessions with your spiritual and philosophical beliefs.

Saturn: When Saturn is in the second house, you may experience financial challenges or limitations. This placement can also indicate a need for financial responsibility and a focus on long-term financial goals.

Uranus: When Uranus is in the second house, you may experience sudden and unexpected changes in your financial situation. You may also have an unconventional approach to money and may be willing to take risks and try new things to achieve financial success.

Neptune: When Neptune is in the second house, you may tend to idealize wealth and may struggle with financial boundaries or limitations.

You may also have a talent for creative or artistic pursuits that can lead to financial gain.

Pluto: When Pluto is in the second house, you may experience a transformation in your relationship with money and material possessions. You may also have a talent for understanding the deeper, more hidden aspects of finance and may be able to use this knowledge to your advantage.

Chiron: When Chiron is in the second house, you may struggle with feelings of unworthiness or insecurity related to financial matters. However, this placement also indicates potential healing and growth as you work through these wounds and learn to value yourself and your talents.

Ceres: When Ceres is in the second house, you may find emotional nourishment through your possessions and financial security. You may also have a tendency to take care of others through financial means and may be generous with your resources. Alternatively, you may struggle with possessiveness or attachment to material possessions and may need to work on finding emotional fulfillment beyond material goods.

Black Moon Lilith: When Black Moon Lilith is in the second house, you may fear poverty or financial insecurity, which can lead to a strong drive to accumulate wealth. Alternatively, you may have a rebellious or non-conformist attitude towards money and may reject societal norms around wealth and material possessions. This placement can also indicate a potential for transformation and growth as you confront and work through your deepest fears and desires around money.

The Third House

The Sun: You strongly desire to express yourself through communication and may enjoy sharing your ideas with others. This placement can also indicate a strong connection to siblings or a desire to connect with your local community.

The Moon: You have a natural curiosity and a desire to learn about various subjects. You may also have a close relationship with siblings or enjoy spending time in your local community. However, this placement can also indicate a tendency toward anxiety and nervousness in social situations.

Mercury: This is a natural placement for Mercury, the planet of communication and learning. You have a quick mind and may enjoy learning and sharing information with others. You may also be skilled at writing, speaking, or teaching.

Venus: You have a charming and friendly communication style that can make you popular in social situations. You may also love art, beauty, and aesthetics and enjoy expressing yourself creatively through writing or speaking.

Mars: You have a competitive and energetic approach to communication, which can make you an effective debater or speaker. However, this placement can also indicate a tendency toward impatience and impulsivity in your communication style.

Jupiter: You have a natural enthusiasm for learning and may enjoy exploring new subjects or ideas. This placement can also indicate a talent for teaching or mentoring others.

Saturn: You may struggle with self-doubt or anxiety around your communication skills, leading to a cautious or reserved approach to speaking or writing. However, this placement can also indicate a potential for developing strong discipline and focus in your mental activities.

Uranus: You have an innovative and unconventional approach to communication and may enjoy exploring new and unconventional ideas. This placement can also indicate a potential for sudden insights or breakthroughs in your learning or mental activity.

Neptune: You have a strong intuition and may be drawn to spiritual or mystical subjects. However, this placement can also indicate a potential for confusion or delusion in your mental activities, so staying grounded in reality is important.

Pluto: You have a strong desire for power and control in your communication and may be drawn to investigative or research-oriented subjects. This placement can also indicate a potential for deep transformation and growth in your mental activities.

Chiron: When Chiron is in the third house, you may have experienced a difficult or traumatic experience related to communication or learning. However, this placement can also indicate a potential for deep healing and transformation through developing your communication skills or exploring new subjects.

Ceres: When Ceres is in the third house, you may enjoy nurturing others through communication, teaching, or mentoring. Alternatively, you may struggle with codependency or struggle to express your own needs in relationships.

Black Moon Lilith: When Black Moon Lilith is in the third house, you may have a deep fear of expressing yourself or struggle with communication in some way. This placement can also indicate a potential for transformation and growth as you confront and work through your deepest fears and desires around communication and learning.

The Fourth House

The Sun: You have a deep attachment to your home and family and may prioritize them above all else. You also desire emotional security and stability.

The Moon: This is a natural placement for the Moon, the planet of emotions and nurturing. You have a deep emotional connection to your home and family and may enjoy cooking, nurturing, or caring for others.

Mercury: You have a strong connection to your roots and family history and enjoy researching or learning about your ancestry. You are also strongly interested in psychology or the mind's inner workings.

Venus: You desire beauty, comfort, and harmony in your home and may enjoy decorating, entertaining, or hosting gatherings for friends and family.

Mars: You want power and control in your home and family relationships. There is a potential for conflict or tension within your family dynamic.

Jupiter: You crave expansion and growth within your home and family life and a spiritual or philosophical exploration within your family dynamic.

Saturn: You possess a strong sense of responsibility or duty towards your family, which can lead to feelings of restriction or limitation. There's the potential for developing strong boundaries or establishing a stable foundation within your home life.

Uranus: You seek freedom and independence within your home and family life. This placement can also indicate unexpected or sudden changes within your family dynamic.

Neptune: You have a strong connection to the spiritual or mystical realm and may find solace in your home or family life. You may experience confusion or illusion within your family dynamic.

Pluto: You desire power and control within your home and family relationships and a chance for deep transformation or upheaval within your family dynamic.

Chiron: When Chiron is in the fourth house, you may have experienced a difficult or traumatic experience related to your home or family life. However, this placement can also offer you deep healing and growth through exploring your family history or nurturing your inner child.

Ceres: You may strongly desire to nurture and care for your family but may struggle with codependency or boundary issues. You can develop strong emotional intelligence and self-care practices.

Black Moon Lilith: When Black Moon Lilith is in the fourth house, you may not feel particularly trusting regarding your family or home life. You'll experience growth as you confront and work through your deepest fears and desires around family and emotional security.

The Fifth House

The Sun: You are likely to have a strong creative drive and may be drawn to art, music, or theater activities. You may also enjoy taking risks and being in the spotlight.

The Moon: Emotions and creativity are closely intertwined for this person, who may find emotional fulfillment through self-expression. You also want to nurture and care for children.

Mercury: This placement suggests a highly communicative person who may enjoy using language creatively. You may be drawn to intellectual pursuits, such as writing or teaching.

Venus: Romance and creativity are closely linked for this person, who may enjoy indulging in romantic fantasies and expressing themselves through art or music. If this is you, you seek to connect with others on a deep emotional level.

Mars: You are highly competitive and may enjoy taking risks in creative pursuits. You also love physical activities such as sports or dance.

Jupiter: You are optimistic and enjoy taking risks in creative endeavors. You want to explore new experiences and may be drawn to adventure and travel.

Saturn: You may experience limitations or restrictions regarding creative expression, but this placement can also indicate the potential to develop discipline and structure in your artistic pursuits. You may also struggle with difficulties or challenges in romantic relationships.

Uranus: You desire innovation and experimentation in your creative endeavors and may be drawn towards unconventional or avant-garde artistic expressions.

Neptune: You have a deep connection to your creative intuition and may find solace in artistic or spiritual pursuits. Look out for confusion or illusion in romantic relationships.

Pluto: You desire power and intensity in your creative endeavors and may be drawn towards transformative or taboo subjects. There is a chance for deep emotional and sexual connections in romantic relationships.

Chiron: When Chiron is in the fifth house, you may have experienced a difficult or traumatic experience related to your creative expression or romantic relationships. However, this placement allows deep healing and growth through exploring your creative talents or developing a healthy sense of self-worth in relationships.

Ceres: Your desire to nurture and care for your romantic relationships is strong, and you may experience codependency or boundary issues. You can develop a strong sense of self-love and independence in relationships.

Black Moon Lilith: When Black Moon Lilith is in the fifth house, you may experience a deep fear or mistrust of your creative expression or romantic relationships. Expect transformation and growth as you confront and work through your deepest fears and desires around creative expression and romantic intimacy.

The Sixth House

The Sun: The Sun in the sixth house can make you very focused on your work and health, and you may take great pride in being of service to others.

The Moon: With the Moon in the sixth house, you may be quite sensitive to the needs of those around you and may need to be careful not to become overly critical or self-critical in your desire to be of service.

Mercury: Mercury in the sixth house can make you an excellent problem solver and communicator, especially in the realm of work and health.

Venus: Venus in the sixth house can give you a talent for creating harmony in your workplace and taking care of your health and wellness needs.

Mars: With Mars in the sixth house, you may be very driven and focused on achieving your goals in your work and health, but you may need to be careful not to overexert yourself.

Jupiter: Jupiter in the sixth house can bring opportunities for growth and expansion in your work and health, but you may need to be careful not to overindulge in food or other pleasures.

Saturn: Saturn in the sixth house can bring a sense of responsibility and discipline to your work and health routines, but you may also struggle with perfectionism or self-criticism.

Uranus: Uranus in the sixth house can bring sudden changes or disruptions to your work and health routines and the potential for innovation and new ideas.

Neptune: Neptune in the sixth house can make it difficult to maintain boundaries and discern what is real in your work and health life, but it also gives you a strong intuitive sense.

Pluto: Pluto in the sixth house can bring intense transformations to your work and health routines but may also bring power struggles or issues with control.

Chiron: Chiron in the sixth house may bring up old wounds or traumas related to your work or health, but it also gives you the opportunity for healing and growth.

Ceres: Ceres in the sixth house may indicate a strong nurturing or caregiving instinct in your work and health life, and you may find fulfillment in helping others.

Black Moon Lilith: Black Moon Lilith in the sixth house can bring up issues related to power and control in your work or health routines, and you may need to confront and release these patterns to find balance.

The Seventh House

The Sun: You may feel more confident and expressive in one-on-one partnerships when the Sun is in your seventh house, but be careful not to let your ego get in the way of compromise.

The Moon: You may be emotionally attuned to your partner's needs and moods when the Moon is in your seventh house, but be aware of codependent tendencies and the need for healthy boundaries.

Mercury: Communication and intellectual compatibility may be important factors in your partnerships when Mercury is in your seventh house, but be cautious of becoming overly analytical and detached.

Venus: You may prioritize harmony and beauty in your relationships when Venus is in your seventh house, but be careful not to compromise too much to avoid conflict.

Mars: You may value assertiveness and passion in your partnerships when Mars is in your seventh house, but be mindful of aggression and the need for healthy communication and negotiation.

Jupiter: You may seek growth and expansion in your relationships when Jupiter is in your seventh house, but be cautious of overcommitting and ignoring red flags.

Saturn: You may experience challenges and lessons in your partnerships when Saturn is in your seventh house, but with patience and commitment, you can build a strong and lasting bond.

Uranus: You may crave freedom and unpredictability in your relationships when Uranus is in your seventh house, but be aware of impulsivity and the need for stability.

Neptune: You may have a romantic and idealistic view of your partnerships when Neptune is in your seventh house, but be careful of disillusionment and the need for clear boundaries.

Pluto: You may experience intense and transformative relationships when Pluto is in your seventh house, but be aware of power struggles and the need for mutual respect and trust.

Chiron: You may encounter wounds and healing opportunities in your partnerships when Chiron is in your seventh house, but with vulnerability and honesty, you can deepen your connection and growth.

Ceres: You may value nurturing and caretaking in your relationships when Ceres is in your seventh house, but be aware of codependency and the need for self-care.

Black Moon Lilith: You may confront issues of power and control in your partnerships when Black Moon Lilith is in your seventh house, but with self-awareness and empowerment, you can transform and heal these dynamics.

The Eighth House

The Sun: The Sun in the eighth house suggests that you may have a deep interest in uncovering hidden truths and exploring the mysteries of life. You may also strongly desire to transform yourself and others through personal growth and self-discovery.

The Moon: The Moon in the eighth house indicates that you may have intense emotional experiences and a strong connection to your subconscious mind. You may also be interested in psychology and exploring the darker aspects of human nature.

Mercury: Mercury in the eighth house suggests that you have a sharp mind and a keen interest in investigating the unknown. You may be great at researching and uncovering secrets, whether in your personal life or work.

Venus: Venus in the eighth house indicates a deep desire for intimacy and connection in your relationships. You should consider exploring the taboo or unconventional aspects of love and sexuality.

Mars: Mars in the eighth house suggests that you have a strong drive to succeed and overcome obstacles, particularly in areas related to power and control. Try a career that involves investigative work.

Jupiter: Jupiter in the eighth house indicates that you have a strong intuition and an interest in exploring spiritual and metaphysical subjects. You may be great at business and finance, particularly in areas related to investments and research.

Saturn: Saturn in the eighth house suggests that you have a serious and disciplined approach to exploring the mysteries of life. Odds are, you have a knack for leadership and management, particularly in finance and business.

Uranus: Uranus in the eighth house indicates that you have a unique and unconventional approach to exploring the unknown. Explore your penchant for technology and innovation, particularly in areas related to research and discovery.

Neptune: Neptune in the eighth house suggests that you have a highly intuitive and empathetic nature. You may enjoy exploring the spiritual and mystical aspects of life, creativity, and the arts.

Pluto: Pluto in the eighth house indicates you have a powerful drive to transform yourself and others. You love exploring taboo subjects and uncovering hidden truths, particularly in areas related to psychology and the occult.

Chiron: Chiron in the eighth house suggests that you have a deep wound related to issues of power and control. You could be among the best in healing and transformation, particularly in areas related to psychology and personal growth.

Ceres: Ceres in the eighth house indicates that you have a strong connection to nature and the cycles of life and death. You are interested in exploring issues related to food and nutrition and nurturing others.

Black Moon Lilith: Black Moon Lilith in the eighth house suggests that you may have a complex relationship with your power and sexuality. You may love exploring taboo subjects and uncovering hidden truths, particularly in areas related to the feminine and the occult.

The Ninth House

The Sun: When the Sun is in the ninth house, you may strongly desire to explore new cultures and belief systems. Your sense of self may be linked to your ability to broaden your horizons and expand your knowledge.

The Moon: The Moon in the ninth house suggests that emotional fulfillment can be found through travel and exposure to different cultures. You may have a strong connection to your spiritual beliefs and find comfort in exploring different ways of understanding the world.

Mercury: When Mercury is in the ninth house, you may have a keen interest in philosophy, religion, or academia. You may enjoy intellectual debates and exploring new ideas.

Venus: Venus in the ninth house indicates that you may be drawn to people from different backgrounds and cultures, affecting your sense of beauty and appreciation of aesthetics.

Mars: Mars in the ninth house suggests a drive to explore new territories, physically or mentally. You enjoy challenging yourself by pushing past your comfort zone.

Jupiter: Jupiter in the ninth house is a natural placement, as it rules this house. This is an excellent placement for expansion, learning, and personal growth. You are fortunate in your travels and have a natural optimism that helps you overcome obstacles.

Saturn: Saturn in the ninth house may indicate a deep respect for tradition and authority. You struggle with conflicting desires to explore the world and stick to familiar, established patterns.

Uranus: Uranus in the ninth house suggests an unconventional approach to philosophy or travel. You are drawn to fringe groups or alternative belief systems.

Neptune: Neptune in the ninth house can bring heightened intuition and a deep sense of spirituality. You may naturally be inclined towards mysticism or feel drawn to spiritual practices.

Pluto: Pluto in the ninth house suggests a transformative experience through travel or philosophical inquiry. You are interested in the workings of power structures and how they affect society.

Chiron: When Chiron is in the ninth house, you may have experienced early wounds related to your beliefs or sense of adventure. You may deeply desire to explore spiritual or philosophical topics and find healing in exploring new ideas and belief systems.

Ceres: With Ceres in the ninth house, you may find nurturing through travel and exposure to new cultures. You are strongly connected to your spiritual or philosophical beliefs and find comfort in exploring new ways of understanding the world.

Black Moon Lilith: Black Moon Lilith in the ninth house suggests a deep mistrust of traditional belief systems and a desire to seek alternative ways of understanding the world. You are drawn to esoteric teachings and reject established dogmas.

The Tenth House

The Sun: With the Sun in the tenth house, you may have a strong drive to succeed in your career or public life. You need to be recognized for your achievements and desire leadership and authority.

The Moon: The Moon in the tenth house suggests a deep emotional connection to your career or public image. Your family or upbringing influences you in your career choices.

Mercury: When Mercury is in the tenth house, you may have strong communication skills and a strategic mindset regarding your career. You can present yourself well in public and have a talent for networking.

Venus: With Venus in the tenth house, you may have a natural charm and grace in your public life. Consider careers involving aesthetics or beauty. You may also have a talent for diplomacy and negotiation.

Mars: Mars in the tenth house suggests a strong drive and ambition regarding your career or public image. You may have a competitive edge and be willing to take risks to achieve your goals.

Jupiter: With Jupiter in the tenth house, you may experience success and good fortune in your career or public life. You have an optimistic attitude toward your goals and are a natural leader.

Saturn: When Saturn is in the tenth house, you may experience delays or challenges in your career or public life. You feel a sense of responsibility and duty towards your goals but may struggle with self-doubt or limitations.

Uranus: Uranus in the tenth house suggests a need for independence and innovation in your career or public image. You love unconventional careers or have a unique approach to achieving your goals.

Neptune: With Neptune in the tenth house, you may want to use your career or public life as a means for spiritual or artistic expression. You seek careers that involve creativity or humanitarianism.

Pluto: Pluto in the tenth house suggests a transformation or intense power struggles in your career or public life. You may have a desire for control and may be drawn to careers that involve power or influence.

Chiron: With Chiron in the tenth house, you may have experienced early wounds related to your career or public image. You feel a deep sense of insecurity or imposter syndrome regarding your achievements.

Ceres: With Ceres in the tenth house, you may find nurturing through your career or public life. You love your work and may feel a sense of purpose or fulfillment through your achievements.

Black Moon Lilith: Black Moon Lilith in the tenth house suggests a rejection of traditional career paths or public images. You enjoy careers that challenge the status quo or struggle with societal expectations of success.

The Eleventh House

The Sun: This is a time of increased socializing and group activities. You love your friends and colleagues and may be more motivated to pursue your long-term goals.

The Moon: With the Moon in the eleventh house, you may experience a strong sense of belonging and connectedness with others. You seek groups or communities that share your values and interests and feel a sense of emotional fulfillment through your social connections.

Mercury: Your communication skills are top-notch in group settings. You find it easier to express your ideas and opinions and enjoy exchanging ideas and information with others.

Venus: You experience increased harmony and enjoyment in your social relationships. You find it easier to connect with others and form mutually supportive friendships.

Mars: You are driven to pursue your goals within a group context. You are competitive in group settings and motivated to take a leadership role within your social circles.

Jupiter: You experience increased opportunities for growth and expansion through your social connections. You are optimistic about your future and feel abundance and generosity in your relationships.

Saturn: With Saturn in the eleventh house, you may feel responsible towards your social networks and work hard to build lasting connections. You choose your friends carefully and take a disciplined approach to your social life.

Uranus: When Uranus is in the eleventh house, you experience sudden changes or disruptions in your social networks. You may feel drawn to unconventional or alternative groups and may be motivated to challenge traditional social norms.

Neptune: You may have a heightened sensitivity to the emotional dynamics within your social circles. You may be more empathetic and compassionate towards others and may seek to connect with those who share your spiritual or creative interests.

Pluto: When Pluto is in the eleventh house, you experience intense power struggles or transformations within your social networks. You are drawn to groups that have a strong sense of purpose or mission and may feel compelled to work toward social change or reform.

Chiron: You struggle with wounds or challenges related to your sense of belonging within groups. You try hard to find your place within social networks or may feel a sense of alienation or rejection from your peers.

Ceres: When Ceres is in the eleventh house, you may experience nurturing and supportive energy within your social networks. You may feel drawn to groups that support your growth and development and may be motivated to give back to your communities.

Black Moon Lilith: With Black Moon Lilith in the eleventh house, you may experience skepticism towards social institutions and networks. You may be drawn to fringe groups or alternative communities and may be motivated to challenge mainstream social norms.

The Twelfth House

The Sun: This placement indicates a strong urge to retreat from the spotlight and seek solitude. It could also suggest a need for introspection and reflection on one's identity and purpose.

The Moon: Individuals with this placement experience intense emotional ups and downs, vivid dreams, and a strong connection to their subconscious. They also have a compassionate and empathetic nature.

Mercury: People with this placement may be drawn to introspective or spiritual topics and may excel in creative or artistic fields. They may also struggle with communication, particularly when it comes to expressing their innermost thoughts and emotions.

Venus: This placement suggests a deep longing for emotional connection and intimacy and a need for creative expression. Individuals with this placement may also struggle with boundaries and self-sacrifice.

Mars: People with this placement have intense and transformative spiritual experiences or are drawn to humanitarian causes. They also struggle with assertiveness and may feel drained by interpersonal conflict.

Jupiter: There is a strong sense of spirituality or interest in religion and a deep desire for personal growth and enlightenment. Individuals with this placement may also tend to indulge in escapism or self-destructive behaviors.

Saturn: People with this placement feel a sense of restriction or confinement in their spiritual or creative pursuits. They struggle with self-doubt and benefit from developing greater self-discipline.

Uranus: This placement suggests a desire for freedom and autonomy in one's spiritual beliefs and creative expression. Individuals with this placement may also tend to resist authority or tradition and may feel a sense of alienation from society.

Neptune: People with this placement may have a heightened sensitivity to spiritual or mystical experiences and a strong intuition and imaginative nature. They may also struggle with boundaries and difficulty distinguishing reality from fantasy.

Pluto: This placement suggests a deep, transformative spiritual journey or interest in esoteric topics. Individuals with this placement may also tend to be secretive or manipulative in their personal relationships.

Chiron: This placement may indicate a need for deep spiritual healing or a desire to help others with their spiritual or emotional struggles. Individuals with this placement may also struggle with feelings of victimization or a sense of inadequacy.

Ceres: People with this placement may strongly connect to the earth or nature and feel a sense of spiritual fulfillment through gardening or other earth-based practices. They may also struggle with feelings of rejection or abandonment in their personal relationships.

Black Moon Lilith: This placement suggests a desire to uncover hidden truths and may indicate a fascination with the darker aspects of spirituality or human nature. Individuals with this placement may also struggle with anger or resentment towards authority figures or societal norms.

Chapter 7: The Planets in the Signs

Now it's time to talk about the planets when they are in each sign of the Zodiac.

The Sun

The Sun in Aries: This dynamic, assertive placement can give you a strong sense of self and a desire to take action and pursue your goals.

The Sun in Taurus: With the Sun in Taurus, you may have a grounded, practical approach to life and a strong connection to nature and the material world.

The Sun in Gemini: This placement can give you a curious, adaptable nature and a love of communication and learning.

The Sun in Cancer: With the Sun in Cancer, you may have a deep emotional sensitivity and a nurturing, protective instinct toward those you care about.

The Sun in Leo: This bold, creative placement can give you a strong sense of confidence and a desire to shine in the spotlight.

The Sun in Virgo: With the Sun in Virgo, you may have a meticulous, analytical approach to life and a desire to serve and help others.

The Sun in Libra: This placement can give you a diplomatic, harmonious nature and a love of beauty and aesthetics.

The Sun in Scorpio: With the Sun in Scorpio, you may have a powerful, intense nature and a deep desire for transformation and growth.

The Sun in Sagittarius: This placement can give you a free-spirited, adventurous nature and a love of exploration and learning.

The Sun in Capricorn: With the Sun in Capricorn, you may have a disciplined, ambitious approach to life and a desire for achievement and success.

The Sun in Aquarius: This placement can give you a unique, unconventional nature and a love of innovation and progress.

The Sun in Pisces: With the Sun in Pisces, you may have a sensitive, intuitive nature and a deep connection to the spiritual realm.

The Moon

The Moon in Aries: You have an impulsive and direct emotional nature, with a need for action and independence. You may struggle with patience and tend to act before thinking things through.

The Moon in Taurus: You need stability and security and find comfort in material possessions and sensual pleasures. You may be resistant to change and value routine and tradition.

The Moon in Gemini: You have a curious and adaptable emotional nature, needing variety and mental stimulation. You battle with emotional depth and tend to intellectualize your feelings.

The Moon in Cancer: You have a sensitive and nurturing emotional nature, with a strong need for emotional security and connection to family and home. You contend with emotional boundaries and can be prone to mood swings.

The Moon in Leo: You have a dramatic and expressive emotional nature, needing attention and recognition. You need to work on emotional generosity and have a tendency towards self-centeredness.

The Moon in Virgo: You have a practical and analytical emotional nature, needing order and efficiency. You think you need emotional perfectionism and can be prone to worry and anxiety.

The Moon in Libra: You have a harmonious and diplomatic emotional nature, needing balance and partnership. You are plagued by emotional indecisiveness and tend to avoid conflict.

The Moon in Scorpio: You have an intense and transformative emotional nature, needing depth and intimacy. Emotional control is not your forte, and you can be prone to jealousy and obsession.

The Moon in Sagittarius: You have an optimistic and adventurous emotional nature, with a need for freedom and exploration. You are emotionally impulsive and tend to avoid emotional depth.

The Moon in Capricorn: You have a disciplined and responsible emotional nature, needing achievement and recognition. You can be cold and prone to repressing your feelings.

The Moon in Aquarius: You have a unique and unconventional emotional nature, needing independence and freedom of thought. You may struggle with emotional detachment and tend towards aloofness.

The Moon in Pisces: You have a sensitive and intuitive emotional nature, with a need for connection to the divine and spiritual realms. You are prone to escapism and addiction.

Mercury

Mercury in Aries: You communicate quickly and directly but may sometimes come across as impatient or argumentative.

Mercury in Taurus: You have a steady and deliberate approach to communication but may resist change or new ideas.

Mercury in Gemini: You are naturally curious and adaptable, with a gift for language and communication.

Mercury in Cancer: You have a sensitive and intuitive communication style but may struggle with letting go of the past or becoming too emotionally attached.

Mercury in Leo: You have a dramatic and confident communication style but may struggle accepting criticism or feedback.

Mercury in Virgo: You are detail-oriented and analytical, with a gift for organization and problem-solving.

Mercury in Libra: You have a charming and diplomatic communication style but may struggle with making decisions or taking a stand.

Mercury in Scorpio: You have a deep and intense communication style but may struggle with trust issues or being too secretive.

Mercury in Sagittarius: You have an adventurous and expansive communication style but may struggle with impulsiveness or being too blunt.

Mercury in Capricorn: You have a practical and disciplined approach to communication but may struggle with being too rigid or closed-minded.

Mercury in Aquarius: You have an innovative and unconventional communication style but may struggle with being too detached or aloof.

Mercury in Pisces: You have a dreamy and intuitive communication style but may struggle with being too vague or unclear.

Venus

Venus in Aries: You are passionate, impulsive, and direct in your relationships, with a tendency towards initiating and taking risks.

Venus in Taurus: You deeply appreciate beauty and pleasure and may enjoy indulging in sensual experiences with a steady and patient approach.

Venus in Gemini: You are charming, witty, and versatile in your relationships, with a natural ability to adapt and communicate effectively with others.

Venus in Cancer: You are nurturing, empathetic, and deeply connected to your emotions and home life, with a tendency toward seeking security and stability in your relationships.

Venus in Leo: You are confident, dramatic, and generous in your relationships, with a desire for attention and admiration from others.

Venus in Virgo: You are practical, detail-oriented, and thoughtful in your relationships, with a focus on service and helping others.

Venus in Libra: You are harmonious, diplomatic, and romantic in your relationships, with a natural ability to create balance and beauty in your surroundings.

Venus in Scorpio: You are intense, passionate, and deeply loyal in your relationships, with a tendency towards seeking deep connections.

Venus in Sagittarius: You are adventurous, optimistic, and free-spirited in your relationships, desiring exploration and personal growth.

Venus in Capricorn: You are responsible, disciplined, and reserved in your relationships, focusing on building long-term stability and security.

Venus in Aquarius: You are unconventional, independent, and intellectually stimulating in your relationships, with a tendency towards seeking progressive and forward-thinking partners.

Venus in Pisces: You are sensitive, romantic, and deeply intuitive in your relationships, with a desire for spiritual connection and emotional depth.

Mars

Mars in Aries: You are assertive and direct in communication and may enjoy a good argument or debate.

Mars in Taurus: You have a deliberate and practical in your communication but may have issues with change or adapting to new ideas.

Mars in Gemini: You are quick-witted and adaptable. You excel in writing, speaking, or teaching.

Mars in Cancer: You are sensitive and emotional in your communication and don't do too well with confrontation or criticism.

Mars in Leo: You communicate dramatically and expressively and enjoy being the center of attention in social situations.

Mars in Virgo: You have a precise and analytical communication style. You do well with research, analysis, or problem-solving.

Mars in Libra: You are diplomatic and charming but not the best at making decisions or asserting yourself.

Mars in Scorpio: You are intense and passionate. You love delving into deep or taboo subjects.

Mars in Sagittarius: You're adventurous and expansive when you share your thoughts. You love exploring new ideas or philosophies.

Mars in Capricorn: You have a disciplined and practical communication style. You're not great at expressing emotions or vulnerability, though.

Mars in Aquarius: You are innovative and unconventional in your communication style.

Mars in Pisces: You have a dreamy and imaginative communication style but may struggle with boundaries or practicality.

Jupiter

Jupiter in Aries: You have a pioneering spirit and enjoy taking risks to achieve success.

Jupiter in Taurus: You have a strong work ethic and may experience material success and abundance.

Jupiter in Gemini: You have a love of learning and enjoy exploring a variety of subjects and ideas.

Jupiter in Cancer: You strongly connect to your family and home and experience emotional fulfillment through nurturing others.

Jupiter in Leo: You have a natural charisma and may enjoy the spotlight and use your talents and creativity to succeed.

Jupiter in Virgo: You have a detail-oriented and analytical mind. You experience success through organization and efficiency.

Jupiter in Libra: You have a strong sense of justice and will have great results in your career through partnerships and collaboration.

Jupiter in Scorpio: You have a powerful intuition. Transformation and deep introspection will take you a long way.

Jupiter in Sagittarius: You'll notice that you feel free and adventurous, and this opens you up to new experiences and growth in every aspect of your life.

Jupiter in Capricorn: Expect greater success and recognition in your career and public life, and you may have opportunities for long-term stability and growth.

Jupiter in Aquarius: There is room for expanding your social and intellectual circles, leading to new insights and a deeper sense of community.

Jupiter in Pisces: You'll discover a greater connection to your intuition and spirituality, leading to a deeper sense of inner peace and fulfillment.

Saturn

Saturn in Aries: You need to look out for impulsiveness, and you may need to develop patience and self-control in your pursuits.

Saturn in Taurus: With this placement, nothing matters more than financial stability, so try to avoid being too rigid in your beliefs and values.

Saturn in Gemini: You may struggle with indecisiveness and need to develop focus and discipline in your communication and learning.

Saturn in Cancer: Emotional security matters deeply to you, and you may find that you're constantly mired by self-doubt and fear of rejection in your personal life.

Saturn in Leo: Be wary of pride and ego. It is important to develop humility and a willingness to collaborate with others.

Saturn in Virgo: There's a tendency to strive for perfection when it doesn't serve you, and you may have difficulty being overly critical of yourself and others.

Saturn in Libra: Balance and harmony may be elusive in your relationships, and you may need to develop a stronger sense of self and boundaries.

Saturn in Scorpio: You may not find it easy to relinquish power as you have issues with letting go in your personal and professional life. Work on developing trust and vulnerability in your relationships.

Saturn in Sagittarius: You are terrified of the unknown. You should definitely work on developing a stronger sense of purpose and direction in your life.

Saturn in Capricorn: This is a natural placement for Saturn, and you may have a strong sense of responsibility and discipline in your personal and professional life.

Saturn in Aquarius: You need to avoid being too rigid in your beliefs. Decide to be open to new and unconventional ideas.

Saturn in Pisces: Boundaries matter. You need to know yourself better and have a clear understanding of your own values and beliefs.

Uranus

Uranus in Aries: You may feel a strong desire for independence and a need to assert your unique identity.

Uranus in Taurus: You experience sudden changes or disruptions in your material world, requiring you to adapt and be flexible.

Uranus in Gemini: You may feel a heightened sense of mental stimulation and innovative ideas, leading to sudden breakthroughs and insights.

Uranus in Cancer: Look out for unexpected shifts in your emotional world, leading to a need for greater personal freedom and expression.

Uranus in Leo: You want nothing more than to break free from limitations and assert your individuality, possibly leading to unconventional creative pursuits.

Uranus in Virgo: Don't be surprised by sudden shifts in your daily routines or work environment, requiring you to be adaptable and flexible.

Uranus in Libra: You have an innovative approach to relationships and partnerships.

Uranus in Scorpio: Expect changes in your life that lead to a deeper understanding of your true self and purpose.

Uranus in Sagittarius: It's time to explore new horizons and break free from limiting beliefs or philosophies.

Uranus in Capricorn: Things could change big time in your career or public image, leading to a need for greater personal authenticity and expression.

Uranus in Aquarius: You're known for your eccentricity and uniqueness.

Uranus in Pisces: You'll have sudden breakthroughs in your intuitive abilities or spiritual practice, leading to greater personal liberation and freedom.

Neptune

Neptune in Aries: You are drawn to spiritual practices emphasizing self-discovery and self-awareness.

Neptune in Taurus: You have a strong connection to nature and appreciate the beauty and abundance of the physical world.

Neptune in Gemini: You possess a natural curiosity and an interest in a wide variety of subjects but may struggle with focus and concentration.

Neptune in Cancer: Your intuition is strong, and you have a natural ability to nurture others. You may have trouble with emotional boundaries and taking care of yourself.

Neptune in Leo: You strongly desire creative self-expression and are drawn to the performing arts or other forms of creative expression.

Neptune in Virgo: Your mind is critical and analytical, but you must contend with perfectionism and self-criticism.

Neptune in Libra: You possess a strong sense of justice and enjoy activism or other forms of social justice work.

Neptune in Scorpio: You may have a natural ability to delve deeply into the mysteries of life and death.

Neptune in Sagittarius: You love adventure and desire spiritual or philosophical exploration. However, you have to contend with feeling trapped or limited.

Neptune in Capricorn: You prefer practical and disciplined approaches to spirituality or other forms of personal growth. You do have to work on your rigidity or fear of change.

Neptune in Aquarius: You are a visionary. You choose the unconventional approach to spirituality or personal growth and are very involved in social justice work or other forms of activism.

Neptune in Pisces: This is the natural placement for Neptune and can indicate a deeply spiritual or mystical nature and a natural sensitivity and empathy towards others.

Pluto

Pluto in Aries: You desire power and control in your life.

Pluto in Taurus: You have the potential for transformation and growth in areas related to material possessions and security.

Pluto in Gemini: You find deep transformation and growth in your communication and intellectual pursuits.

Pluto in Cancer: You are emotionally intense and desire emotional security.

Pluto in Leo: You desire power and control in creative expression.

Pluto in Virgo: In areas related to work, health, and service, you do phenomenally well.

Pluto in Libra: You strongly desire power and control in relationships, which can lead to positive changes and growth in this area.

Pluto in Scorpio: You possess a deep intensity and desire for power and transformation in all areas of life.

Pluto in Sagittarius: You are very concerned with the thoughts of the collective, especially in terms of belief systems that serve as the foundation of society.

Pluto in Capricorn: When it comes to your career, you want to be in control. You think it's important for you to carve a place for yourself in society.

Pluto in Aquarius: Expect profound growth in social justice, innovation, and unconventional thinking areas.

Pluto in Pisces: You have a deep sensitivity and desire for spiritual transformation and growth, which can manifest in various ways in your life.

Chiron

Chiron in Aries: You may struggle with expressing your individuality or identity.

Chiron in Taurus: You may have difficulty feeling secure and grounded.

Chiron in Gemini: Communication or feeling understood may be an issue for you.

Chiron in Cancer: You may have deep wounds related to your family and home.

Chiron in Leo: Expressing your creativity or uniqueness will be challenging.

Chiron in Virgo: You may have difficulty with perfectionism or feeling inadequate.

Chiron in Libra: Your obstacles include finding balance and harmony in your relationships.

Chiron in Scorpio: You may have deep wounds related to power and control.

Chiron in Sagittarius: Your hurdle is all about finding meaning and purpose in your life.

Chiron in Capricorn: You may have deep wounds related to authority and structure.

Chiron in Aquarius: You may feel like an outsider or struggle with feeling connected to society.

Chiron in Pisces: The main issue you'll face concerns boundaries or feeling overwhelmed by your emotions.

Ceres

Ceres in Aries: Ceres in Aries can indicate a nurturing style that emphasizes independence, assertiveness, and taking action toward fulfilling personal needs.

Ceres in Taurus: Providing for yourself and loved ones through material comforts and pleasures can bring a sense of deep emotional satisfaction.

Ceres in Gemini: Ceres in Gemini suggests a need for diverse mental stimulation and curiosity in your approach to nourishing yourself and others.

Ceres in Cancer: With Ceres in Cancer, there may be a deep emotional connection to home and family and a desire to create a sense of belonging and security in these areas of life.

Ceres in Leo: You strongly need creative self-expression and a desire to be recognized for one's unique talents and abilities.

Ceres in Virgo: You focus on practical self-care and a desire to create a healthy, organized environment.

Ceres in Libra: Nothing matters to you more than harmony in relationships and partnerships and a desire to help others grow through cooperation and diplomacy.

Ceres in Scorpio: Ceres in Scorpio shows you have a deep desire for intense experiences that allow for emotional catharsis and growth.

Ceres in Sagittarius: There may be a tendency to seek emotional fulfillment through exploring new perspectives and ideas and expanding one's horizons.

Ceres in Capricorn: You are focused on establishing practical and structured ways of providing and receiving care, support, and nourishment.

Ceres in Aquarius: You want nothing more than to foster a sense of community and belonging through unconventional or innovative means.

Ceres in Pisces: This represents a deep emotional connection to the cycles of nature and a spiritual approach to nourishment and sustenance.

Black Moon Lilith

Black Moon Lilith in Aries: You tend to be impulsive or aggressive, especially in relationships.

Black Moon Lilith in Taurus: You may struggle with possessiveness or fear losing what you value most.

Black Moon Lilith in Gemini: You have difficulty communicating and expressing your needs in relationships.

Black Moon Lilith in Cancer: You have deep emotional wounds related to family or home life, leading to a fear of vulnerability in relationships.

Black Moon Lilith in Leo: You constantly contend with power and control issues in relationships or fear being seen as weak.

Black Moon Lilith in Virgo: You are quite the perfectionist, creating challenges in relationships, leading to feelings of inadequacy.

Black Moon Lilith in Libra: You have to deal with codependency or difficulty setting boundaries in relationships.

Black Moon Lilith in Scorpio: You worry about being controlled or manipulated in relationships, leading to intense emotional reactions.

Black Moon Lilith in Sagittarius: You aren't very brave regarding commitment or struggle with finding meaning in relationships.

Black Moon Lilith in Capricorn: The fear of failure plagues you. You have a tendency towards workaholism that creates challenges in relationships.

Black Moon Lilith in Aquarius: Your major concern involves losing your independence or individuality in relationships or struggling to connect emotionally.

Black Moon Lilith in Pisces: You may tend towards escapism or victimhood in relationships or struggle to assert your own needs and desires.

Chapter 8: Solar Return Aspects I — The Major Ones

Did you know your solar return chart can tell you everything you need to know about your future? You can tell what the stars have in store for you by looking at how the planets interact with one another during your solar return. So, getting into the nitty-gritty of the different aspects of solar return is important. In this chapter, you're going to learn about the ones that matter the most. They are:

- The Conjunction
- The Sextile
- The Square
- The Trine
- The Opposition

The Conjunction

In astrology, a conjunction is an aspect between two or more planets located in close proximity to each other in the same zodiac sign or degree. This aspect is considered one of the most important aspects of astrology because it represents the merging of energies between the planets involved.

Sun-Sun: The Sun-Sun conjunction reinforces solar energy and can indicate strong self-identity, willpower, and leadership potential.

Sun-Moon: Sun-Moon blends conscious and unconscious aspects and can indicate emotional depth, sensitivity, and intuition.

Sun-Mercury: Sun-Mercury connects the rational mind and the self, indicating good communication skills, mental agility, and creativity.

Sun-Venus: Sun-Venus blends personal values and aesthetics, indicating a charming, sociable, and artistic nature.

Sun-Mars: Sun-Mars represents strong will and physical vitality, indicating passion, competition, and being action-oriented.

Sun-Jupiter: Sun-Jupiter broadens the self, indicating optimism, generosity, and a desire for growth and expansion.

Sun-Saturn: Sun-Saturn represents duty, responsibility, and discipline, indicating a serious, mature, and cautious nature.

Sun-Uranus: Sun-Uranus represents individuality and rebellion, indicating a unique, unconventional, and freedom-loving nature.

Sun-Neptune: This conjunction represents a blending of the spiritual and creative aspects of the self and can indicate sensitivity, intuition, and artistic talent.

Sun-Pluto: Sun-Pluto represents transformative, intense energy, indicating a powerful will, deep insight, and potential for personal transformation.

Moon-Moon: A reinforcement of lunar energy in a person's chart. It can indicate emotional intensity, sensitivity, and a strong connection to the feminine.

Moon-Mercury: The blending of emotional and rational energies; it shows good communication skills, a strong intuition, and a deep understanding of human psychology.

Moon-Venus: A strong connection between emotions and the aesthetic sense. It reveals a love of beauty, harmony, and the arts.

Moon-Mars: This conjunction represents a strong connection between emotions and the will and can indicate a passionate, impulsive, and action-oriented nature.

Moon-Jupiter: There's a blending of emotional depth and expansive, optimistic energy. This conjunction shows a generous, open-hearted, and philosophical nature.

Moon-Saturn: You demonstrate emotional sensitivity and a sense of duty or responsibility, revealing a serious, reserved, and cautious nature.

Moon-Uranus: Your emotions run deep. You desire freedom, change, and innovation and are unique, unconventional, and sometimes unpredictable.

Moon-Neptune: You possess a deep connection to the spiritual realm, artistic talent, psychic ability, and a strong intuition.

Moon-Pluto: Not only do you feel things intensely, but you also carry transformative energy and have a deep insight into human psychology, personal transformation, and the potential for emotional rebirth.

Mercury-Venus: You have a deep love of beauty, harmony, and the arts, as well as good communication skills in relationships.

Mercury-Mars: You are rational and assertive. You've got a quick mind, a strong will, and good communication skills in conflict situations.

Mercury-Jupiter: You are expansive in your thinking, and this shows you have a philosophical nature, good communication skills, and a talent for teaching and sharing knowledge.

Mercury-Saturn: Not only are you mostly rational, but you are also well disciplined. Your organizational skills, practicality, and serious approach to communication are impressive.

Mercury-Uranus: Your mind is constantly innovative, and you've got a knack for quick, original thinking, as well as an interest in science and technology.

Mercury-Neptune: This conjunction represents a blending of rational and spiritual energies and can indicate a talent for art, music, and writing, as well as good intuition and psychic ability.

Mercury-Pluto: This conjunction is a combination of rational and transformative energies and can indicate a talent for research and investigation, a deep understanding of human psychology, and a potential for personal transformation through communication and writing.

Venus-Mars: You are passionate and creative, as well as talented at dancing, acting, and other forms of performance art.

Venus-Jupiter: You love travel, adventure, and learning. You're known to be generous and optimistic.

Venus-Saturn: You have a practical and realistic approach to beauty and relationships and a sense of responsibility and duty in matters of the heart.

Venus-Uranus: You enjoy freedom, independence, and originality. You have a talent for modern and unconventional art forms.

Venus-Neptune: This conjunction indicates a talent for music, dance, and other forms of artistic expression, as well as sensitivity and compassion in matters of the heart.

Venus-Pluto: Psychology and counseling are your forte. Not only that, you have the potential for deep transformation and renewal in matters of love and relationships.

Mars-Jupiter: You are bold and adventurous. You are good at risk-taking and leadership.

Mars-Saturn: You have a strong sense of responsibility, hard work, and potential for frustration and anger.

Mars-Uranus: You are extremely good at original thinking and creative problem-solving and love technology and science.

Mars-Neptune: You have a potential for psychic ability, a love of mysticism and spirituality, and a potential for addiction or escapism.

Mars-Pluto: There is a strong potential for deep transformation, a talent for investigation and research, and a potential for anger and power struggles.

Jupiter-Saturn: This represents a strong sense of responsibility, hard work, and potential for conservatism or caution.

Jupiter-Uranus: The odds are you enjoy technology, science, and social change, as well as rebellion or restlessness.

Jupiter-Neptune: Your life is deeply rooted in mysticism, spirituality, and charity, as well as a potential for escapism or deception.

Jupiter-Pluto: Nothing is more important to you than deep transformation, research, and investigation. There is also the potential for power struggles or obsession.

Saturn-Uranus: You are very at home with thinking outside the box and have no issues being all on your own on any particular topic if no one else will support you.

Saturn-Neptune: You have a strong connection with all things spiritual, as well as a potential for confusion, delusion, or addiction.

Saturn-Pluto: Be very careful because your desire for power could become quite obsessive. Channeled correctly, this can be a tool for deep transformation for the better.

Uranus-Neptune: You are no stranger to mystical experiences and spiritual insights. There is also a potential for confusion or disillusionment.

Uranus-Pluto: With this conjunction, you can expect that there will be a complete and total revolution of the things that are not desirable in your life.

Neptune-Pluto: You have extremely powerful psychic abilities that you can use to your benefit should you choose to develop them.

The Sextile

In astrology, a sextile is an aspect between two planets that are 60 degrees apart from each other. This aspect is considered harmonious and beneficial, as it allows the planets involved to work together positively and be supportive.

Sun-Sun: Sextile between the Sun and Sun represents a harmonious exchange of energy between two individuals with similar identities, promoting mutual support and cooperation towards common goals.

Sun-Moon: Sun-Moon sextile fosters a smooth energy exchange between the conscious and unconscious parts of the self, promoting emotional stability and the ability to integrate feelings into rational decision-making.

Sun-Mercury: Sun-Mercury sextile reflects a harmonious flow of energy between the conscious and rational minds, promoting effective communication, sharp intellect, and sound decision-making abilities.

Sun-Venus: Sun-Venus sextile embodies the connection between the conscious self and aesthetic values, promoting a natural charm, appreciation for beauty, and harmonious relationships.

Sun-Mars: Sun-Mars sextile represents the thread that binds the awareness to the drive for action, promoting motivation, energy, and a strong will.

Sun-Jupiter: This sextile indicates optimism, confidence, and a sense of abundance.

Sun-Saturn: This sextile shows practicality, responsibility, and a strong sense of purpose.

Sun-Uranus: You are at home with originality, independence, and a desire for change.

Sun-Neptune: You have great sensitivity, creativity, and a desire for spiritual growth.

Sun-Pluto: You can confront challenges, personal power, and a desire for deep change.

Moon-Moon: This sextile is all about mutual understanding, emotional support, and a deep emotional bond.

Moon-Mercury: This sextile is all about emotional intelligence, effective communication of feelings, and the ability to express oneself through writing or speaking.

Moon-Venus: You deeply love beauty, emotional connection in relationships, and a desire for harmonious environments.

Moon-Mars: This sextile is about your motivation, assertiveness, and strong will.

Moon-Jupiter: This sextile reveals optimism, generosity, and a sense of abundance.

Moon-Saturn: You possess emotional maturity, responsibility, and a strong sense of boundaries.

Moon-Uranus: Your emotional intelligence is off the charts. The way you express yourself is very authentic, and there is nothing you desire more than change.

Moon-Neptune: You are a very sensitive person who has no trouble empathizing with others. One of the things that matter the most to you is spiritual growth.

Moon-Pluto: Your emotions run very deep and you are well aware of the power you carry to affect any change you desire in life. You can transmute it into something better whenever you notice an emotional pattern that does not serve you.

Mercury-Venus: With this sextile, it is obvious that the thing that matters to you the most is the ability to communicate clearly and effectively with your partner in a relationship.

Mercury-Mars: You are very assertive whenever you communicate with others and have the drive to make things happen, moving them from ideas to implementation.

Mercury-Jupiter: You have a natural joy for learning new things. There is nothing that excites you more than gaining more knowledge on a variety of topics.

Mercury-Saturn: You possess clear, structured thinking, practical communication, and a strong sense of responsibility.

Mercury-Uranus: You have no trouble effectively communicating new and creative ideas, and you also have a desire for change and progress.

Mercury-Neptune: You are the one people can count on to take abstract concepts and make them grounded in reality. This makes you an effective spiritual teacher should you decide to follow that path.

Mercury-Pluto: The things that matter to you the most are personal growth and evolution.

Venus-Mars: This sextile represents a love of physical activity, effective communication of desires and passions, and a desire for balance and harmony between love and assertiveness.

Venus-Jupiter: You love to learn and travel. You have a desire for growth and progress in relationships and an ability to find joy and pleasure in the world around you.

Venus-Saturn: You enjoy structure and stability, effective communication in relationships, and a desire for commitment and responsibility in love.

Venus-Uranus: You are the person who tends to have unconventional ideas in relationships and a desire for freedom and independence in love.

Venus-Neptune: Nothing excites you more than a deep spiritual, emotional connection with other people. You also enjoy everything beautiful around you.

Venus-Pluto: You believe in love as a vehicle for personal growth and evolution. And your love is not ordinary because it is very intense and true.

Mars-Jupiter: You find nothing more exciting than the chance to go on an adventure. You love to take risks because you realize that that is exactly how you can grow in life. Conquering personal challenges and challenges at work gives you a thrill because you feel satisfied with each achievement.

Mars-Saturn: You enjoy structure and routine, effective communication in business and personal life, and a desire for success and recognition through hard work and perseverance.

Mars-Uranus: What you seek the most are change and excitement, effective communication of new and unconventional ideas in business and personal life, and a desire for freedom and independence in action.

Mars-Neptune: You believe in making the spiritual practical by taking action. You love applying spiritual laws in the practical aspects of life, like business, relationships, health, etc. You are also very in touch with your creative side.

Mars-Pluto: You are constantly on the lookout for any experience that will transform your life into something greater than it already is.

Jupiter-Saturn: You believe that growth and progress can only come through hard work and constantly keeping your nose to the grindstone. More often than not, this mindset pays off.

Jupiter-Uranus: You can effectively communicate new and unconventional ideas in your personal and business life, and often these ideas lead to growth and evolution.

Jupiter-Neptune: This sextile represents growth and spirituality and can indicate a love of creativity and artistic pursuits, effective communication of spiritual and abstract concepts in business and personal life, and a desire for growth and progress through personal growth and evolution.

Jupiter-Pluto: You crave intensity and power, effective communication of complex emotions in business and personal life.

Saturn-Uranus: To you, your life is basically a big science experiment. You love to take a look at unconventional ideas and see if they will actually pan out successfully in real life. You are the one person who has no problem adapting to the situation, no matter what it's like.

Saturn-Neptune: You have a deep love for the application of metaphysical concepts in business and personal life and a desire for progress and success through personal growth and evolution.

Saturn-Pluto: You possess a disciplined approach to power, intensity, and effective communication of complex emotions in business and personal life.

Uranus-Neptune: You have a talent for creative visualization and manifestation, a desire for mystical experiences and spiritual growth, and a willingness to break free from limiting beliefs and perceptions.

Uranus-Pluto: You desire personal and collective evolution, are willing to break free from oppressive systems and structures, and have a talent for leading and inspiring others toward radical change.

Pluto-Neptune: You've got an amazing talent for transformative and visionary manifestation and a willingness to break free from limiting beliefs and perceptions.

The Square

In astrology, a square is an aspect that occurs when two planets are separated by 90 degrees or three signs apart in the zodiac. This aspect is considered a challenging or hard aspect, as it creates tension and conflict between the energies of the two planets involved.

Sun-Sun: The clash of two strong wills leads to power struggles and a need to establish dominance.

Sun-Moon: A conflict between the individual's conscious desires and emotional needs, leading to inner turmoil and difficulty finding emotional balance.

Sun-Mercury: A challenge in communication and self-expression, leading to misunderstandings, arguments, and difficulty getting one's point across.

Sun-Venus: A struggle to balance one's desire for love and harmony with the need for independence and self-expression, leading to relationship challenges and difficulty finding common ground.

Sun-Mars: A clash between the individual's desire for action and assertiveness and their need for harmony and cooperation, leading to impulsive behavior and conflict with others.

Sun-Jupiter: A tendency to overreach or take on more than one can handle, leading to unrealistic expectations, wastefulness, and the need to learn moderation.

Sun-Saturn: A challenge in establishing oneself and achieving one's goals, leading to self-doubt, fear of failure, and a tendency to be overly critical or restrictive.

Sun-Uranus: A conflict between the individual's need for freedom and their desire for stability and security, leading to impulsiveness, rebellion, and unpredictability.

Sun-Neptune: A struggle to maintain clarity and focus, leading to confusion, delusion, and a tendency to be overly idealistic or escapist.

Sun-Pluto: A clash of wills between the individual and others or with one's own subconscious, leading to power struggles, manipulation, and a need for control.

Moon-Moon: Emotional clashes and mood swings between two individuals or within oneself, leading to hypersensitivity, neediness, and a lack of emotional stability.

Moon-Mercury: Difficulty expressing one's emotions and understanding others' emotions, leading to misunderstandings, arguments, and emotional distance.

Moon-Venus: A struggle to reconcile one's emotional needs with one's desire for love and harmony, leading to emotional turbulence in relationships and a need for balance between intimacy and independence.

Moon-Mars: A propensity to act impulsively based on emotional impulses, leading to conflict and aggression, and a need to balance emotional expression with self-control.

Moon-Jupiter: The temptation to overindulge in emotional pleasures or idealize emotional experiences leads to unrealistic expectations, wastefulness, and the need to learn emotional moderation.

Moon-Saturn: A tendency to restrict one's emotional expression or to feel emotionally blocked, leading to feelings of isolation, loneliness, and a need to develop emotional resilience.

Moon-Uranus: A need for emotional freedom and independence, leading to unpredictable emotional behavior, rebellion, and a need to find emotional stability and consistency.

Moon-Neptune: A constant tendency to blur the lines between reality and fantasy, leading to confusion, escapism, and a need to develop emotional boundaries and clarity.

Moon-Pluto: A struggle to confront and transform deep emotional issues and patterns, leading to power struggles, emotional manipulation, and a need to develop emotional self-awareness and healing.

Mercury-Sun: An endless fight to express oneself effectively and confidently, leading to misunderstandings, ego clashes, and a need to balance self-expression with active listening.

Mercury-Moon: Difficulty communicating one's emotions and understanding others' emotions, leading to misunderstandings, emotional distance, and a need to develop emotional intelligence.

Mercury-Venus: Constant misinterpretation of social cues and messages in relationships, leading to misunderstandings, conflicts, and a need to develop better communication skills.

Mercury-Mars: A tendency to argue, debate, or act impulsively based on thoughts and ideas, leading to conflicts and misunderstandings and a need to balance thought and action.

Mercury-Jupiter: The exaggeration and oversimplification of ideas and beliefs, leading to misunderstandings, overconfidence, and a need to develop critical thinking skills.

Mercury-Saturn: A natural bent towards being overly critical or self-critical, leading to pessimism, self-doubt, and a need to develop positive self-talk and constructive feedback.

Mercury-Uranus: Being overly rebellious or unconventional in one's thinking – leading to misunderstandings, impulsiveness, and a need to develop more strategic thinking.

Mercury-Neptune: Leaning a little too heavily towards idealism or being unrealistic in one's thinking, leading to confusion, deception, and a need to develop a more grounded perspective.

Mercury-Pluto: Extreme intensity and obsession in one's thinking, leading to power struggles, manipulations, and a need to develop more detachment and self-awareness.

Venus-Mars: A tendency to be overly assertive or passive-aggressive in relationships, leading to conflicts and misunderstandings, and a need to develop assertiveness and healthy communication.

Venus-Jupiter: Being too optimistic or indulgent in relationships – leading to unrealistic expectations, overconfidence, and a need to develop realistic expectations and boundaries.

Venus-Saturn: Excessive pessimism, self-doubt, and a need to develop positive self-talk and constructive feedback.

Venus-Uranus: Choosing to be unconventional in relationships – leading to misunderstandings, impulsiveness, and a need to develop more empathy and understanding.

Venus-Neptune: Unrealistic expectations in relationships – leading to confusion, deception, and a need to develop a more grounded perspective.

Venus-Pluto: Power struggles, manipulations, and a need to develop more trust and vulnerability in relationships with others.

Mars-Jupiter: An inability to control impulsive or reckless behavior, leading to overextension, conflicts, and a need to develop more caution and strategic thinking.

Mars-Saturn: Being critical to the point of self-restraint, leading to frustration, self-doubt, and a need to develop more self-confidence and assertiveness.

Mars-Uranus: A rebellious spirit, leading to restlessness, accidents, and a need to develop more patience and self-control.

Mars-Neptune: Deception, confusion, and a need to develop more clarity and self-awareness on account of being out of touch with reality.

Mars-Pluto: Obsession leading to power struggles, manipulation, and a need to develop more trust and healthy boundaries.

Jupiter-Saturn: Frustration due to rigid expectations and a need to develop a more balanced approach to one's goals.

Jupiter-Uranus: Impulsiveness, restlessness – leading to a need to develop a more grounded perspective and respect for tradition.

Jupiter-Neptune: More clarity and critical thinking are needed to avoid constantly falling prey to deception.

Jupiter-Pluto: Here, expressing trust and having healthy boundaries is important to stay out of unnecessary power struggles.

Saturn-Uranus: You must be more flexible and adaptable to avoid disappointment and frustration.

Saturn-Neptune: A tendency to be overly fearful or delusional, leading to confusion, self-deception, and a need to develop more clarity and self-awareness.

Saturn-Pluto: You may become obsessed with power. For this reason, you need to know which lines not to cross with others.

Uranus-Neptune: You can sometimes be delusional or unrealistic. This makes you feel confused, and you get lost trying to escape the real world. Develop more self-awareness and grounding.

Uranus-Pluto: You're not very open to change. You must learn to be more accepting and find a way to make the new changes in your life work with and for you.

Neptune-Pluto: You can be rather secretive, to the point where it's detrimental for you. Do your best to share your thoughts with others, as this will allow for more growth and expansion in your life.

Trines

In astrology, a trine is an aspect that occurs when two planets are approximately 120 degrees apart, creating a harmonious and flowing energy between them. It is considered one of the most positive and beneficial aspects of astrology. Trines are associated with ease, cooperation, and creativity. They are often seen as a natural talent or gift that a person possesses rather than something that needs to be worked hard for.

Sun-Sun: A harmonious aspect that promotes self-confidence, creativity, and vitality.

Sun-Moon: A supportive aspect that enhances emotional balance, understanding, and deep inner harmony.

Sun-Mercury: A beneficial aspect that helps with communication, mental clarity, and the ability to express oneself effectively.

Sun-Venus: A harmonizing aspect that encourages social harmony, cooperation, and a sense of aesthetic beauty.

Sun-Mars: A dynamic aspect that enhances energy, passion, and assertiveness and promotes positive action toward goals.

Sun-Jupiter: A fortunate aspect that promotes optimism, growth, and abundance and enhances confidence and generosity.

Sun-Saturn: A grounding aspect that promotes discipline, responsibility, and a practical approach to life and helps you set boundaries and achieve long-term goals.

Sun-Uranus: An innovative aspect that promotes change, progress, and a willingness to take risks and enhances originality and creativity.

Sun-Neptune: An intuitive aspect supporting sensitivity, imagination, and creativity and promoting a spiritual or mystical approach to life.

Sun-Pluto: This aspect promotes personal power, intensity, and regeneration and enhances the ability to face challenges and overcome obstacles.

Moon-Moon: Expect emotional security, nurturing, sensitivity, and a sense of inner peace and contentment.

Moon-Mercury: Here, you experience superb communication, mental agility, and adaptability – and it promotes an understanding of one's own emotional needs and those of others.

Moon-Venus: A harmonious aspect that propagates emotional connection, intimacy, and creativity and promotes a sense of beauty and harmony in relationships.

Moon-Mars: This aspect fosters emotional assertiveness, passion, and initiative and promotes positive action toward goals.

Moon-Jupiter: A fortunate aspect that allows emotional optimism, growth, abundance, a sense of generosity, and expansiveness.

Moon-Saturn: A grounding aspect. It fosters emotional discipline, responsibility, and a practical approach to life and helps set emotional boundaries and achieve long-term emotional goals.

Moon-Uranus: You'll experience emotional freedom, independence, and a willingness to take emotional risks. You will have a tendency to express originality and emotional creativity.

Moon-Neptune: Sensitivity, imagination, and creativity reign supreme here. This is the aspect that promotes a spiritual or mystical approach to life.

Moon-Pluto: With this aspect, you can expect emotional intensity, personal power, and emotional regeneration, and it helps with emotional transformation and healing.

Mercury-Venus: A harmonious aspect that will boost your social skills, diplomacy, and creativity and also develops a sense of beauty and harmony in relationships.

Mercury-Mars: You'll experience enhanced mental agility, assertiveness, and initiative. Not only that, you'll take positive action toward your goals.

Mercury-Jupiter: Enjoy mental growth, optimism, and abundance. You will have a greater sense of generosity and expansiveness.

Mercury-Saturn: Your mental discipline, focus, and practical approach to life receive a boost. This aspect also helps with setting mental boundaries and achieving long-term mental goals.

Mercury-Uranus: An innovative aspect that enhances mental freedom, originality, and a willingness to take mental risks and promotes creativity and intellectual curiosity.

Mercury-Neptune: Your spiritual and creative paths will bloom and prosper with this aspect.

Mercury-Pluto: Here, you have mental depth, personal power, and mental regeneration. This aspect helps with mental transformation and healing.

Venus-Mars: Enjoy adventure in relationships and take positive action toward romantic goals.

Venus-Jupiter: Expect more abundance, optimism, and a sense of enjoyment and pleasure in life. The odds are you'll have a generous and expansive attitude toward love and relationships.

Venus-Saturn: This aspect brings stability, enhances commitment, responsibility, and a practical approach to love and relationships, and helps set boundaries and achieve long-term relationship goals.

Venus-Uranus: This is no ordinary aspect. It enhances independence, originality, and a willingness to take risks in love and relationships and promotes a sense of excitement and spontaneity.

Venus-Neptune: Expect enhanced sensitivity, empathy, and a spiritual or mystical approach to love and relationships. You'll also have a sense of idealism and a deep connection with others.

Venus-Pluto: This aspect boosts passion, personal power, and emotional regeneration and helps with relationship transformation and healing.

Mars-Jupiter: You will enjoy optimism, energy, and a willingness to take risks, and it promotes success in personal and professional endeavors.

Mars-Saturn: Your perseverance, determination, and strong sense of responsibility will receive a boost here. This aspect helps with achieving long-term goals through focused effort.

Mars-Uranus: Enjoy an increase in individuality, innovation, and a capacity for change and evolution. This aspect allows proactive and creative problem-solving skills.

Mars-Neptune: You will have greater empathy and compassion and positive action toward spiritual and artistic goals.

Mars-Pluto: With this aspect, you will have more personal power, determination, and capacity for profound transformation and help with healing and transformation through focused effort.

Jupiter-Saturn: A disciplined aspect that enhances a sense of responsibility, practicality, and a capacity for focused effort and helps achieve long-term goals through persistence and hard work.

Jupiter-Uranus: An innovative aspect that enhances a sense of adventure, individuality, and a capacity for change and evolution and promotes positive and transformative growth and expansion.

Jupiter-Neptune: A spiritually attuned aspect that enhances intuition, creativity, and a sense of empathy and compassion and promotes positive and inspiring spiritual and artistic endeavors.

Jupiter-Pluto: This aspect will do wonders regarding your personal power, growth, and capacity for profound transformation, and it helps with healing and transformation through spiritual and psychological work.

Saturn-Uranus: A stabilizing aspect that enhances a sense of independence, innovation, and a capacity for change and evolution and promotes a balance between stability and change.

Saturn-Neptune: A grounding aspect that enhances practicality, self-awareness, and a capacity for compassion and empathy and promotes grounded and realistic spiritual and creative endeavors.

Saturn-Pluto: This aspect gives you more depth of character and will help you heal your psyche so that it is easier for you to handle the challenges that life sends your way.

Uranus-Neptune: With this aspect, you will experience increased intuition, compassion, and a capacity for spiritual and creative evolution. This aspect also promotes success in creative, artistic, or spiritual fields.

Uranus-Pluto: This is one aspect that makes it possible for you to find extreme success in the most innovative fields.

Neptune-Pluto: Expect stronger intuition, insight, and a capacity for profound spiritual transformation. This aspect will promote success in fields related to spiritual or psychological healing or in transformative and innovative fields.

The Opposition

In astrology, the opposition is an aspect that occurs when two celestial bodies are exactly 180 degrees apart from each other. This means that they are on opposite sides of the zodiac circle. The opposition is considered a major aspect of astrology, as it represents a point of tension and potential conflict between the two energies involved.

Sun-Sun: This opposition can bring about power struggles and conflicts with authority figures, as well as a need for balance between the desire for self-expression and the needs of others.

Sun-Moon: Expect tension between your emotions and sense of self-identity and a need to balance the desire for independence with the need for emotional support and nurturing.

Sun-Mercury: You will notice a fair bit of conflict between your thoughts and how you communicate them and your desire to find some sort of balance intellectually with how you express your thoughts to only bring harmony to your social circles.

Sun-Venus: You may notice that your values and desires are not aligned. Therefore, it becomes important for you to realize that as you go about the process of self-gratification, you must do so in a way that brings harmony in your relationships.

Sun-Mars: This opposition can bring about conflicts between one's personal will and desire for action, as well as a need to balance the desire for self-assertion with the need for compromise and cooperation.

Sun-Jupiter: There is a lack of alignment between your beliefs and your sense of morality. While seeking to expand in many ways is natural, you must also ensure you are grounded in reality.

Sun-Saturn: You want to be successful by any means necessary but also understand that you are responsible to yourself and others. It would help you to find a way to balance your self-discipline with freedom and spontaneity.

Sun-Uranus: The conflict with this opposition lies in the difference between your sense of individuality and your desire to be free and rebel against the status quo. You seek change, but you also desire stability in your life.

Sun-Neptune: Your sense of self, identity, and spiritual or artistic aspirations are at loggerheads. As creative as you are, you need to find a way to ground your wild imagination in the practical, realistic world.

Sun-Pluto: This opposition can bring about conflicts between one's desire for power and transformation and a need to balance the desire for control and intensity with the need for acceptance and to let go.

Moon-Moon: A clash of emotions, the potential for heightened sensitivity and mood swings, and the need for compromise and understanding in relationships.

Moon-Mercury: Conflict between emotions and logical thinking, difficulty expressing emotions or finding the right words to communicate.

Moon-Venus: Tension between emotional needs and desires in relationships, potential for intense emotions and passion, and the need to balance giving and receiving love.

Moon-Mars: Potential for emotional outbursts and conflict, difficulty controlling impulses and aggression, need for self-control and emotional regulation.

Moon-Jupiter: You may experience emotional excess and indulgence, the need to find a balance between emotional well-being and practical considerations.

Moon-Saturn: Tension between emotional needs and responsibilities, the potential for feelings of loneliness or isolation, the need for self-discipline, and emotional maturity.

Moon-Uranus: Watch out for emotional unpredictability and sudden changes, the need for flexibility, and adaptability in emotional responses.

Moon-Neptune: You will notice heightened emotional sensitivity and confusion, a tendency towards idealization and emotional escapism, and the need for grounding and clarity in emotional experiences.

Moon-Pluto: Potential for intense emotional experiences and power struggles, the need for emotional transformation and healing.

Mercury-Venus: Conflicts in relationships or social situations, possible miscommunications, or lack of understanding in matters of love or pleasure.

Mercury-Mars: Disagreements in decision-making or taking action, the potential for impulsiveness or aggression in communication.

Mercury-Jupiter: Challenges in balancing details and the big picture, potential for overestimating one's abilities, or making unrealistic plans or promises.

Mercury-Saturn: Delays or obstacles in communication, potential for negative self-talk or self-doubt, possible conflicts with authority figures.

Mercury-Uranus: There is the potential for unpredictable behavior or unusual ideas.

Mercury-Neptune: Possible confusion or misunderstandings in communication, the potential for deception or unclear thinking, a tendency towards daydreaming or escapism.

Mercury-Pluto: Tendency towards power struggles or manipulation in communication, the potential for obsession or fixation on certain ideas or topics.

Venus-Mars: You may notice increased sexual attraction and desire for excitement in your relationships, but it also creates conflicts and power struggles. You may need to find a way to balance your assertiveness and passion with cooperation and compromise.

Venus-Jupiter: You experience abundance, optimism, and generosity in your relationships, but also exaggeration and overindulgence. You may strongly desire love, pleasure, and adventure, but you must avoid becoming too extravagant or unrealistic.

Venus-Saturn: You contend with challenges, limitations, and delays in your relationships but also opportunities for growth and commitment. You may feel a sense of responsibility, duty, or seriousness in your love life but also fear rejection, loneliness, or inadequacy.

Venus-Uranus: You are used to sudden changes, surprises, and unconventional experiences in your relationships, but also instability and unpredictability. You may feel a need for freedom, experimentation, and authenticity in your love life but also fear commitment, boredom, or rejection.

Venus-Neptune: You will enjoy romantic idealism, imagination, and spiritual connection in your relationships but also experience confusion, deception, and disillusionment. You may feel a strong urge to merge with your partner or experience a soulmate connection, but you must be aware of your boundaries and avoid becoming too dependent or unrealistic.

Venus-Pluto: This aspect can bring intense passion, transformation, and power dynamics in your relationships, but also obsession, control, and manipulation. You may feel a deep emotional connection or attraction to someone but must be aware of hidden motives or destructive patterns.

Mars-Jupiter: The desire for success and achievement may lead to overconfidence and taking unnecessary risks.

Mars-Saturn: There may be frustrations and obstacles in achieving one's goals, leading to feelings of resentment or a sense of being held back.

Mars-Uranus: A sudden change of plans or unexpected events can lead to impulsive and reckless actions.

Mars-Neptune: Confusion and uncertainty can lead to misunderstandings and unrealistic expectations.

Mars-Pluto: Power struggles and manipulation may occur, leading to intense confrontations or even violence.

Jupiter-Saturn: This aspect can indicate a period of growth and expansion in career or personal ambitions but may also bring a sense of restriction or limitations that need to be overcome.

Jupiter-Uranus: You may find sudden opportunities for growth and expansion, but they may also lead to impulsiveness and a lack of consideration for the long-term consequences of one's actions.

Jupiter-Neptune: This aspect can bring a sense of spiritual or creative growth but may also lead to unrealistic expectations or a tendency to overlook practical considerations.

Jupiter-Pluto: This aspect can indicate a period of powerful transformation and growth but may also bring power struggles and a tendency to be controlling or manipulative in one's pursuits.

Saturn-Uranus: This can bring a clash between traditional and innovative or unconventional approaches, leading to instability or disruption and an opportunity for creative problem-solving and restructuring.

Saturn-Neptune: You feel a sense of confusion or disillusionment, leading to a period of doubt or disappointment, but also a chance to develop greater clarity, discernment, and spiritual maturity.

Saturn-Pluto: Expect a sense of intensity, crisis, or transformation, leading to a period of deep change or challenge, but also an opportunity for inner strength, resilience, and personal power.

Uranus-Neptune opposition: This aspect can create a desire for spiritual and mystical experiences. The individual may be drawn to unconventional forms of spirituality and may have psychic abilities or intuitive insights. However, this aspect can also create confusion and a lack of clarity around personal beliefs and values.

Uranus-Pluto opposition: This aspect can bring sudden and intense transformative experiences. The individual may be drawn to power and may want to challenge authority figures or traditional power structures. This aspect can also create a tendency towards extremism and a desire to push boundaries beyond what society considers acceptable.

Neptune-Pluto: This can indicate a deep transformational journey towards spiritual or psychological growth and a tendency towards intense emotional experiences and crises.

Chapter 9: Solar Return Aspects II — The Minor Ones

In astrology, minor aspects are less commonly used or discussed than major ones. Some of the minor solar return aspects include:

Semisextile

You get a semisextile when both planets are 30 degrees away from each other. This aspect can indicate a slight tension or adjustment between two planets or points in a chart.

Sun-Moon: Potential for inner conflict or challenges balancing the ego and emotions.

Sun-Mercury: Heightened communication and intellectual abilities.

Sun-Venus: Potential for artistic talent or harmonious relationships.

Sun-Mars: Drive and determination towards personal goals and ambition.

Sun-Jupiter: A balance between confidence and overconfidence, the potential for luck and opportunities.

Sun-Saturn: A need for structure and discipline, potential for self-doubt or fear of failure.

Sun-Uranus: A need for independence and freedom, potential for unconventional thinking and unique ideas.

Sun-Neptune: Heightened intuition and imagination, potential for artistic or spiritual pursuits.

Sun-Pluto: Transformative and powerful energy, potential for personal growth and evolution.

Moon-Mercury: Intuitive understanding and communication.

Moon-Venus: Emotional connection and appreciation of beauty.

Moon-Mars: Inner drive and emotional energy working together.

Moon-Jupiter: Positive emotional outlook and expansive feelings.

Moon-Saturn: Emotional discipline and responsibility.

Moon-Uranus: Emotional breakthroughs and unconventional feelings.

Moon-Neptune: Emotional sensitivity and imaginative capacity.

Moon-Pluto: Deep emotional transformation and intensity.

Mercury-Venus: Artistic talent and social charm may also lead to superficiality or indecisiveness.

Mercury-Mars: Strong opinions and persuasive skills may also lead to arguments or impatience.

Mercury-Jupiter: A broad perspective and optimism - but it may also lead to overconfidence or exaggeration.

Mercury-Saturn: A practical and disciplined approach to problem-solving - but may also lead to pessimism or rigidity.

Mercury-Uranus: Innovative and original thinking, which may also lead to impulsiveness or erratic behavior.

Mercury-Neptune: Intuition and creative inspiration may also lead to confusion or illusion.

Mercury-Pluto: The ability to delve deeply into complex issues may also lead to obsession or power struggles.

Venus-Mars: Passionate desires and strong attraction can lead to disagreements or competitiveness.

Venus-Jupiter: Generosity and a love of pleasure may also lead to overindulgence or extravagance.

Venus-Saturn: A serious and responsible approach to relationships - but it may also lead to emotional distance or loneliness.

Venus-Uranus: A desire for freedom and independence in relationships may also lead to unpredictability or sudden changes.

Venus-Neptune: Romantic ideals and creative inspiration may also lead to confusion or disappointment.

Venus-Pluto: Intense desires and the ability to transform oneself and relationships – but can also lead to power struggles or obsession.

Mars-Jupiter: Ambition and the drive to succeed may also lead to overconfidence or impulsiveness.

Mars-Saturn: The discipline and determination to achieve goals may also lead to frustration or restriction.

Mars-Uranus: A rebellious and innovative spirit – but it can also lead to unpredictability or sudden changes.

Mars-Neptune: A creative and imaginative drive – but it may also lead to confusion or deception.

Mars-Pluto: Intense energy and the ability to transform oneself and situations – but can also lead to power struggles or destructive tendencies.

Jupiter-Saturn: A balance of expansion and limitation may also lead to conflicts between tradition and progress.

Jupiter-Uranus: A willingness to take risks and embrace change – but may also lead to restlessness or rebellion.

Jupiter-Neptune: Spiritual and artistic inspiration – but may also lead to delusion or escapism.

Jupiter-Pluto: A desire for power and transformation may also lead to obsession or manipulation.

Saturn-Uranus: A desire for change and innovation may also lead to conflict between tradition and progress.

Saturn-Neptune: A need for practicality and structure may also lead to disillusionment or a lack of imagination.

Saturn-Pluto: A need for control and power may also lead to obsession or paranoia.

Uranus-Neptune: A desire to transcend the mundane and a heightened sensitivity to the collective unconscious may also lead to confusion or escapism.

Uranus-Pluto: An intense desire for change and a need to transform oneself and society may also lead to extremism or radicalism.

Neptune-Pluto: The ability to transform and transcend on a deep spiritual level – but it may also lead to confusion or a loss of ego boundaries.

Sesquiquadrate

This aspect has both planets 135 degrees apart from each other and can indicate a sense of discord or tension between two planets or points in a chart.

Sun-Moon: The potential for compulsive behavior.

Sun-Mercury: Mental strain, difficulty in communication or decision making.

Sun-Venus: Tension between personal values and relationships, potential for creative self-expression.

Sun-Mars: Inner conflict between willpower and action, the potential for impulsiveness or aggression.

Sun-Jupiter: Possible overindulgence or grandiosity.

Sun-Saturn: Excess self-doubt or restriction.

Sun-Uranus: Rebelliousness, sudden change, a desire for a shift in the status quo.

Sun-Neptune: You may experience confusion or deception.

Sun-Pluto: There is an opportunity for transformation here or a tendency towards manipulation.

Moon-Mercury: Mental anxiety, difficulty in understanding or expressing emotions.

Moon-Venus: Strain between emotional needs and relationships, potential for mood swings or emotional manipulation.

Moon-Mars: No alignment between emotions and action, the potential for impulsiveness or aggression.

Moon-Jupiter: The likelihood of overindulgence or emotional excess.

Moon-Saturn: Emotional repression or isolation is possible here.

Moon-Uranus: The strain of contending with one's emotions and individuality can lead to sudden emotional detachment.

Moon-Neptune: In the battle of finding a balance between your spiritual and emotional lives, the odds are, you'll experience confusion or excessive emotional sensitivity.

Moon-Pluto: But there is the chance to experience intense emotional experiences or to be manipulated.

Mercury-Venus: Difficulty in expressing thoughts or ideas in relationships, potential for misunderstandings or miscommunication.

Mercury-Mars: Mental tension between thoughts and actions, potential for impulsive or reckless behavior.

Mercury-Jupiter: Difficulty reconciling the details with the big picture, potential for overconfidence or exaggeration.

Mercury-Saturn: Mental strain, difficulty in decision-making, and the potential for negative thinking or self-doubt.

Mercury-Uranus: There is a battle in your mind between conventional and unconventional thinking and the potential for sudden insights or rebelliousness.

Mercury-Neptune: Confusion and difficulty in distinguishing reality from fantasy, potential for deception or escapism.

Mercury-Pluto: Mental tension and power struggles, the potential for manipulation or obsession.

Venus-Mars: You may experience a fair bit of conflict and emotional volatility in your relationships.

Venus-Jupiter: Be very careful of the temptation to be extravagant or overindulge.

Venus-Saturn: You may struggle with feelings of loneliness or self-doubt.

Venus-Uranus: You struggle to find the balance between your personal values and your individuality. This could leave you open to sudden changes or end up in unconventional relationships.

Venus-Neptune: In the process of sorting out your spiritual values, you may be open to confusion or being deceived.

Venus-Pluto: Tension between personal values and power dynamics in relationships, potential for intense emotional experiences or manipulation.

Mars-Jupiter: You'll find yourself struggling to keep up with your ambitions while ensuring not to cross any moral lines. Be careful because you may give in to reckless behavior or feel a little too confident and take on more than you can handle.

Mars-Saturn: When achieving your goals, you may experience some difficulty and frustration along the way.

Mars-Uranus: You will feel an overwhelming desire to act impulsively. It would be best if you could keep this in check.

Mars-Neptune: In the process of finding your spiritual truth, be careful that you do not wind up deceiving yourself.

Mars-Pluto: As you take constructive action towards your goals, you may find yourself plopped in the middle of power struggles. You need to be aware of being susceptible to manipulation.

Jupiter-Saturn: You need to find the balance between your personal values and practical considerations as you achieve your dreams.

Jupiter-Uranus: There is the potential for you to experience good things, but you must be prepared for the unexpected or for your usual routine to be disrupted.

Jupiter-Neptune: As admirable as it is that you are diving deeper into spiritualism and are optimistic about your path, you need to be careful so that you do not wind up losing touch with reality.

Jupiter-Pluto: You may find yourself optimistic about a particular project or person to the point of obsession. Depending on your decisions, this could be a good or bad thing.

Saturn-Uranus: On the one hand, you desire to maintain the status quo, and on the other hand, there is nothing you would love more than to shake things up. You need to find the balance between both desires.

Saturn-Neptune: You may feel disappointed or disillusioned if you do not find the difference between illusion and reality.

Saturn-Pluto: Here is a unique opportunity to change for the better or give yourself over to corruption.

Uranus-Neptune: You are finding your true identity within your spiritual path. In the process, you may find yourself full of unconventional beliefs that may not serve you when it comes to practical living.

Uranus-Pluto: There's the opportunity for radical change and for you to have the upper hand regarding power dynamics.

Neptune-Pluto: Beware of the people around you and their possible hidden agendas. You can also expect to experience great change through your spiritual journey.

Quincunx

Quincunx has both planets 150 degrees apart from each other. This aspect can indicate a need for adjustment or realignment between two planets or points in a chart.

Sun-Moon: A need to adjust between ego and emotions can lead to tension or uncertainty.

Sun-Mercury: Trying to balance self-expression and communication can lead to misunderstandings or anxiety.

Sun-Venus: Seeking the sweet spot between self-worth and relationships can lead to indecision or conflict.

Sun-Mars: You may feel some frustration or impulsiveness as you seek to find the balance between your will and your actions.

Sun-Jupiter: If you are not careful, you will be susceptible to unrealistic expectations or a little too much optimism if you do not take the time to find the alignment between your values and beliefs.

Sun-Saturn: In the process of expressing yourself and being a responsible person, you may find yourself succumbing to fear or doubting your abilities.

Sun-Uranus: Beware of suddenly giving in to impulsiveness or rebellion while trying to find the balance between your individuality and self-expression.

Sun-Neptune: While your love for spirituality is admirable, you need to be careful of giving in to idealism and finding yourself in a situation where you are all talk and no action.

Sun-Pluto: You need to be aware that you are very susceptible to manipulation or control, especially as you find a way to adjust between your ego and power dynamics.

Moon-Mercury: With the Moon and Mercury in this aspect, it is natural to expect mood swings or miscommunication to be the norm. So be very careful what you say or how you interpret whatever someone tells you.

Moon-Venus: With this aspect, finding a balance between your relationships and the emotions they cause you to experience could possibly lead you to codependency or emotional turbulence.

Moon-Mars: A need to adjust between emotions and actions can lead to impulsiveness or emotional outbursts.

Moon-Jupiter: There is a great chance that you may become overindulgent or have unrealistic expectations, especially as you consider your personal values and how you feel from moment to moment.

Moon-Saturn: If you do not find a healthy way to handle your responsibilities and address your emotions, you may feel emotionally detached from life or struggle with depression.

Moon-Uranus: The desire to balance emotions and individuality can lead to emotional instability or rebelliousness.

Moon-Neptune: You may experience emotional confusion or escapism.

Moon-Pluto: You may be susceptible to emotional manipulation or control.

Mercury-Venus: Make it a point of duty to avoid misunderstandings or imbalances in your relationships with others.

Mercury-Mars: You may get sucked into arguments or make impulsive decisions that you later regret.

Mercury-Jupiter: While being optimistic is a desired trait, you need to be very careful not to exaggerate the possible results that you may get out of a project or whatever it is you are working on.

Mercury-Saturn: When faced with the energies of Mercury and Saturn in opposition, you need to be careful because you may struggle with self-doubt or inhibitions, especially as you figure out how to communicate effectively with others.

Mercury-Uranus: Mercury and Uranus and opposition tend to lend to the energy of impulsivity in eccentricity. This could be a good thing or a bad thing. You just need to be aware and do things in moderation.

Mercury-Neptune: While it is understandable that you need to make adjustments between your communication style and spirituality, you also need to be aware that there is a chance for deception or confusion in the process.

Mercury-Pluto: Mercury and Pluto in opposition are the perfect recipe for obsession or manipulation to develop.

Venus-Mars: Throw Venus and Mars in opposition to each other, and you may experience a lot of imbalance in your relationships.

Venus-Jupiter: Be careful because there is a tendency for you to have unrealistic expectations and indulge in things more than you should when these two planets, Venus and Jupiter, are in opposition.

Venus-Saturn: Being in love is beautiful, but there is always a tendency to forget yourself and your responsibilities. Therefore you need to watch out for that so you do not experience emotional attachment or become deathly afraid of intimacy.

Venus-Uranus: You may find yourself in the most unconventional relationships or experience sudden changes that you just never anticipated.

Venus-Neptune: The fact that you were finding a balance between your love for someone and your love for spirituality is a great thing. But you need to be aware that you might fall into the trap of deception or idealize this other person to your own detriment.

Venus-Pluto: With Venus and Pluto in opposition to each other, you need to be careful because there is a huge chance that you may give in to obsessive thoughts.

Mars-Jupiter: In opposition to each other, Mars and Jupiter is the perfect recipe for getting too confident and acting recklessly. Please be careful so you do not have to face consequences that you regret later.

Mars-Saturn: Mars and Saturn and Opposition will drive you to take action and to be responsible for yourself, but the problem is in the process, you may experience a lot of frustration, especially as it feels like your goals are so far out of reach.

Mars-Uranus: You may feel a little impulsive in response to sudden changes around you, but it is important to take your time and think things through before taking any action.

Mars-Neptune: Mars and Neptune and opposition provide the possibility that you may deceive yourself on a very important matter, so you need to prioritize being honest with yourself.

Mars-Pluto: There is a huge chance you may be caught in a power struggle, so you must ensure you do not give in to this temptation. Otherwise, it puts you in the perfect position to be manipulated into a situation that you do not find desirable at all.

Jupiter-Saturn: You may find balancing your practical considerations with your personal beliefs to be especially tough.

Jupiter-Uranus: You may feel a little rebellious or thinking unconventionally due to trying to find the alignment between what you value and your sense of individuality.

Jupiter-Neptune: Jupiter and Neptune in opposition is another aspect that makes it possible for you to be deceived. This deception could either be self-deception or from someone else.

Jupiter-Pluto: Because you want what you want, no matter the cost, there is a chance that you may find yourself abusing power. Be mindful of that.

Saturn-Uranus: You may find yourself in a tug of war between choosing to do the responsible thing and sticking to tradition versus choosing to be your individual self and progressing in the process.

Saturn-Neptune: Be careful regarding this opposition because there is a chance that you will find yourself mired in confusion, especially regarding your spiritual practices.

Saturn-Pluto: As you attempt to find the balance between your responsibility and power dynamics, you may find yourself in a unique position where you can either abuse power or change for the better.

Uranus-Neptune: While everyone generally finds their sense of spirituality by going along with everyone else in the beginning, you need to note that at some point in time, you must find your own true path. If you do not, you will struggle with confusion or idealizing the wrong things.

Uranus-Pluto: With Uranus and Pluto in opposition to each other, you might find yourself on a bit of a rebellious streak. You want to be careful that this does not lead you down a path you will regret later.

Neptune-Pluto: A need to adjust between spirituality and transformation can lead to intense spiritual experiences or obsession with power.

Quintile

The quintile has both planets 72 degrees apart from each other. This aspect involves creativity and unique abilities.

Sun-Moon: Creative solutions to emotional conflicts.

Sun-Mercury: Innovative thinking and problem-solving.

Sun-Venus: Expression and aesthetic appreciation.

Sun-Mars: Confidence and inspiration.

Sun-Jupiter: Finding opportunities and expanding your vision.

Sun-Saturn: Discipline, focus, and hard work.

Sun-Uranus: Originality and innovation.

Sun-Neptune: Artistic expression and spiritual vision.

Sun-Pluto: Transformative power and regeneration.

Moon-Mercury: Intuition and imaginative thinking.
Moon-Venus: Emotional connection and harmonious relationships.
Moon-Mars: Instinctual action and self-preservation.
Moon-Jupiter: Emotional generosity and growth.
Moon-Saturn: Emotional maturity and responsibility.
Moon-Uranus: Emotional independence and progressive thinking.
Moon-Neptune: Emotional sensitivity and artistic expression.
Moon-Pluto: Emotional intensity and transformation
Mercury-Venus: Creative communication and social grace.
Mercury-Mars: Persuasive communication and assertive action.
Mercury-Jupiter: Expansive thinking and persuasive communication.
Mercury-Saturn: Disciplined thinking and intellectual focus.
Mercury-Uranus: Innovative thinking and communication.
Mercury-Neptune: Creative thinking and spiritual insight.
Mercury-Pluto: Penetrating insight and transformative communication.
Venus-Mars: Creative passion and harmonious action.
Venus-Jupiter: Expansive creativity and joyous self-expression.
Venus-Saturn: Disciplined creativity and perseverance.
Venus-Uranus: Unique and unconventional expression.
Venus-Neptune: Artistic expression and spiritual love.
Venus-Pluto: Emotional transformation and healing.
Mars-Jupiter: Inspired action and expansion.
Mars-Saturn: Disciplined action and focus.
Mars-Uranus: Original and innovative action.
Mars-Neptune: Inspired action and creative expression.
Mars-Pluto: Transformative action and personal power.
Jupiter-Saturn: Practical vision and disciplined expansion.
Jupiter-Uranus: Visionary innovation and unconventional growth.
Jupiter-Neptune: Spiritual growth and artistic expression.
Jupiter-Pluto: Deep personal growth and transformation.
Saturn-Uranus: Balancing tradition with innovation and change.
Saturn-Neptune: Disciplined spiritual practice and compassionate service.

Saturn-Pluto: Profound transformation through hard work and self-discipline.

Uranus-Neptune: Visionary ideas and creative imagination.

Uranus-Pluto: Radical change and transformational breakthroughs.

Neptune-Pluto: Spiritual transformation and regeneration.

Chapter 10: Interpreting a Solar Return Chart

A solar chart is created by casting a chart for the exact moment when the Sun returns to its natal position each year. The position of the Sun at that moment is the foundation of the chart, which is then calculated for the location where the individual will be living during the year.

The solar chart is calculated using the same astrological data as a natal chart, including the positions of the planets, the angles between them, and their positions in the twelve houses. The chart is usually interpreted in the context of the individual's natal chart to see how the coming year may affect their overall life path.

It's important to note that the solar chart is not a replacement for the natal chart but rather a complementary tool to gain insight into specific themes and challenges that may arise during the year.

The Importance of the Natal Chart

The natal chart is the foundational astrological chart representing the planetary positions at the time of an individual's birth. It is the starting point for all astrological interpretation and analysis, including the interpretation of a solar return chart. The solar return chart is created by calculating the exact moment when the transiting Sun returns to the same position it occupied at the time of an individual's birth. This occurs once a year, on or around the individual's birthday. The resulting chart represents the astrological influences that will be present in the individual's life during the following year.

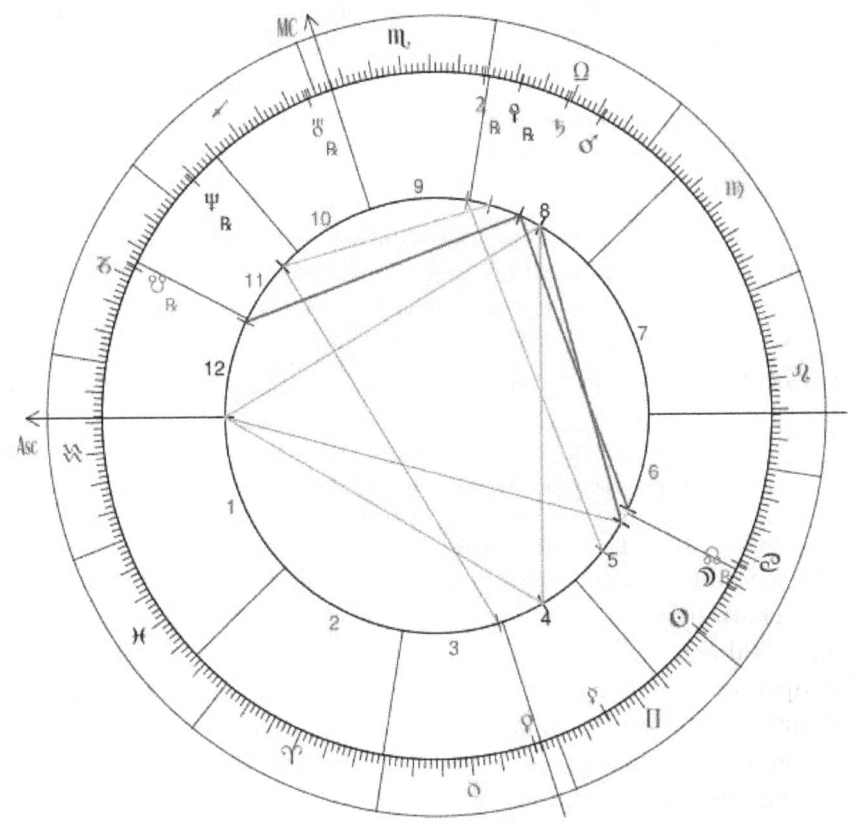

An example of what a natal chart looks like.
Mom, CC BY-SA 3.0 <https://creativecommons.org/licenses/by-sa/3.0>, via Wikimedia Commons
https://upload.wikimedia.org/wikipedia/commons/4/43/Natal_Chart_-_Adam.svg

However, interpreting a solar return chart in isolation can be limited since it only considers the planetary positions at a particular moment in time. To fully understand the meaning and significance of the planetary positions in a solar return chart, astrologers also compare and contrast them with their corresponding positions in the individual's natal chart.

For example, let's say the solar return chart shows that Mars is in the 10th house of career and public image. This placement may indicate a year of increased ambition and assertiveness in the professional realm. However, to fully understand the potential impact of this placement, an astrologer would also consider the position of Mars in the individual's natal chart.

If Mars is in a challenging aspect of the natal chart, such as a square or an opposition, it could indicate that this increased ambition and assertiveness will lead to conflict or challenges in the individual's professional life. However, suppose Mars is in a harmonious aspect, such as a trine or a sextile, with another planet, such as Jupiter. In that case, it may suggest that this growth and success will be more expansive and beneficial, leading to greater success and opportunities.

By examining the relationship between the solar return chart and the natal chart, astrologers can better understand the areas of life that will be most impacted during the upcoming year and the overall themes and challenges that may arise. This holistic approach to interpretation is essential to create a nuanced and accurate assessment of the individual's astrological influences.

The Ascendant and Its Ruler

The Ascendant and its ruling planet are important factors to consider when interpreting a solar return chart. The Ascendant sets the stage for the entire chart, indicating the overall energy and focus of the coming year. The ruler of the Ascendant represents the individual's personal approach to the upcoming year and how they will navigate its challenges and opportunities. Examining the Ascendant's placement, aspects, and house position and ruler can provide valuable insights into the individual's overall experience in the year ahead.

The Significance of the Sun and the Moon

The Sun and Moon are two of the most important factors in any astrological chart, including the solar return chart. The placement of the Sun represents the individual's focus and the areas of life that will be highlighted in the coming year. The placement of the Moon indicates the individual's emotional needs and how they will seek to meet them in the year ahead. Examining the placement, aspects, and house position of the Sun and Moon can provide insight into the individual's overall experience in the year ahead and any potential challenges or opportunities they may face.

Identifying the Important Aspects and Configurations

Aspects and configurations in the solar return chart can provide important information about the individual's experience in the coming year. For example, challenging aspects between planets may indicate areas of difficulty or conflict, while harmonious aspects may indicate areas of ease and opportunity. Configurations such as stelliums or grand trines may indicate areas of particular focus or strength in the individual's life during the upcoming year. Examining the aspects and configurations in the chart can provide valuable insight into the individual's experience in the year ahead and help identify potential areas of growth and challenge.

The Impact of Planetary Transits

Planetary transits can significantly impact the experience indicated by the solar return chart. Examining the transits that will occur throughout the year can provide insight into potential challenges and opportunities that may arise during specific periods. For example, suppose a challenging transit is indicated for a particular month. In that case, it may be helpful to plan accordingly or take steps to mitigate any potential difficulties. Similarly, if a beneficial transit is indicated, it may be a good time to take advantage of opportunities or make significant progress in certain areas of life. Understanding the impact of planetary transits can help individuals make the most of the information provided by the solar return chart and navigate the coming year with greater insight and awareness.

Interpreting House Placements

Interpreting the house placements in the solar return chart is an important aspect of understanding the areas of life highlighted during the upcoming year. Each house in the chart corresponds to a specific area of life and can reveal important information about what to expect in those areas. Here are some tips for interpreting the house placements in the solar return chart:

Start by identifying the house where the solar return Sun is located. This area of life will be the focus for the upcoming year, and it will be important to pay close attention to any aspects made to this planet.

Look at the house where the solar return Moon is located. This will give insights into the year's emotional focus and potential changes in the home or family life.

Examine the house where the solar return Ascendant is located and the planet ruling the Ascendant. This will give insights into the individual's personal focus and self-expression for the year.

Pay attention to any stelliums or clusters of planets in a particular house. This can indicate a concentration of energy in a particular area of life and can reveal important themes for the year.

Look at any planets located in the angular houses, particularly the first, fourth, seventh, and tenth houses. Planets in these houses will strongly influence the individual's life during the year.

Consider the rulers of each house and any aspects made to them. This can give insights into how each area of life will be affected during the year and can reveal important themes and opportunities.

Examining the Progressed Chart in Relation to the Solar Return Chart

Examining the progressed chart in relation to the solar return chart can provide valuable insights into the overall astrological climate for the upcoming year.

The progressed chart is a chart that is created by advancing the natal chart forward in time. Each day after birth represents a year of progression in the progressed chart. For example, if someone is 30, their progressed chart would be for the 30th year after their birth.

When examining the progressed chart in relation to the solar return chart, it is important to look at the angles, such as the Ascendant, Midheaven, and Descendant, and the progressed Moon, as they indicate key areas of focus for the year. Suppose significant transits or progressions are occurring in these areas. In that case, they will likely have an impact on the solar return chart.

Additionally, it can be helpful to look at the progressed chart's planetary placements and compare them to the solar return chart's placements. Any significant conjunctions, squares, or oppositions between the progressed and solar return planets may indicate major themes for the year.

It is also important to note that while the solar return chart represents the astrological climate for the upcoming year, the progressed chart provides a more gradual and long-term perspective. Therefore, analyzing both charts together can give a complete understanding of the overall astrological influences at play.

A Sample Solar Return Chart for Rihanna in 2021

The first thing to note is that Rihanna's solar return chart for 2021 has the Sun in Pisces in the 4th house, indicating that this will be a year focused on home and family matters, and she may seek more privacy and seclusion. The Moon is in Aquarius in the 3rd house, suggesting that communication and networking will be important themes for her this year.

The Ascendant is in Taurus, indicating that she may take a more practical and grounded approach to her goals this year and focus on building stability and security. The ruler of her Ascendant, Venus, is in Pisces in the 4th house, further emphasizing the themes of family and home and suggesting that she may find comfort and solace in creative and artistic pursuits.

In terms of important aspects, there is a stellium in Pisces with the Sun, Venus, and Neptune all in conjunction, suggesting that creative expression, spirituality, and emotional sensitivity will be strong themes for her this year. Additionally, there is a square aspect between the stellium in Pisces and Mars in Gemini in the 7th house, indicating that there may be conflicts or tensions in her partnerships and relationships.

Looking at the progressed chart in relation to the solar return chart, we can see that her progressed Sun is in Aquarius, suggesting that her focus may shift towards innovative and unconventional ideas and pursuits this year. Her progressed Moon is in Scorpio in the 11th house, indicating that friendships and social connections may be important areas of growth and development for her.

Overall, Rihanna's solar return chart for 2021 suggests a year focused on home, family, and creative expression, with potential conflicts in partnerships and relationships. The combination of the stellium in Pisces and progressed Sun in Aquarius also suggests a strong emphasis on spirituality and unconventional thinking, with potential for growth in social connections and friendships indicated by the progressed Moon in Scorpio.

Conclusion

In conclusion, solar returns are a powerful tool in predictive astrology that can provide insight and guidance for the year ahead. As you have found throughout this book, the Sun's return to its natal position each year provides a snapshot of the energies and themes present in your life for the next 12 months.

You have learned how to create a solar return chart, interpret the placements of the Sun, Moon, planets, and houses in the chart, and identify important aspects and configurations that can provide clues to the events and experiences you may encounter. You have also explored the impact of planetary transits on the solar return chart and how to use the progressed chart in relation to the solar return chart for a deeper understanding of the year ahead.

The importance of the natal chart in the creation and interpretation of the solar return chart cannot be overstated. It is essentially a snapshot of the energies that will be active in the upcoming year, but the natal chart provides the foundation and context for these energies. It is important to remember that astrology is not a deterministic practice, and the chart is not a fixed destiny you are bound to experience. Rather, it is a map of the energies and opportunities that will be available to you, and how you choose to work with these energies is up to you.

As you have seen in the example of Rihanna's chart, each chart is unique and provides a personalized map of the energies and themes that will be present in your life for the year ahead. The interpretation requires technical knowledge, intuition, and experience, and it is important to consider all factors to gain a comprehensive understanding of the chart. It is also important to remember that the solar return chart is not the only tool available in predictive astrology, and it should be used in conjunction with other techniques and methods for a more holistic understanding of the year ahead.

In conclusion, studying solar returns is valuable for anyone interested in predictive astrology. It provides a powerful way to gain insight into the energies and themes that will be present in our lives for the year ahead. By using the techniques and methods outlined in this book, you can gain a deeper understanding of your own charts and use this knowledge to navigate the challenges and opportunities that come your way with greater wisdom and clarity.

Glossary of Astrological Terms and Symbols

Planetary Symbols and Abbreviations

Sun: ☉, abbreviated as "SUN"

Moon: ☽, abbreviated as "MOO" or "MON"

Mercury: ☿, abbreviated as "MER"

Venus: ♀, abbreviated as "VEN"

Mars: ♂, abbreviated as "MAR"

Jupiter: ♃, abbreviated as "JUP"

Saturn: ♄, abbreviated as "SAT"

Uranus: ♅, abbreviated as "URA"

Neptune: ♆, abbreviated as "NEP"

Pluto: ♇, abbreviated as "PLU"

Sign Symbols and Abbreviations

Aries: ♈, abbreviated as "ARI"

Taurus: ♉, abbreviated as "TAU"

Gemini: ♊, abbreviated as "GEM"

Cancer: ♋, abbreviated as "CAN"
Leo: ♌, abbreviated as "LEO"
Virgo: ♍, abbreviated as "VIR"
Libra: ♎, abbreviated as "LIB"
Scorpio: ♏, abbreviated as "SCO"
Sagittarius: ♐, abbreviated as "SAG"
Capricorn: ♑, abbreviated as "CAP"
Aquarius: ♒, abbreviated as "AQU"
Pisces: ♓, abbreviated as "PIS"

Other Symbols and Abbreviations

Ascendant: ASC
Midheaven: MC
North Node: ☊
South Node: ☋
Retrograde: Rx
Direct: D

Extra: Your Solar Return Charts

This extra chapter provides a useful tool for recording and analyzing your solar return charts. After studying the principles of solar returns and learning how to interpret them, you can use these blank templates to create your own personalized solar return charts. These templates can be photocopied and added to your journal or book of shadows alongside your notes and interpretations. As you make predictions and observe how the events of the coming year unfold, you can use these charts to reflect on what came true and what did not.

By creating your solar return charts and using them to make predictions, you can deepen your understanding of astrology and gain valuable insights into your life. Whether you are a beginner or an experienced astrologer, these templates can help you to harness the power of solar returns and unlock the secrets of the year ahead. Don't hesitate to use these templates to record your solar return charts and reflect on your predictions as the year progresses. With practice and patience, you can learn to use the ancient wisdom of astrology to guide you on your journey through life!

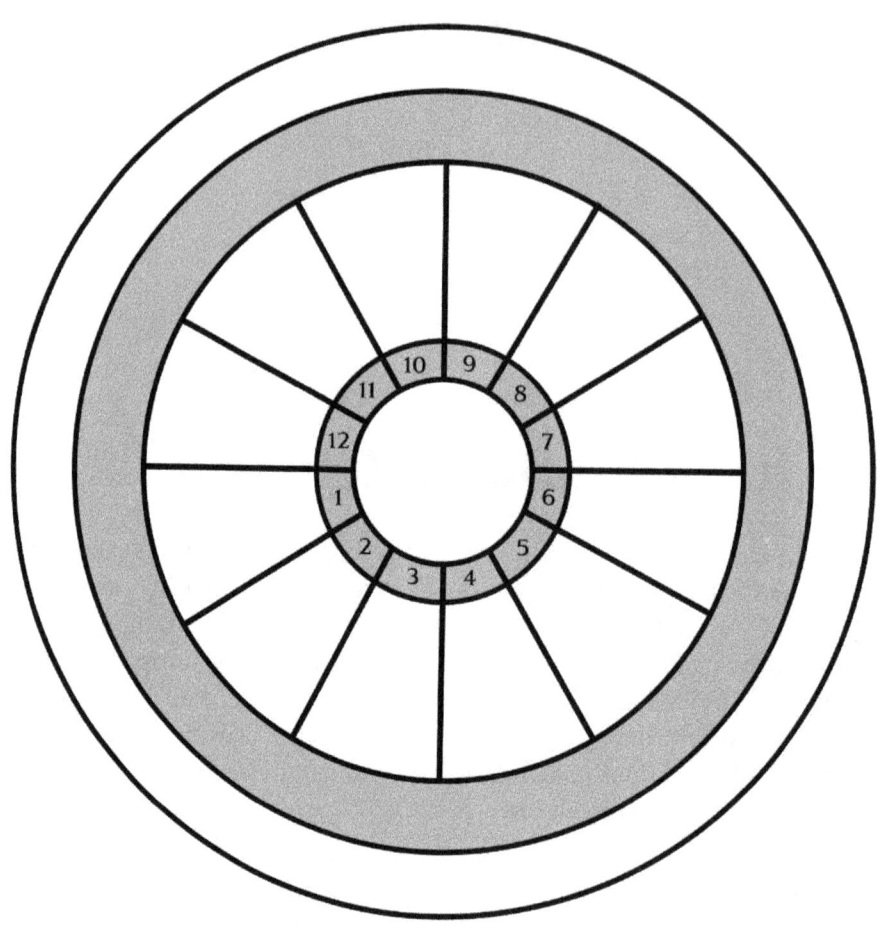

Horoscope Data Sheet

Name: _____

Place: _____

Lat.: _____

Long.: _____

Birth date: Month: _____ Day: _____ Year: _____

Hr.: _____

Min.: _____ A.M.   P.M. (Std. Time)

Std. Time: Eastern Central   Mountain Pacific

<u>**Cross out all time zones except your own**</u>

True Local Time: _____

Cale. Sid. Time: _____

Nearest Sid. Time: _____

Greenwich Mean Time: _____

Adj. Cale. Date: _____

Elements	Planets	Planets' Deelination	Aspects						
Cardinal									
Fixed									
Common									
Fiery									
Earthy									
Airy									
Watery									
Essentially Dignified									
Exalted									
Detriment									
Fall									
Angular									
Critical									

Here's another book by Mari Silva that you might like

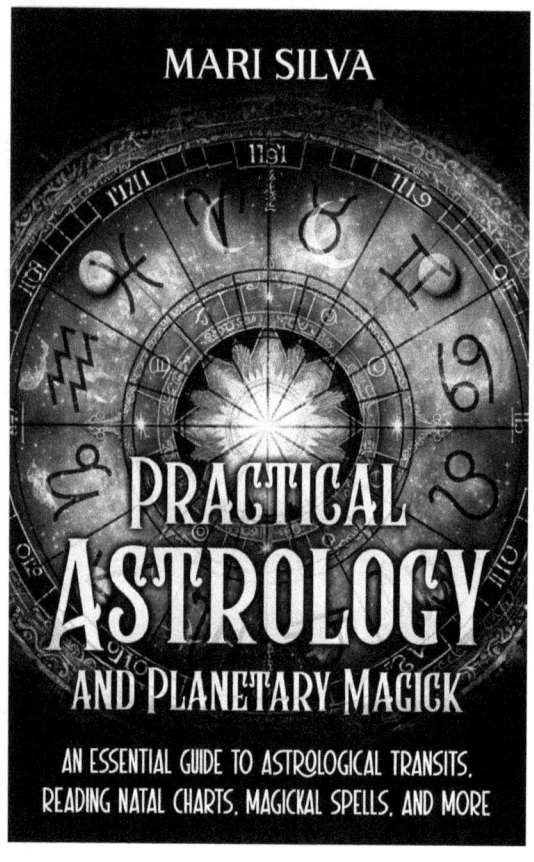

Your Free Gift
(only available for a limited time)

Thanks for getting this book! If you want to learn more about various spirituality topics, then join Mari Silva's community and get a free guided meditation MP3 for awakening your third eye. This guided meditation mp3 is designed to open and strengthen ones third eye so you can experience a higher state of consciousness. Simply visit the link below the image to get started.

https://spiritualityspot.com/meditation

Or, Scan the QR code!

References

(N.d.). Symbolspy.com. https://www.symbolspy.com/zodiac-symbols-text.html

"A Brief Introduction to Astrology: Aspects." n.d. Astro.com. . https://www.astro.com/astrology/in_aspect_e.htm.

"Aquarius Papers - Global Astrology." n.d. Aquarius Papers - Global Astrology. . https://www.aquariuspapers.com/astrology/2018/05/astrology-class-on-the-specializing-aspects-pt-1-the-quintile-and-biquintile.html.

"Horary Astrology Lesson 4, Aspects and Their Perfection." n.d. Tripod.com. . https://mithras93.tripod.com/lessons/lesson4/lesson4.html.

"Minor Aspects - Meaning." 2011. Astrologers' Community. February 13, 2011. https://www.astrologyweekly.com/forum/index.php?threads/minor-aspects-meaning.33323/.

"The Aspects." n.d. Astrograph.com. . https://www.astrograph.com/learning-astrology/aspects.php.

"The Aspects." n.d. Astrograph.com. . https://www.astrograph.com/learning-astrology/aspects.php.

"The Meaning of the Aspects in Astrology." 2015. Cafeastrology.com. Cafe Astrology .com. April 15, 2015. https://cafeastrology.com/articles/aspectsinastrology.html.

"The Most & Least Lucky Aspects to Have on Your Zodiac Chart, from Astrologers." 2022. Mindbodygreen. April 19, 2022. https://www.mindbodygreen.com/articles/aspects-in-astrology.

Aries 101: Everything you need to know about the kickstarter of the zodiac. (2021, March 26). Mindbodygreen. https://www.mindbodygreen.com/articles/aries-sign-101

Aries traits. (2021, October 4). GaneshaSpeaks. https://www.ganeshaspeaks.com/zodiac-signs/aries/traits/

Astrogle. (2009, September 6). FAQs about combust planets and their effects. Vedic Astrology & Ayurveda. https://www.astrogle.com/astrology/faqs-about-combust-planets-and-their-effects.html

Astrologernyc. (n.d.). Livejournal.com. https://astrology8.livejournal.com/1513.html

Beare, K. (2007, May 2). Zodiac signs and the words that describe them. ThoughtCo. https://www.thoughtco.com/zodiac-personality-4122956

Brennan, C. (n.d.). The planetary joys and the origins of the significations of the houses and triplicities. Hellenisticastrology.com. https://www.hellenisticastrology.com/the-planetary-joys.pdf

Broadwater, A. (2023, February 13). Mental restriction can be a major roadblock for intuitive eating – here's what helps. Well+Good. https://www.wellandgood.com/mental-restriction/

Brown, M. (2021a, October 11). A guide to air signs: Gemini, Libra, and Aquarius. InStyle. https://www.instyle.com/lifestyle/astrology/air-signs

Brown, M. (2021b, November 17). A guide to fire signs: Aries, Leo, and Sagittarius. InStyle. https://www.instyle.com/lifestyle/astrology/fire-signs

Brown, M. (2022, May 25). What each zodiac sign can expect while Mars is in Aries. Yahoo Life.

Bunch, E. (2020, January 21). The zodiac wheel is divided by extroverted and introverted energy – here's what it means for you. Well+Good. https://www.wellandgood.com/polarity-in-astrology/

Campbell, S. (2022, June 7). StyleCaster. StyleCaster. https://stylecaster.com/body-parts-zodiac/

Campbell, S. (2022, September 16). What does retrograde mean? How each planet's retrograde affects you. StyleCaster. https://stylecaster.com/feature/what-does-retrograde-mean-1134829/

Dictionary.com. (2022, January 21). Zodiac signs: Learn the names, symbols, and more! Dictionary.com. https://www.dictionary.com/e/horoscope-meaning/

Ep. 145 Transcript: The Origins of Horary Astrology. (2022, December 29). The Astrology Podcast. https://theastrologypodcast.com/transcripts/ep-145-transcript-the-origins-of-horary-astrology/

Finding the answers with Horary astrology. (2009, November 19). WellBeing Magazine. https://www.wellbeing.com.au/mind-spirit/Finding-the-answers-with-Horary-astrology.html

Getting started with horary astrology. (2018, October 5). Soul Friend Astrology. https://soulfriendastrology.com/2018/10/04/entries-into-horary-astrology/

Grabianowski, E. (2005, May 26). What Is Astrology? HowStuffWorks. https://entertainment.howstuffworks.com/horoscopes-astrology/question749.htm

Horary: Where is it? by Deborah Houlding. (n.d.). Skyscript.co.uk. https://www.skyscript.co.uk/wit.html

Houlding, D. (n.d.). Skyscript: Horary Love Charts. Skyscript.co.uk. https://www.skyscript.co.uk/relationships.html

Houlding, Deborah. n.d. "An Introduction to Aspects and Chart Shaping in Natal Astrology by Nicholas Campion." Skyscript.co.uk. . https://www.skyscript.co.uk/aspects2.html.

How to thrive as A water sign (looking at you, Cancer, Scorpio & Pisces). (2021, August 5). Mindbodygreen. https://www.mindbodygreen.com/articles/water-signs

How to thrive as an air sign (shoutout Gemini, Libra & Aquarius). (2021, September 13). Mindbodygreen. https://www.mindbodygreen.com/articles/air-signs

Ht, P. L. C., & More, R. (2022, March 3). What Is Horary Astrology? Complete Beginner's Guide. LoveToKnow. https://horoscopes.lovetoknow.com/astrology-basics/what-is-horary-astrology-complete-beginners-guide

Johnson, S. (n.d.). The essentials of essential dignities. Seeingwithstars.net.

Kahn, Nina. 2019. "What Conjunction, Trine, Square, Opposition, and Sextile Mean in Astrology & Birth Charts." Bustle. January 26, 2019. https://www.bustle.com/life/what-conjunction-trine-square-opposition-sextile-mean-in-astrology-birth-charts-13108526.

Katee, A. (2023, January 7). The 4 essential dignities of planets in astrology the keys to understanding your strengths and weaknesses. Well+Good. https://www.wellandgood.com/essential-dignities-planet-astrology/

Kelly, A. (2018, February 2). The personality of a Cancer, explained. Allure. https://www.allure.com/story/cancer-zodiac-sign-personality-traits

Libra zodiac sign: Symbols. (2019, June 18). Cafeastrology.com; Cafe Astrology .com. https://cafeastrology.com/libra-symbols.html

Mahtani, N. (2021, March 15). Horary Astrology Is Like a Q&A Session About Your Chart – Here's What To Know About it. Well+Good. https://www.wellandgood.com/horary-astrology/

Miller, K. (2019, July 20). What it means if you're A cardinal sign in astrology, according to experts. Women's Health. https://www.womenshealthmag.com/life/a28280252/cardinal-signs/

Miller, K. (2020, October 29). The zodiac's fire signs: Aries, Leo, and Sagittarius personality traits, explained by astrologers. Women's Health. https://www.womenshealthmag.com/life/a34329807/fire-signs-zodiac-traits/

Muniz, H. (n.d.). The 7 fundamental Cancer traits and what they mean for you. Prepscholar.com. https://blog.prepscholar.com/cancer-traits-personality

New insights into Mutual Reception. (2016, November 1). Sky Writer. https://skywriter.wordpress.com/2016/11/01/new-insights-into-mutual-reception/

Padmadeo, B. B. (n.d.). Astroturf. The Pioneer. https://www.dailypioneer.com/2017/sunday-edition/astroturf--the-precision-of-horary-astrology.html

Padmadeo, B. B. (n.d.). Astroturf. The Pioneer. https://www.dailypioneer.com/2017/sunday-edition/astroturf--the-precision-of-horary-astrology.html

Robinson, K. (2022, June 9). Decans (Decantes): Definition, Zodiac Signs, How to Find. Astrology.Com. https://www.astrology.com/article/decans-astrology/

Rose, K. (2020, August 22). What does the Aries symbol & glyph mean? YourTango. https://www.yourtango.com/2020336399/aries-symbol-zodiac-sign-glyphs-meanings

Rose, K. (2021, April 9). What does the Capricorn symbol & glyph mean? YourTango. https://www.yourtango.com/2020336299/capricorn-symbol-zodiac-sign-glyphs-meanings

Rose, M. (2022, August 17). StyleCaster. StyleCaster. https://stylecaster.com/different-types-of-each-zodiac-sign/

Rose, M. (2022a, December 29). Air signs, explained: Here's what it means to be a Gemini, Libra, or Aquarius. Glamour. https://www.glamour.com/story/zodiac-air-signs

Rose, M. (2022b, December 29). Earth signs, explained: Here's what it means to be a Taurus, Virgo, or Capricorn. Glamour. https://www.glamour.com/story/zodiac-earth-signs

Ross, H., Clarke, J., Young, E., & Bishop, K. (2018, December 18). What is my ruling planet, according to the zodiac, and what does it mean for me? Repeller. https://repeller.com/ruling-planets-and-what-they-mean-for-you-according-to-the-zodiac/

Sam, T. +., & Wander, T. (2021, June 7). What Are The 12 Houses In Astrology - . Two Wander x Elysium Rituals. https://www.twowander.com/blog/what-are-the-12-houses-astrology

Sam, T. +., & Wander, T. (2022, August 15). How To Read A Horary Astrology Chart - . Two Wander x Elysium Rituals. https://www.twowander.com/blog/how-to-read-a-horary-astrology-chart

Sam, T. +., & Wander, T. (2022, February 7). Planetary dignities and joys - . Two Wander x Elysium Rituals. https://www.twowander.com/blog/planetary-dignities-and-joys

Sidharth, A. (2016, February 29). Horary astrology Hindu traditional system. The Astrology Online | Best Astrologer in India, Online Astrologer in India, KP Experts in India; Astrologer Sidharth. https://theastrologyonline.com/horary-astrology/

Sloan, E. (2021, October 16). Here's what the modality of your zodiac sign actually means, according to an astrologer. Well+Good. https://www.wellandgood.com/modality-astrology/

Spanner, H. (2023, January 4). Retrograde motion of the planets: Everything you need to know. BBC Science Focus Magazine. https://www.sciencefocus.com/space/retrograde/

Stardust, L. (2020a, March 12). Cardinal signs: The CEOs of your group chat. Cosmopolitan. https://www.cosmopolitan.com/lifestyle/a31434873/cardinal-signs-zodiac-astrology-meaning/

Stardust, L. (2020b, August 12). Everything you need to know about earth signs. Cosmopolitan. https://www.cosmopolitan.com/lifestyle/a33588028/earth-signs-astrology/

Stardust, L. (2021, October 15). Introduction to Horary Astrology: What Is It and How to Use It. Astrology.Com. https://www.astrology.com/article/what-is-horary-astrology/

Stardust, L. (2021, October 15). Introduction to Horary Astrology: What Is It and How to Use It. Astrology.Com. https://www.astrology.com/article/what-is-horary-astrology/

Stardust, L. (2021, October 15). Introduction to horary astrology: What is it and how to use it. Yahoo Life. https://www.yahoo.com/lifestyle/introduction-horary-astrology-235556300.html

Stardust, L. (2021, October 15). Introduction to horary astrology: What is it and how to use it. Yahoo Life. https://www.yahoo.com/lifestyle/introduction-horary-astrology-235556300.html?guccounter=1&guce_referrer=aHR0cHM6Ly93d3cuZ29vZ2xlLmNvbS8&guce_referrer_sig=AQAAADqIUemWCHLj9rVLm09sQ2l6nkP1vHgARcd4VQ_da5MxxoZ9g153UVQc1gDQj-4ABeWWfPZdZ_K-QAh08kG77IOb2Ccm5cFZWbWrnS-gbkyAWlj1I-zIrGKBsP6TCnytlUcvUUnY6OYBX91jUxue4zDji1gJTJLqwVOWv0d56MLI

Surtees, K. (2018, May 28). What is horary astrology? We take an in-depth look at the planets. WellBeing Magazine. https://www.wellbeing.com.au/mind-spirit/astrology/what-is-horary-astrology-we-take-an-in-depth-look-at-the-planets.html

Surtees, K. (2018, May 28). What is horary astrology? We take an in-depth look at the planets. WellBeing Magazine. https://www.wellbeing.com.au/mind-spirit/astrology/what-is-horary-astrology-we-take-an-in-depth-look-at-the-planets.html

Surtees, Kelly. 2018. "What Is Horary Astrology? We Take an in-Depth Look at the Planets." WellBeing Magazine. May 28, 2018. https://www.wellbeing.com.au/mind-spirit/astrology/what-is-horary-astrology-we-take-an-in-depth-look-at-the-planets.html.

Tarot.com Staff. (2017, February 9). Your Zodiac Sign's Power Color. Tarot.Com. https://www.tarot.com/astrology/zodiac-sign-colors

The 12 Houses of Astrology - The Astrological Houses and Your Natal Chart. (2020, August 14). Labyrinthos. https://labyrinthos.co/blogs/astrology-horoscope-zodiac-signs/the-12-houses-of-astrology-the-astrological-houses-and-your-natal-chart

The 12 zodiac signs: Traits, meanings, symbols, colors, and more! (n.d.). Tarot.com. https://www.tarot.com/astrology/zodiac

The Astrology Dictionary. (2012, July 24). The Astrology Dictionary. https://theastrologydictionary.com/d/decans/

The astrology dictionary. (2012, September 12). The Astrology Dictionary. http://theastrologydictionary.com/j/joys/

The Axis In Astrology – Ac, Ic, Dc And Mc. (2021, January 14). Star Sign Style. https://starsignstyle.com/astrology-axis-points-four-angles-explained/

Thiessen, A. (2017, November 2). The ASCENDANT and DESCENDANT Axis – . Canary Quill Astrology. http://www.canaryquillastrology.com/articles/2017/9/26/the-ascendant-and-descendant-axis

Thomas, Kyle. 2021. "Your Guide to Planetary Aspects." Cosmopolitan. August 18, 2021. https://www.cosmopolitan.com/lifestyle/a37341996/astrology-aspects-list/.

Time Nomad. 2019. "Minor Astrological Aspects and the Domain of Magic." Time Nomad. May 30, 2019. https://timenomad.app/posts/astrology/philosophy/2019/05/30/minor-aspects-domain-of-magic.html.

TIMESOFINDIA.COM. (2021, August 16). What does the symbol of each zodiac sign mean? Times of India. https://timesofindia.indiatimes.com/life-style/relationships/love-sex/what-does-the-symbol-of-each-zodiac-sign-mean/photostory/85349448.cms?picid=85349511

Transits: Predictions, Dates and Timings. (n.d.). Astrosage.com. https://www.astrosage.com/transits/

Wroskopos's blog. (2010, February 13). Wroskopos's Blog. https://wroskopos.wordpress.com/2010/02/13/starting-with-horary-the-basic-steps

Brady, B. (1998). Predictive Astrology: The Eagle and the Lark. Weiser Books.

Clow, B. H. (1987). Chiron: Rainbow Bridge Between the Inner and Outer Planets. Llewellyn Worldwide.

DeVore, N. (2005). Encyclopedia of astrology. Astrology Center of America.

Fagan, C., & Firebrace, R. C. (2008). Primer of Sidereal Astrology (No. 1). American Federation of Astr.

Forrest, S. (1986). The Changing Sky: A Practical Guide to the New Predictive Astrology. Bantam Books.

Frawley, D. (1992). The Astrology of Seers: A Comprehensive Guide to Vedic Astrology. Motilal Banarsidass Publisher.

Gerwick-Brodeur, M., & Lenard, L. (2003). The Complete Idiot's Guide to Astrology. Penguin.

Laishley, L. (2007). Astrology as Religion: Theory and Practice. Journal for the Study of Religion, Nature & Culture.

Orion, R. (2011). Astrology for dummies. John Wiley & Sons.

Page, S. (2002). Astrology in medieval manuscripts. University of Toronto Press.

Robson, V. E. (2010). A Beginner's Guide to Practical Astrology. Astrology Classics.

Simmonite, W. J. (2009). Horary Astrology. American Federation of Astr.

Sutherland, P. (2012). How Astrology Saved My Life. Clarion Reviews.

Teal, C. (2009). Predicting Events with Astrology. Llewellyn Worldwide.

Woolfolk, J. M. (2012). The Only Astrology Book You'll Ever Need: Now with an Interactive PC-and Mac-Compatible CD. Taylor Trade Publications.

www.ingramcontent.com/pod-product-compliance
Lightning Source LLC
Chambersburg PA
CBHW051855160426
43209CB00006B/1311